Adventures in Paradise
MEMOIRS OF AN ENTREPRENEUR IN THE YUCATAN

Gus Gordon

Copyright © 2010 Gus Gordon
All rights reserved.

ISBN: 1453801936
ISBN-13: 9781453801932

For

Los Gansos

Acknowledgements

This book would not have been possible without the help of many people. First and foremost are the characters I met on my adventure. Milton Burton was incredibly helpful as an editor. The same is true for Dana Adams who also did the artwork for the cover.

Most importantly, the adventure was consummated and became a dream fulfilled as a result of the extraordinary efforts of my colleagues in the business, Operadora Ganso Azul. Ganso Azul means Blue Goose and the reason for the name is explained in the book. Ganso Azul would not exist were it not for Michael Blauer who is the president of Blauer Manufacturing, our customer.

Finally, were it not for the actions of Tyrone Black, David Duhon and Linda Brogan the adventure would never have been possible.

CHAPTER ONE
Mexico:
Myth, Romance and Reality

Mexico is truly a land of contradictions and mysteries. Hollywood has helped to create a stereotype of Mexico that is part myth and part romance with only a dash of reality thrown in. My perspective is somewhat unique in that I moved to Mexico to begin a legitimate business that has been successful to date. I believe I have become culturally competent and not just fluent in the language. Becoming culturally adept was more difficult than I had anticipated, but it has given me additional insight beyond what the average foreign resident in Mexico would have. I am hopeful that my perspective and insight will be helpful, not only to those interested in pursuing business in Mexico, but also those who have an interest in retiring there.

The reality is that Mexico is a socialist country masquerading as capitalist. Maybe the U.S. is now doing the same, but the effects in Mexico have created a status quo that benefits a very fortunate few at the expense of a great majority. Furthermore, the Mexican government seems completely disinterested in changing the situation. Perhaps this is due to the fact that most of the fortunate few are made more fortunate each day thanks to some connection with the government, either direct or indirect.

Corruption is rampant at every level of government and also pervades everyday life. It is unavoidable and must be dealt with if you choose to live or do business in Mexico.

Until recently most Mexicans have thought of corruption as an innocuous part of daily life, while most foreigners living in Mexico have joked about it in the same terms. Often the deleterious effects of corruption on business efficiency have been downplayed. However, the recent violence associated with President Calderon's admirable attempt at wresting control from the drug cartels has shown that this supposedly "humorous" corruption has a very dirty underbelly.

Mexico is like Colombia was fifteen years ago. Colombia solved many its problems to a great extent through U.S. military technology, intelligence and advice. Mexico will most likely have to do the same to resolve its crisis. But Mexico has a love-hate relationship with the U.S. and may not overtly invite U.S. military assistance until it is completely unavoidable and this will only make the cure even more difficult.

Mexican society seems quite disorganized in most respects. While this is frustrating, it has some advantages. For one, it creates an anything goes philosophy and with this comes the idea that anything is possible. And this is part of what contributes to the romance of the country.

Hollywood has helped with the romantic views of Mexico. Numerous films have depicted life in Mexico as easy and wonderful. And it often is for the very rich and for those vacationing in five star resorts.

Various movies have shown American adventurers going to Mexico in search of fortune and romance. The Treasure of the Sierra Madre starring Humphrey Bogart is a famous movie that most people do not know was based on a novel written by Bruno Traven. Traven himself was a mysterious figure who came to Mexico from Germany. He wrote a number of novels in the 1930's and 1940's, but little is known about him.

Pancho Villa, perhaps the most famous Mexican outside of Mexico, is normally shown by Hollywood to be a romantic adventurer. The same is true for many other Hollywood creations, some fictional and some historical.

I always had a romantic vision of Mexico beginning with my childhood. My grandfather had gone to Mexico as a roughneck in the early 1900's. He had some interesting stories. He was there during the Mexican Revolution. His stories only flamed my interest.

Mexico has always been known as a place that one can go and disappear from authorities. Part of this is due to the disorganized nature of Mexican society. Another part is due to corruption—identities are easily obtainable and secrets easily hidden.

For this reason some Americans find refuge in Mexico. The Yucatan is one of the most isolated parts of Mexico so it is a destination of choice of those who may wish to "disappear" and I write about of couple of those characters that I met.

There are some places in the world that have a special appeal and attract fascinating people. Merida,

Yucatan, where this story is set, is one of those places. Some of the interesting people stay permanently and some stay for only a short time. Some come and go over a period of decades, like a comet that maintains its fiery orbit around what many think is the center of the universe—Merida.

One such example is Lee Richards. I tell part of Lee's story here to give the reader some initial flavor of the characters that Merida attracts.

I cannot remember when I first met Lee Richards[1]. Most probably we first met in Pancho's, which is the prime watering hole for ex pats in Merida. Not so much anymore, but in the old days the bar would be full of an interesting mix of locals, tourists, and ex pats living in Merida during Happy Hour.

At any rate, at some point Lee indicated he had a boat for sale since he was going to return to the States. I had owned two sailboats in the States and had always thought a power boat would be easier and less work. We went out to the marina in Progreso to see the boat.

The boat was a classic: a forty-two foot Owens with a mahogany hull. It was built in 1970, as I remember, and had that classic, sexy profile of boats of that era. I fell in love with it instantly. The boat was powered by twin gas-guzzling Chryslers each of which produced 330 horse power for a total of 660! Those motors had that deep rumble that can only be reproduced on the water by incredibly powerful engines or on land by a big Harley Davidson. It had two cabins that slept four and a main cabin with a galley. There were two heads with electric toilets. I was accustomed to pumping by hand in my other boats,

---
1   I am using a fictitious name for a real person

so I considered this an incredible luxury. The decks were teak, and the interior was beautiful mahogany. Lee was leaving some simple electronics like GPS and VHF radio. The boat also had dual stations. I was in love and you would have been, too. Especially at the price of $10,000.

I took a second trip on the boat with Lee on the first visit of Michael, my customer, to Merida. A picture memorializing that trip is still on my desk at the office.

I knew the boat needed some work and also thought Lee did not really have much time to market the boat as he needed to return to Detroit for urgent business. I negotiated and ultimately bought the boat for $5,000—the only condition was that Lee would not accept a check because, I learned later, he did not have a bank account. He wanted greenbacks. He got them and I got the boat.

Lee is a very interesting character. He is six-foot-five inches tall and relatively slim, but not skinny. It was 1999, and I believe he told me he was about 60 years old. However, he lived the life of a much younger man. He had a great personality and was very jovial.

He was gray-haired with a gray beard that was trimmed fairly close. When he spoke, he had the voice of Marlon Brando in *The Godfather*. I doubt that this whispering, gritty voice was helped much by his chain-smoking. He wore great big aviator eyeglasses.

Lee's physical appearance, which I think was a cultivated almost bum-like look, belied his intellect. He could speak intelligently on many subjects with a fine-tuned reason behind his dialogue. He was incredibly articulate and wrote eloquently. After we made the boat deal by email (I was in the States and he in Cancun on the boat), he wrote in an email of the last voyage he made on what was to become my boat. That voyage was a trip from Cancun to Merida, and Lee described the voyage and his sentiments about this boat in such a poetic fashion that it almost moved me to tears.

He had bought the boat, which he had named *The Blind Pig*, somewhere in the Great Lakes region more than a year before. He motored through the Great Lakes to the Intra-Coastal Canal on the U.S. Eastern Coast. From there, he travelled to the tip of Florida and ultimately to Cuba. He stayed awhile in Cuba, illegally under U.S. law, and then crossed the Yucatan Channel to Merida.

He had lived part of the time on the boat in a marina in Progreso and part of the time in the hotel in which he usually lodged in Merida. He told me he had been coming to Merida for the last twenty years or so. Lee had been in Mexico several months when he needed to return to the States for his business.

I had only known Lee as an interesting acquaintance to talk to in Pancho's. So, on the trip to Progreso with him to see *The Blind Pig* for the first time I started asking the normal make-conversation-type questions. "Lee", I asked, "What is the boat's name?" Lee had kind of an odd accent that affected the sound of certain words and coupled with his Godfather-like voice sometimes it was hard to comprehend the words. I thought he responded, "*The Blind Peg*". "Lee", I asked, "What's a blind peg"? "No, no," he said, "a blind PEG". Well, we were at a standoff. Eventually I determined he was saying "pig."

Clarifying the annunciation difference between "peg" and "pig" still did not help my comprehension. If I am not mistaken, a blind pig is a euphemism for a sort of business he claimed he managed—and here I am certain of the annunciation and the specific words he used: "I run a quasi-legal gambling establishment in Chicago". [2]

My next question was, "Lee, what is a *quasi*-legal gambling establishment"? He said, "You pay off the Sergeant on the beat, then you operate with 'legal' protection"!

"Oh," I said. This sounded interesting so I continued to question him.

"I have partners and they are Italian," he explained. This seemed an unnecessary explanation, and he said it in that implying tone that would indicate there was some additional protection for his business that originated in the Sicilian part cf Italy.

Lee continued, "I only work for about a year and then I take a year off. In the year I work I can usually generate about $200,000 – $250,000 and I use that for the year I am travelling."

I remarked, "Lee, that sounds like a lot of money but it also sounds pretty risky, not withstanding the 'protection' you have."

"Well," he said, "I also have security at the building."

I was very curious. "Lee, how does all this work"?

"Well, I spread the word that I am back in town, and my customers come back to our location. I have

---

[2] The city that Lee named was not Chicago, but I think it best not to use the name of the actual city where his business was located.

a three-story building with an apartment on the top floor. Security is on the bottom floor and on the second floor is where the gaming occurs."

"Do you have crap tables, blackjack, and all those kinds of games?" I wanted to know.

"No, its pure poker, and we take a percentage of each pot. We usually have several tables going at the same time."

"You must not have competition," I asked.

"Oh no," he responded, "there are other blind pigs around Chicago".

"So, you go off for a year and come back and your clientele comes back with you. What is it about your operation that creates such a loyalty in your clientele"? I asked.

"We run a tight ship," he responded. "We have good security and we never let a problem develop. We nip potential problems in the bud. Also, we serve good drinks and make everyone comfortable."

"Ahh. . ."

"I really don't want to go back right now," he volunteered, "but my partners are insisting on it". Again, he used that tone that implied that if his partners were insisting upon it, he better pay attention.

Before Lee went back to the States to deal with his business and his partners, I got to know him much better. He began to tell me about some of his past experiences. These stories were always interesting. He had been in the Navy as a young man and travelled around a good bit. He'd been an enlisted man, and I believe he said he had been in for about twelve years. Apparently, after leaving the Navy he decided that there were better ways to make a living and also figured out that his disposable income would be greater if he did not pay taxes. He claimed, proudly, not to have filed a tax return after some point in the 1970s.

Somewhere along the line, Lee picked up a trade–he was a printer. At some point, he told me, he decided to print counterfeit collectible comic books.

"Why comic books?" I asked.

"There's lots of money in collectible comic books", he said. "We had a good deal going. We would print maybe fifty copies of a collector's edition. I had a team I worked with on the East Coast. I would give a copy to each one of them in different cities. Each of us would then go to the local store that bought and sold these old comic books."

His eyes were lighting up, and he became very animated. "At each store our story would be the same to the store owner or manager: 'hey, I was cleaning out my attic and found this old comic book. I really don't know how much it is worth but I don't have any need for it and thought I could pick up a few bucks.'"

He laughed heartily and continued, "Of course, we knew exactly what it was worth if it had been the real McCoy. We would watch as the owner would look it up in the reference guide and often his eyes would get big, and he would try to hide his excitement with a straight face. Some of them would really low-ball us. We might try and negotiate a little, but usually we just accepted the offer, said thanks and left with our hard-earned money." He laughed really loudly at this point.

He continued, "The *coup de grace* was planned for a comic book convention where these geeks were gathering to buy and sell from one another as well as discuss whatever the hell comic book geeks discuss when they get together. Me and my buddy had about ten copies of the same counterfeit comic book that we were going to sell to the highest bidder. We had spent all morning discretely talking to various buyers at the convention. We told each one that there was only one comic book and that it would go to the highest bidder. Then, of course, we were going to approach each one separately and tell each one of them the good news: they had been the highest bidder and each one would walk off with a comic book! It was a good plan."

"We went up to our room in the hotel to rest after a hard day's work of selling in the morning. After resting we came down late in the day and went to the first bidder who was going to be the first winner of ten. He told us there was some excitement going on as two FBI agents were at the convention trying to find some counterfeiters. We agreed it was exciting, told him unfortunately he was not the highest bidder, and immediately left by the side door." He punctuated this last sentence with a big laugh.

I asked, "Lee, how did you get away with it so long?"

He said, "None of the store owners ever wanted to admit that they had been conned so they never reported anything. It would have been too embarrassing for them. However, I guess someone at the convention smelled something and called in the FBI."

"Did you ever counterfeit money"?

He seemed taken aback and exclaimed, "Of course not! Why, that would be fraud!"

"Lee," I retorted, "What is counterfeiting comic books if not fraud?"

He said, "Oh, that's just taking advantage of other peoples' greed." I guess his logic did make some sense.

Lee's real identity is not Lee Richards. He never told me his true name. On another occasion he told me the story of a different type of counterfeiting. He had made a living for a period of time helping others get fake identities. "It's real easy," he said. "You start first with the driver's license and from there you can get all the other documents."

While he would not tell me why he had a fake identity, he did tell me that he used more than one identity to scam the government out of welfare checks.

"Yeah, while I was living in Boston, I had a big house that went from one street in the front of the house all the way to the next block on the street running parallel at the back. The house actually had two front doors and two separate addresses. I think it had been two houses at one time. So it occurred to me that I could get two separate welfare checks. I was between jobs at the time." He finished the last statement off with a thunderous laugh.

"All I needed," he continued, "was to become two different people and that was easy enough. So I became two different people, at least as far as the government was concerned. I applied for welfare under each name and I was successful. One welfare check arrived in one name to the address at the front of the house and another arrived in another name at the address at the back of the house. I doubled my income," he laughed. "And the same postman delivered both checks. It was great."

Lee had another story of how he had lived in a commune in the seventies up in Oregon. There were thirty to forty people living there during the summer. However, Lee claimed that in the winter it got too cold for these hippies, and they always disbanded, went their respective ways and came back in the Spring.

This was Lee's first year with them, and he did not understand why they would be participating in a part-time commune. He told them, "I don't feel a need to leave. Do you have a problem if I stay through the winter?"

The leader of the commune was a woman, and she agreed to his proposition. She had about fifteen dogs living with them that she usually took back for her winter hiatus from the commune. She asked if Lee would mind taking care of the dogs through the winter. He agreed. Lee also convinced a couple of the guys in the commune to stay for winter.

Lee said, "Yeah, I was really enjoying this commune with nature thing. They had told us that you can't get food supplies in the dead of winter and that made it even better from my perspective. After all, this is the wilds of Oregon in the middle of nowhere with lots of wildlife. We had guns and would simply kill our food. I was really excited."

"Once the dead of winter arrived, I began to understand why they all left," he explained. "It was really, really cold, and the snow was really deep. I don't know if all the damn wildlife was hibernating or what, but we never saw anything to shoot. Then we ate up all the supplies we had and realized we could not get any more supplies as the roads, such as they were, were un-passable."

"How did you survive?" I asked.

"We really didn't have a choice – we had to start shooting the dogs they had left and eat them. They really weren't that bad."

"Anyway," he continued, "the commune leader made it back in the Spring and when she asked how her dogs were, we had to give her the bad news. She was not amused. She asked me about one in particular." Once he finished laughing he explained, "Hell, I knew this was over anyway, so I told her, 'Yeah, he was the best-tasting of all.' And, you know, he really was, but now she was even less amused." He laughed some more.

As a dog lover, I sided with the commune leader on this one.

After Lee sold me his boat and returned to Chicago to his "quasi legal gambling establishment," he eventually bought another boat. This was a steel-hulled sailboat he found in Alaska. As I recall it was about sixty feet long. He spent a good bit of time and, undoubtedly, a great deal of his money earned at the establishment in Chicago getting the boat shipshape.

Once done, he sailed down the West Coast of the U.S., Mexico and Central America, finally crossing through the Panama Canal. He would send emails about his travels and experiences. I was fortunate enough to be on his list.

Most of the time his emails were very entertaining, describing scrapes with various Coast Guards and government agencies in various banana republics. The common thread always seemed to have as a theme some combination of drink, drugs and women. There was one interesting story concerning a U.S. ex pat who had married a local in one of these countries who was eventually shot by the jealous wife. Lee's friend wanted to keep partying at the bar and the new wife wished to return back to their boat. When the friend did not agree, she went back to the boat and retrieved a pistol, returning to the bar and spraying shots randomly into the bar from outside. Everyone ducked behind the bar and considered the next step. Finally, the new husband said, "I'll go talk to her and settle her down."

The next thing Lee heard after only a couple of words were exchanged was a gunshot and then silence. Lee and the rest went outside to find the girl standing over the man, who had a gunshot wound in his stomach. They loaded the victim into a taxi and took him to the hospital. As the orderlies were rushing him to the operating room, his last words were, "Take care of my dog." He clearly did not know of the care that Lee had given the dogs in Oregon.

Fortunately, he survived, and Lee, true to his word, took care of the dog and boat while the victim recuperated in the hospital. Then, to everyone's annoyance, the wounded husband took back the wife once he got out of the hospital and they moved back on his boat together. Lee said, "We were all really pissed off. I mean, we had visited this guy every day in the hospital and took care of his dog and boat. Then he takes this crazy bitch back."

Occasionally Lee would embark on a political diatribe. As one might imagine, he was not a Republican, but neither was he a Democrat. He is a self-proclaimed anarchist. Lee had worked in Cuba in the 1970s in something he called "The Sugar Cane Brigades". He had a special love for Fidel and reserved a special disregard for anyone who did not love Fidel. (I think he made an exception for me.) This seems to be a characteristic of many ex pats and logic will not intervene. Lee thought Fidel Castro a great man. He was proud of his service to Fidel. My visits to Cuba, on

U.S. government-sanctioned and approved business, led me to believe that the Cuban people would revolt in a heartbeat if they were not living in abject fear and had weapons. But Lee had a different opinion.

Lee and I did not agree on much with respect to politics, but it never made any difference to us. We could share our opinions without rancor, which is more than I can say for many of the ex pats in Merida. He always has a well-thought logic to support his positions.

Lee would come back to Merida from time to time and word got around. You could always find him in Pancho's.

On one trip after I bought his boat, I saw Lee the closest that I had ever seen him to worry. He told me, "You know, Gus, next year I turn sixty-two and I will be eligible for social security. I wonder if I am going to get it?" he asked rhetorically.

"Well, Lee, I don't know but didn't you tell me you had not filed a tax return since the 1970s?"

"Yeah, that's true but I had worked enough up to that point to have qualified."

I have not seen Lee since that conversation and so I don't know the answer to his question. But I have a feeling that Lee is probably receiving at least one social security check under at least one name, real or assumed.

After Lee bought the other boat, the first year he left the boat in Panama and returned to Chicago. While he was in Chicago, I never remember receiving many emails from him. After about a year of "work", he would return to his boat and stay on it for about a year, and the emails would resume. He visited Merida a couple of times after he bought the new boat.

However, on these trips he would leave the boat somewhere down south and fly from there to Merida.

Lee always maintained that his plans were to ultimately arrive in Merida with the new boat. I would joke with him that I would agree to buy the new boat for the same price I had bought *The Blind Pig*. Lee always responded, "Gus, I might sell it to you, but it won't be for that price!"

At some point, I stopped receiving emails from Lee. I was very disappointed. Also, Lee has not been seen in Merida for about three years as of this writing. That is also a disappointment. Given his life and lifestyle, one could conjure up a number of different scenarios running the gamut for where he is and/or what has happened to him. If he is no longer among the living, I know one thing for sure – he died a happy man.[3]

---

3   At the time I originally wrote Lee's story, I thought his death to have been a real possibility. Fortunately, I was mistaken and Lee re-appears in a later chapter.

CHAPTER TWO
The Adventure Begins

My adventure began before I knew it began. I was a university professor and the Director of Graduate Business Studies at the University of Southern Mississippi when approached by the Administrator of the Study Abroad Program. He had already done the ground work and established an itinerary for a Business Program for students in Merida, Mexico. He came to me to essentially chaperone the students to Merida as he knew I spoke Spanish. I had traveled throughout Mexico but had never been to Merida. So, I agreed.

Merida is unlike any other part of Mexico. I was in love with the place instantly. After returning from three weeks there, I knew I would go back. The next summer I was awarded a grant with the government to work for three months in the Yucatan. After those three months I was head over heels in love with Merida, the Yucatan and its people. I had always loved Mexico, and knew I had to find a way to live in Merida.

When I returned to the States after my grant, I began to write some articles on doing business in Mexico in general and the Yucatan in specific. NAFTA had recently passed, and there was a good deal of interest in Mexico. Out of the blue I soon received an email from the president of a manufacturing company, a man named Michael, who was interested in closing his six sewing factories in the United States and moving all of his production to Mexico. He wanted to know if I could help with various issues associated with the move. I jumped at the chance.

Actually I had just married a Mexican woman who was operating a small factory for an American owner. I thought she would be a natural choice to run his new factory.

Over a period of several months Michael and I continued in email contact discussing numerous issues. His large family business that had begun over sixty years prior manufactured uniforms for Federal, State and Local law enforcement agencies in all fifty states and Canada. Finally we made plans to meet in the Miami Airport and fly together to Merida. Since we had never seen one another, we described ourselves and set a meeting place within the terminal. I shall always remember seeing Michael walking down the terminal. He has a distinctive walk and did not look as he had described himself.

We shook hands, and with that both of us embarked on an adventure. Michael liked what he saw. He soon brought his father, the Chairman of the Board of the company for his opinion. I had just gone on sabbatical from the university. It was May, 1999.

They toured Merida and met with government officials. I left them in the hands of the government officials. We met the last day of their trip at 5:00 P.M. in the bar of the Fiesta Americana Hotel, where they were staying. That conversation and image of our surroundings will forever be emblazoned in my mind.

They decided that it would be impossible to do business under the conditions present in the Yucatan. Because Claudia, my wife at the time, knew the sewing business, I leaped into the breach (sometimes I think foolishly) and asked them if I put up the money to start a small factory and prove that it could be done using Claudia to run the operation, would they then agree to buy me out and move their factories to Merida? I remember the immediate response: "I like that idea".

I liked it too, at first. I had no idea what I was getting myself into. While I thought I understood Mexican laws, I really did not. While I thought I understood Mexican culture, I really did not.

I began investing what little money I had based on a handshake. Thank God I was dealing with honest people. Soon, we received a contract. And relatively soon, I ran out of money. My customer began loaning money to the company so that we could continue. There have been many key players in our success, and one of those is Michael. He believed in us and probably stuck with us longer than I would have had our roles been reversed. I am grateful that he maintained his vision for his own company and his trust in our ability.

Things did not go well at first. Our first order of some two hundred pairs of pants took an interminable time to finish. Once shipped, every garment failed the inspection done by the customer's auditors. The entire order was classified as seconds. I was disheartened, to say the least, especially since I was running out of money and would soon have to go into debt. My customer reassured me that this was normal for the first shipment, but that there was no doubt we needed to improve.

The customer's standards are very high. Professionals in law enforcement want to present an image that reflects quality in all dimensions. And the word "uniform" means just that—every garment must look exactly alike in every detail including the number of sewing stitches per inch, for example.

Mexican craftsmanship had a certain stereotypical image in the States. I knew we had to overcome this image through assuring our customer we could prove our ability to reach the required standards and even surpass them. I stressed quality first, production second with our team.

We slowly became better. Now our customer tells us we have the best quality of any of his suppliers. I found out just how high our quality standards were when we subcontracted with a factory that produced high-fashion and very high-priced garments to fulfill some orders that were backlogged. The factory that produced high fashion could not reach our standards. We had to reject their garments and produce them ourselves, despite our backlog.

In these early days, I thought that if we grew to a hundred employees I would consider our operation a success. It never occurred to me that within eight years we would have over five hundred employees.

CHAPTER THREE

The History of Merida and the Odd Ball Ex Pats Who Live There

Merida lays claim to a part of world history that not many know about. It is surmised that the dinosaurs were wiped off the face of the earth by an enormous meteor that struck the earth, changing the climate overnight. There is a huge crater on the sea floor just off the coast of the little fishing village of Chicxulub, Yucatan, about twenty miles from Merida. Scientists believe that the crater is the result of the impact of a huge meteor. It is known as the Chicxulub Crater.

I was told by a relatively important Yucatecan government official that the silicon in the sand on the Yucatecan coast has much more highly conductive properties than normal silicon as a result of the heat that was created when the meteor struck. However, I have since called into question his credibility as he also told me that it was an established fact that the moon was actually a Russian satellite. He followed that up with a rather long and involved story about the subterranean city below New York that is inhabited by some twenty-five thousand lizard men.

Well after the formation of the Chicxulub Crater, the ancient Mayan civilization occupied the Yucatan and other parts of Southern Mexico and Guatamala from around the time of Christ until as late as 1200 A.D. This civilization was extremely advanced and well versed in astronomy. One of the pyramids in Chichen Itza was built in such a fashion that only on the day of the equatorial solstice, as the sun travels across the sky, the side of the pyramid creates a shadow on the steps of the pyramid so that it appears that the serpent carved into the steps is actually moving. I don't think I could accomplish that task with computers, heavy equipment and existing knowledge today.

Merida is the capital of the Yucatan, one of three states located on the Yucatan Peninsula. As the Maya civilization was dissolving and disintegrating, the Spaniards arrived. There was a pre-existing Maya city on the site occupied today by Merida. Francisco de Montejo is credited with founding the modern day city on January 6, 1542.

Montejo ordered the Mayan edifices dismantled and many of the stones were used to construct churches which still stand today. Supposedly, one of these churches, the Cathedral of San Idelfonso, is the oldest cathedral on the American continent. Construction began in 1561.

The State of Yucatan sought independence from Mexico in the early 1840's. Obviously, it was unsuccessful, but the Peninsula was then split into 3 states, including Yucatan, to dissipate power. The other two states are Campeche and Quintana Roo. Chetumal is the capital of Quintana Roo, but the most famous city of that state is Cancun.

The War of the Castes began around 1850 and lasted for about 50 years. This was an uprising led by Mayans who had a very bad plight in those days. The first few years of the war were incredibly bloody. Ultimately, the battles were fewer and fewer in between and the war sort of fizzled out.

At one time, the Yucatan was the residency for many of the world's richest families. This is because an indigenous plant, called hennequin, was used to make rope. This is a plant that looks like a spiny cactus and is a cousin to the agave plant, from which tequila is made. The leaves of the hennequin plant are smashed into a fibrous material that is then dried in the sun. These fibers are subsequently spun together to make rope. The material from which the rope is made is sometimes called hemp or sisal.

The invention of nylon was disastrous for this region. Almost overnight, hemp ropes became obsolete. However, in recent years, sisal has made a comeback in the form of fashionable carpets and rugs.

As a result of the hennequin industry, many fabulous homes were constructed on the hennequin ranches, called haciendas. The Yucatan is littered with these old homes which have gone into disrepair. Nevertheless, it has become fashionable for wealthy foreigners to restore the old haciendas and outbuildings that come with them. Some of these haciendas are used as hotels and spas, and some are part or full-time residences for the owners.

During the heyday of hennequin, many of the rich hacienda owners in the Yucatan found it easier to travel to Europe and the U.S. than the Mecca of Mexico, Mexico City. For this reason the architectural influence of Europe, particularly France, is very strong. Many of the huge mansions that were the city homes for the hacienda owners reflect this European influence. The most spectacular of these homes are located on the central boulevard of the city, Paseo de Montejo.

In the old days, Meridians had a good bit of contact with New Orleans. New Orleans is only six hundred miles due north across the Gulf of Mexico. The contact with the rest of Mexico was limited due to the geographic isolation of Merida. The roads were not particularly good. I am told there was no railroad connecting with Mexico City until the 1950s.

Merida is known for its tranquility and the warmth of the people. Today, Mexicans are fleeing Mexico City and Northern Mexico to come to Merida and its relative tranquility. The city is growing rapidly.

Tourism is also increasing. Merida has the advantage of being located in the midst of many interesting ruins. The city is only twenty miles from the Coast. There are three universities located within Merida and it has been a cultural center since the heyday of hennequin.

Besides the more well-known ruins of Chichen Itza, Uxmal, and Dzibixaltun, there are many other less well-known but also interesting ruins. These include Abala, Mayapan, Acanceh, Cacalchen, Oxkintok and the Grutas de Loltun, among others. Oxkintok has a small building that contains a labyrinth inside.

Other interesting ports besides Progreso are Telchac Puerto, Sisal and Celestun. Sisal was the major port during the hennequin heyday. A small fort still exists at the port of Sisal, although it is very small town with no commercial shipping at this time.

From about October through March, the weather in this corner of paradise is incredibly nice. However, beginning in April, it starts to heat up quickly. May is the hottest month. I remember one Saturday in May a few years ago when the temperature reached 116 degrees (in the sun). I spent the entire afternoon in the pool. But after a time one becomes accustomed to the heat.

Average temperature year-round is reported to be 26 degrees centigrade or about 88 - 89 degrees Farenheit. However, the evenings are nearly always pleasant with a nice breeze coming in off the Gulf of Mexico.

Once the rainy season begins in June, things cool off a bit. The downside is that humidity increases and after the cooling afternoon showers, you get the sensation of being in a steam room. Rains can be torrential. It is not uncommon in the downtown area for water to accumulate and rise above the street curbs. However, the water dissipates fairly quickly. The rainy season ends around November or December. It rains very rarely after December until the next June.

During the dry season, fires in the jungle and low lying growth around Merida become a problem, particularly in May, the height of the dry season. But regardless of dry season or not, smoke wafts through the air often, as the custom of burning trash still seems fairly prevalent.

All in all, Merida is a very nice place to live. It certainly has its disadvantages, as does any city, but the advantages far outweigh the disadvantages. The people, for the most part, are very warm and friendly. The city is quite clean. As mentioned, it is located in the midst of very interesting Mayan ruins and the city government promotes cultural activities, most of them free. On Sundays, downtown Merida is closed and street vendors hawk their goods. Sometimes there are entertainment troupes in the streets. Large numbers of locals and a few tourists stroll the downtown area buying, selling and people-watching.

Carnaval is a local tradition. While not as raucus as New Orleans or Rio, the Paseo de Montejo is packed with fun-loving people watching parades for about 10 days straight.

In short, I have enjoyed Merida and think anyone wanting to travel or live in Mexico would also find Merida enjoyable and interesting. Life in Merida is not always easy, but it is fun.

ODDBALLS IN PARADISE

Ex-pats are odd. At least, that is my conclusion. I conclude that as an ex-pat myself. And its not just those in Mexico. Friends who have lived in other countries say the same about the ex-pat community in other countries. In many respects the ex-pat community here is a microcosm of any other social community in the U.S. or Canada. It is just that the average participants in this social community are nearly all exaggerations in one or several ways in comparison to the average participant in a U.S. or Canadian society.

There has to be a reason why ex-pats are odd. I believe it has to do with a type of self-selection. Each of these individuals, through his own decision-making logic, arrived at the decision to leave his/her country for some reason. I think that the set of reasons manifests a cognitive process that reflects some degree of an inability to fit in with their home country. Despite this, most ex-pats I find to be very interesting—some in good ways and others in less good ways. A few, as in all communities, are boring.

I would categorize ex-pats in Merida into several groups. First, there is the Retired Group. There are retirees who have retired from all interesting thought, as well as professional life. Their hobby seems to be gossip, especially about other ex-pats. Most of them seem to live physically close to each other and not venture far from the circle of ex-pats from which they feed on for their gossip.

There is another group of retirees who are retired but remain intellectually curious. They go to a foreign country for the experience. They are not retired from life at all and often have other homes in other countries. They seem to have been successful in their past professional life. It is probably uncharitable to describe this group as "oddballs." They no doubt did "fit in" in their home country.

Another group of ex-pats are the type that just sort of materialize out of nowhere. It is as if a Jimmy Buffet song just finished playing on the radio about someone moving to a Banana Republic to escape the IRS or a woman and you round a corner and this character begins to strike up a conversation with you. They may be a fugitive, con man, or just a ne'er-do-well. Of course, they are always interesting and I do write about some of them.

The number of entrepreneur wanna-be's is astounding. It seems many of these frustrated be-your-own-boss types arrive with the same thought: that they are going to teach these Mexicans how to do business right. It is clear they arrive with visions of becoming rich quickly by instituting efficiency and cost savings schemes and/or selling something that the market is lacking.

Their approach, more often than not, is *UGLY AMERICAN* and the result is preordained. They see no need in *selling* their ideas nor in taking into consideration deep seated cultural differences that affect the way business is done. They start from the premise that the U.S. economy is the most powerful in the world and so the American Way is The Way and The Answer. Their disgust for Mexican business protocols is barely hidden and their style is "my way or the highway." Often it is these ex-pats who ultimately take the highway.

There are those who are successful entrepreneurs. This is a small group, admittedly. They have open minds, are flexible and persevere—the same traits needed for successful entrepreneurship anywhere. They have an adventurous spirit and interesting life experiences. I write about Bob and Wayne. Their stories are easy to tell and interesting. There are a couple of others that I wanted to write about, but I, unfortunately, was requested not to do so as they want to maintain a low profile. Since I want to maintain their friendship, I am not able to share their experiences.

There are those who come to Paradise in search of romance. It is sort of like one of those internet dating web sites – you have categories of men seeking women, men seeking men, women seeking men, including one type seeking either sex. The locals who enter that scene are almost always looking for someone to throw them a financial life line and pull them into veritable luxury and comfort. There are the inevitable age differences that are sometimes so great as to be grotesque.

Those who come solely for romance are not that interesting. They are one-dimensional and their conversation reflects it. Things usually don't end well for them. A case in point is Frank, who was a retired Navy enlisted man. Frank was about seventy and found a Mexican local, Ruby, who agreed to marry him. Ruby was about thirty-five. Ruby ended up with the house, the furniture, the Mexican bank account, and Frank ended up with a number of legal problems, most of them probably trumped up. It took no more than about two years for the *denoument.* Last I heard, Frank was in Thailand living with an eighteen-year-old girl. I wish him well.

Lastly, there is a group that is a hodge podge and can't really be categorized. Some are sort of latter day hippies. Some are just non-categorizable misfits. All of the ex-pats in this group I am certain I would not have met if I were living in the States. Our paths just never would have crossed due to our personal likes and dislikes. It is at Pancho's I met most of this group, just as I met Lee Richards.

I would have to say that I like this group. Again, I know I would never have met them in the States, so my life has been enriched through their acquaintance in ways it never would have been in the States. My closest friends from this group are Lyman and Cheryl. I don't write about them, as most of what I would have to say about them is too personal to share and I doubt I would do a very good job of capturing their unique essence.

A characteristic that transcends all of the groups is alcoholism. I suspect that the rate of alcoholism is much higher per capita in the ex-pat community than it is in the home country society. I believe most of the cause is due to boredom and I know it is easy to fall into this trap. I, myself, noticed upon arrival my inclinations to go to bars as a type of entertainment. I have the benefit of having to go to work and be lucid and feeling well the next day. Many ex-pats are retired and more easily trapped by alcoholism.

AS I mentioned earlier, there are some places in the world that just seem to attract interesting people. Merida is one of those places. Some of the interesting people come and go over time. For example, Chuck. Chuck spent three tours in Viet Nam as a Navy pilot. He went to law school afterwards and clerked for William Rhenquist at the Supreme Court. As a result, Rhenquist and Chuck became personal friends.

Later, Chuck became a Federal Magistrate. He taught law for awhile and subsequently began consulting for the World Bank on a project to install a western-style legal system in Eastern Europe. Chuck's stories about this experience are interesting and humorous.

Chuck lived in Merida for almost a year and returned to the States, although he comes back to Merida for visits from time to time. He makes cameo appearances in other stories told later in the book.

All types of characters and personalities are attracted. Nearly everyone who comes to Merida falls in love with it. Another interesting friend, who does not want his story told, won his property south of the border in a Boo Ray card game in Louisiana.

There are still more ex-pats that are interesting and fun that I don't write about in detail. These are friends of mine that, besides the people I do write about, you would encounter at Pancho's or at parties given by any of us who live here. They are an interesting cultural mix and I briefly describe some of them below, not in any particular order and I am not using last names.

The amiable Jake is originally from Holland. He moved to Canada at age twenty-one and began to look for ways to make money. Apparently, Jake did fairly well and has now retired early, moved to Merida and begun buying and selling beach property.

The hilariously funny John Lawless is from Great Britain. He has been living in Merida for close to 20 years as a manufacturer's rep for a company based in England. For awhile, John also was a sales rep for a well-known scotch whiskey made in Scotland. As a British citizen, he has no legal barrier to do business with Cuba and so he began selling this scotch in fairly great quantities to the Cuban government. However, once the Cuban government stopped paying for the scotch, John wisely decided to stop selling to them.

Another friend is Peter Munro, a fun-loving Welshman with a Welsh brogue that is very difficult for me to understand. Peter married his Mexican wife about twenty-five years ago. He has spent most of his Mexican professional career working in the ocean shipping business.

Regina is from New York. Almost thirty years ago she married a local artist, Francisco. Regina administers a language school.

Jennifer began a very successful internet real estate business about six years ago. She is originally from England, but became a naturalized U.S. citizen years ago. She had worked for the last twenty years before moving to Merida in the real estate business in San Antonio.

Cactus, whose real name is Lou and who will not be happy that I have divulged this news, is from

Oregon. Cactus retired early about ten years ago. Shortly after his retirement, he had an accident that left him in a wheel chair. I have enormous respect for Cactus for many reasons, not the least of which is that he is more independent in his wheel chair than most people without disability. He has maintained a great, positive attitude that we could all learn from. Shortly after he was injured, he lost his wife of over twenty years to cancer. A couple of years ago Cactus married the beautiful Darlean, a Canadian.

Bob and Jeannie are a very sweet couple originally from Connecticut. They retired early about ten years ago from the insurance industry. Jeannie is the only person Bob ever dated. People sometimes tell me that I must have married everyone I ever dated. While that is an exaggeration, in Bob's case it is a very precise statement.

Brian is a Canadian, a successful computer type who retired early. During the 1970s, Brian was a professional boat racer. He married Astrid, a beautiful Mexican lady who speaks perfect English. That worked out well, as Brian speaks only a smattering of Spanish.

Then there is Jim (a false name I have given him), a Canadian married to a pretty Australian. I have given Jim this name as I was told by a relatively unreliable source that Jim is wanted by the Canadian version of the IRS. I rather doubt it, but it makes a good story.

Giovanni is an Italian who has previously lived in Argentina and the U.S. Prior to moving to Merida, he was a golf pro on a cruise ship. He met Andrea, a pretty Mexican who is an incredible athlete, while on a trip to Merida. He stayed and now they have a company doing real estate and house remodeling.

Jose (pronounced Joe-say) is a Belgian married to Elizabeth, an American. Jose and Elizabeth both have a great sense of humor and are a joy to be around. Jose worked in Europe and Florida doing real estate development for many years. He is now doing the same in Merida.

Corvado is an Italian married to Echey, a Panamanian. Echey is a medical doctor that was schooled in Cuba. Echey is the most beautiful doctor I have ever seen. I call the two of them, Beauty and the Beast.

Admittedly, my description of these groups and individuals may be unfair to some extent and lacking to a great extent. But some flavor, hopefully, has been imparted that reflects the mix of characters that are living in this corner of Paradise. These groups exist in the States, but their effect and coloration of the societal scenery is highly diluted. The self selection that is drawing us together, albeit for different reasons, infuses the entire atmosphere with oddities and odd characters. The high concentration of odd people, and mostly interesting odd, has a mutual and collective effect on one another and the environment in which we interact only serves to compound the oddness. But, again, in a good way for the most part. I sometimes feel as if I am living in a novel co-written by Jimmy Buffet and Elmore Leonard that is being played out on the set of *One Flew Over the Cuckoo's Nest*.

The end result of living life in this context has provided me with a rich and robust experience that could never have been duplicated in the United States or anywhere else on Earth. I am a better person for having lived amongst these Odd Balls in Paradise. I thank each and every one of them for having touched and enriched my life in ways I would never have imagined.

CHAPTER FOUR

J. W. BARNES[4]

---

[4] This story is meant to entertain. The events are actual events that occurred but names and places have been changed in many instances to protect the identity of those involved, but not necessarily their innocence.

Mérida, Yucatán, México – July 4, 2004.

Once J.W.Barnes stopped talking in his loud and raspy voice, raucous laughter followed. As always, J.W.was the life of the party. J.W.was a former Navy pilot and wanted to celebrate American Independence Day with other expatriates living in Merida and some Mexican friends.

It was a hot, but beautiful, day in the Yucatan. We were all gathered at J.W.'s house right around the corner from the bullring. The house was fairly modest for a successful businessman, but comfortable nonetheless. There were Mexicans, Americans and Canadians, a true NAFTA mix.

I had arrived early at his request to help put up the shade tent between the patio where the hamburgers would be grilled and the pool. J.W. hired bartenders and waiters for the occasion. They were dressed in clean, pressed white shirts and black pants. After getting everything ready for the guests, we tested the bartender's expertise before the others arrived. The rum was good, the cokes cold, and the limes fresh – we were having Cuba Libres, which translates to "a free Cuba," or as they say in Havana when Fidel is not listening, *una mentira* (a lie).

Once the other guests began arriving, J.W. wasted no time in encouraging the ladies to don their bikinis and take a dip. His encouraging words were for naught. Despite the heat and the inviting coolness of the water, not a single lady accepted the invitation.

I had not known J.W. for very long. As the afternoon progressed into early evening, I noticed he was drinking in prodigious quantities. At some point he eased into a state of inebriation. I was somewhat surprised as my experience with successful people is that the discipline that has made them successful works in their favour in other areas of their life most of the time. However, there is no question that he remained entertaining. I assumed he was just letting his hair down. Upon reflection, I should have noticed that he really did lack discipline, although he hid that fault well.

✼

Havana, Cuba September 24, 1997

John W. Bailey was seated in at a conference table in the offices of Carlos Lage, a high-level Cuban government official. Lage's official title was First Vice President and Economic Minister. To most of the outside world Raul Castro, brother of Fidel, is considered to be Fidel's right-hand man. However, many of those in the know believe that Sr. Lage may really be Fidel's right-hand man and one of the more likely to succeed as the next *Lider Maximo* in Cuba.

Bailey was extremely satisfied. He had just signed a deal with the Cuban government to develop a free trade zone in the area around the port of Mariel. The other signatory to the Letter of Intent was Hector

Gonzalez Perez, representing Almacenes Universales, S. A. While presumably a private company, Bailey knew that in Cuba all businesses are State-owned.

The Letter of Intent outlined plans for development of the port, leasing port facilities, charging for labor and services, as well as maintenance of the seaport, airport, land, and warehouses. Also included in the Letter of Intent were plans to establish the Port of Mariel as a *Zona Franca*, or Free Trade Zone. In the process, Bailey would work with the Cuban government to modernize the facilities of the port. Mariel, Cuba is just south of Key West about 100 miles and is probably best known to Americans as the port of embarkation for Cuban refugees that the Carter Administration accepted in the 1970s. Included in the supposed political refugees were criminals and the mentally insane. Fidel was relieved of the cost of housing and feeding these unproductive citizens; this cost was transferred to U.S. citizens. Fidel had to have been very satisfied with himself for this scam.

Bailey signed the agreement in his position as CEO of Port Development International Holdings, Ltd. As part of the agreement, Port Development International was to invest approximately one million dollars and to seek additional foreign investors. He knew that once Cuba was open to U.S. trade there would be a flood of business, products, and investment. The Port of Mariel was perfectly positioned geographically to take advantage of this trade. Presumably, once Fidel was out of the picture a wave of investment would begin. At about age seventy, Fidel's tenure and hold on the country could not continue for much longer.

Port Development International would be strategically positioned to take full advantage of the situation. The development would be done by Port Development International and in the process Bailey would be making business and professional contacts with foreigners interested in investing in Cuba. At the same time, he would be solidifying his connections within the Cuban government. Therefore, he would probably be the most well-connected foreigner in Cuba and would profit immensely once U.S. sanctions were lifted.

It was a good plan. And really, it was quite a coup. Not everyone could have pulled this agreement off, much less an American. After all, it is illegal for Americans to do business in Cuba. Later the law was amended to allow U.S. government-sanctioned transactions of a humanitarian nature by U.S. citizens, including sales of limited products. These limited products are essentially restricted to food and medical supplies.

However, Bailey believed he had found a loop hole in the existing law. If the expenses of doing business were borne by a non-U.S. host, that is, a foreign country or foreign corporation, then the operation would not be in violation of U.S. laws. He was justifiably satisfied with the work he had done.

Everyone agreed I knew J.W. better than anyone else in Merida. It is true that J.W. and I were the best of friends. We hit it off right from the start. He seemed to have a great work ethic, was serious, and responsible. He had a great sense of humour and was always entertaining in social settings. Most days we spoke and/or saw one another several times a day. We became business partners for a period of time. I think, therefore, I am best-placed to tell his story.

We met through a mutual friend in Merida. My friend, Chuck, was a former Navy pilot. He and J.W. had that in common. Chuck was a retired lawyer and a former judge. He had been a consultant for the World Bank and was in Merida for an extended vacation.

Chuck is a bright and forthright guy with whom I have had many philosophical and political conversations. We mostly agreed with one another about politics and philosophy. Chuck was humorously self-deprecating especially about his Vietnam experiences and service for the government after Vietnam. I had great respect for him as a person and respected his judgement. He introduced me to J.W., describing him as a "good guy." Shortly after the introduction, Chuck returned to the U.S.

Before I was actually introduced to J.W., Chuck told me that J.W. had an unfortunate disagreement with his housekeeper several months prior. The disagreement had resulted in J.W.'s throat being slashed on both sides with a razor blade as well as a long gash along the rib cage on his left side. It was amazing that J.W. survived. He did receive several hundred stitches.

Chuck and I both commented that it is startling that a Yucatecan housekeeper could react that strongly and aggressively. Yucatecans, for the most part, are a pretty even-tempered group. What could possibly have caused this, we both wondered?

Once J.W. and I became close friends, he indicated the slashing had actually been done by a girlfriend who took his decision to break up a little hard, to say the least. That made a little more sense, but only a little bit, and still seemed an awfully harsh reaction. People who I met later who were called to the hospital that night by J.W. referred vaguely to still other sets of facts, but more on that later.

J.W. was a patriot. On Veterans Day he always sent out emails speaking to the meaning of Veterans Day and how much we should give thanks and honor to those who had died in defense of our freedom. Of course, we all agreed, and this seemed perfectly in character for J.W. He often regaled us with humorous Navy jet fighter pilot stories. He had flown Vigilantes while in the Navy.

He described harrowing experiences of landing on the moving deck of an aircraft carrier while at sea. He explained that the Vigilante had been initially designed as a fighter-bomber. His job, however, had been to fly photo reconnaissance missions over Cuba using a Vigilante specially retro-fitted for this purpose.

Once he showed me once a photo of a Vigilante in flight with him in it as the pilot. I could only see the pilot in silhouette. He explained the photo was taken by a Cuban pilot in a MIG while in flight over Cuba; the MIG was monitoring his flight. The call letters of the Vigilante were clearly visible, and he said this was his plane. He mentioned that by coincidence he later met this Cuban pilot, and they became friends. The photo was signed by "Eddie," as I recall. It was addressed to "John" with a handwritten reference to a flight over Cuba. I noted that some people called him "John," instead of "J.W."

On the anniversary of September 11, J.W. wanted to celebrate the memory of those who perished on that fateful day. He was from New York originally, and this was evident in his accent. He said he had a number of close friends who died in the World Trade Center. He always seemed to be a generous type and said he had contributed a significant sum to a fund set up for the surviving children of his friends who died in the WTC.

His September 11 party was typical J.W. The booze was flowing freely. J.W. grilled fajitas, his favorite outdoor meal. All had a great time, and J.W. was his usual entertaining self.

J.W. told me had three children, and, unhappily, he had divorced. Apparently, he caught his wife in an uncompromising position with a male stripper. This, he said, was the last straw. He said she had been acting strangely prior to that point, and he also caught her taking illicit drugs. He claimed to have been devastated by the divorce.

I mentioned that he must have wanted to fight for the custody of his kids under these circumstances. He said, no, that it was really better for his kids to grow up with their mother. He was a busy and successful entrepreneur who travelled often and did not believe that would be good for the kids if he was constantly travelling internationally. Without any fight, he had given his ex-spouse his expensive home so that his kids had a comfortable and pleasant home to grow up in. Also, while not happy about having to pay some $6,000 to his wife in monthly child support and alimony, he wanted his kids to be well-cared for. He made it clear he was happy to make these financial sacrifices for his kids.

With respect to his children, he was sad, obviously, that he was not able to see them much with his living out of the country and working so hard in his ventures. Nevertheless, he explained that every other Christmas he had visitation rights and spent a great deal of quality time with them. Certainly, one Christmas he did leave and told us he picked them up in Georgia at his wife's home and flew them to New York to be with his mother, the children's grandmother.

After J.W. told me the story about the kids, I told him, "J.W., I haven't noticed any photos of the kids in your house."

He said, "Yeah, of course, I've got photos of the kids. I just don't display them in the living areas of the house. I keep them in the bedroom. I mean I really feel like that is kind of private." I thought the response a little strange since most people liked to brag about their kids, but I accepted it.

He spoke most often of the oldest son, Stephen. When I first met J.W., Stephen was in boarding school in Switzerland. This was quite costly, but J.W. thought it worth the money. At some point over the next couple of years, J.W. informed us all that Stephen had graduated, returned to Georgia, and was accepted into an Ivy League school, Princeton, I believe. J.W. was very proud. For having done so well, J.W. bought his son a new BMW Z4 sports car.

Nassau Bahamas November 7, 1997

John Bailey was travelling with his friend, Alan Wilson, another U.S. citizen, from Havana to Nassau. The two were exhilarated about the possibilities of the port deal that Bailey had signed in his capacity as

CEO of Port Development International. They were aboard a Cuban commercial airliner.

Bailey, a pilot himself, was joking with his friend about the flight capabilities of the airliner. It was an old Russian-built airliner and not in very good shape. Both travellers felt it was something of an adventure. The flight landed without incident, thankfully, in Nassau.

Under federal statues, Cuba is considered an enemy of the United States. U.S. Customs is charged with the responsibility of enforcing the Trading With the Enemy Act. In addition to that U.S. Customs Service has the responsibility to enforce laws and regulations concerning violations of the Cuban Asset Control Regulations put in place by the Office of Foreign Assets Control (OFAC) office, which is part of the U.S. Department of Treasury. OFAC does issue travel licenses to those individuals who are engaged in U.S. government-sanctioned business with Cuba; it is unlawful for a U.S. citizen to travel to Cuba without an OFAC-issued travel license.

For these reasons Customs officers were interested in any U.S. citizen arriving from Cuba. When Bailey and Wilson entered the U.S. Customs pre-clearance facility, they were questioned about the purpose of their trip. Both Bailey and Wilson claimed the purpose of the trip was to attend an International Trade Show in Havana. While Bailey did not have with him a travel license issued by OFAC, he apparently indicated he was travelling legally to Cuba.

The explanation was accepted by Customs agents, but both individuals and their belongings were searched. Bailey had in his possession various documents indicating that the real purpose of his trip to Cuba was to negotiate a contract to develop a seaport and airport at Mariel, Cuba. These documents included a signed Letter of Intent and a construction timetable.

Bailey and Wilson were released to continue their trip with a final destination of Augusta, Georgia. However, OFAC was contacted by Customs to determine the status of Bailey's travel license. OFAC indicated that Bailey had received no U.S. government permission to travel to Cuba, nor any license permitting authorized business dealings with the Cuban government or Cuban nationals. As a result, OFAC requested that Customs begin an investigation.

※

February 2, 1998 Augusta, Georgia

As a result of OFAC's request of the Customs Department to investigate John Bailey, Customs officers obtained an appointment with Bailey and his attorney. Bailey's residence and business offices were located in Augusta. Therefore, the Atlanta office of U.S. Customs was assigned the case. Two Customs agents met with Bailey and his attorney.

Once down to business, the two Customs agents explained the purpose of the visit was to make sure there were no misunderstandings concerning U.S. laws and the embargo of Cuba established by Congress almost 40 years prior. The Cuban Assets Control Regulations were explained to Bailey. The agents explained in no uncertain terms that it was illegal to travel to Cuba without a license. They also mentioned that it was illegal to do business or even attempt to do business without a license. They specifically explained that it was illegal to enter into any type of business transactions with Cuban officials or Cuban nationals. To make sure that Bailey understood, they gave him a pamphlet produced by OFAC explaining all of this in detail so that he would be able to read and analyze the law at his leisure.

Bailey was asked if he understood. He responded he did. He was asked if he was previously aware of the embargo of Cuba. He responded he was. He was asked if he had a license or any authorization to travel and/or do business in Cuba. He responded that he did not have any license regarding travel or business in Cuba.

He was asked if he had a copy of the OFAC Regulations on travel and doing business in Cuba. He said he had a copy.

The Customs agents seemed satisfied that they had made their point. Then, Bailey voluntarily offered his reasoning as to why he had travelled to Cuba and also contracted with Cuban government officials to build the seaport. Bailey stated that it was his understanding that if he spent no money in Cuba and if all his expenses were paid by a host or host corporation that he could travel to Cuba and remain within the laws of the United States.

The agents did not seem impressed with his rather specious reasoning. The agents asked Bailey, "Who or what is the host paying your expenses in Cuba?"

Bailey responded, "Port Development International Holdings Ltd, a corporation registered in the Cayman Islands, a country which has no prohibition against doing business with Cuba."

They asked Bailey, "What is your relationship with this Cayman Islands corporation?"

He responded, "I am on the Board of Directors, and I also work for that corporation doing trading and development consulting".

In their investigation the agents had discovered that Bailey was doing business in offices in Augusta in the name of Port Development International Inc. "What is your relationship to a corporation called Port Development International, Incorporated?"

Bailey responded, "I am the sole corporate officer of this company; it is a U.S. registered corporation." Bailey continued in his defense of his travel to Cuba stating, "Even if I did enter into a business deal with a Cuban national and even though my signature is on this Letter of Intent and it is in English, a deal has not been consummated." He continued, "I have not entered into any business transaction with the Cuban government or any Cuban national."

The agents were somewhat stunned at his denial of what appeared to be very obvious facts. After all, it was his signature on a letter of intent found in his possession. The agents stated, "Mr. Bailey, a letter of intent describes *intentions*, it is true, but it seems more than clear that you intended to consummate a deal if you have not already done so. You have actually broken the law just by signing a letter of intent, regardless of your actual intentions." The agents stated in no uncertain terms, "Mr. Bailey, business dealings with any Cuban national or Cuban official is illegal, including the Letter of Intent that you and a Cuban national signed." When the agents left the meeting, they were certain that their point had been made and understood.

J.W. had the ability to pay for foreign boarding schools, Princeton, and fancy cars for his teenaged children because he had been quite successful in business. He had been a bank executive in New York. He had done well and when the bank was bought out he had a golden parachute that enabled him to retire to Atlanta, Georgia at age 36.

However, he soon grew tired of early retirement. He began to look for something to do that was entrepreneurial.

His first venture was quite ingenious. He contracted with the U.S. Postal Service to buy their old Jeep mail vehicles. The condition to get the contract was that he had to buy each one that they de-commissioned. However, he only paid $600 for each one.

He then re-conditioned each vehicle and was allowed under some statute to give the vehicle a new Vehicle Identification Number and sell as new. He sold the vehicles to rent car agencies in the Caribbean and called them Fun Cruisers. He also sold one to Burt Reynolds that Burt used on his ranch in Georgia.

His re-conditioning plant was located in Georgia and, as he explained it, he made a deal with the prison system to hire prisoners for low wages. He claimed they did good work, and he certainly had some interesting stories to tell about them.

The Fun Cruiser business did exceedingly well according to J.W. Nevertheless, at some point he grew tired of it and no longer went after the contract from the Postal Service, but moved on to exporting used U.S.-made cars to Europe.

J.W. indicated that there was quite a demand in Europe for certain U.S.-made cars. He started a business to match European buyers to used American-made cars. Apparently the U.S. sports cars were the most in demand, such as the Corvette. Again, he apparently did well.

He also related the story of the sale of medical equipment to the Cuban government as one of his entrepreneurial forays. He explained it is normally illegal for Americans to do business with the Cuban government, but there are exceptions, medical equipment being one. This was another success story as he indicated the Cuban government paid top dollar for these kinds of things.

I had, by accident, the possibility of selling chickens to the Cuban government. My friend Chuck, who originally introduced me to J.W., had described him as a man who had done business in Cuba and had substantial contacts there. This was my initial purpose for getting to know J.W.

The business I was interested in starting with Cuba was totally legal and sanctioned by the U.S. government. I had a travel license issued by the Office of Foreign Assets Control of the U.S. Treasury Department granting U.S. government permission to travel to Cuba for the purpose of negotiating a contract. I had a potential supplier from the U.S. I also had an export license issued by the U.S. government for this purpose.

J.W. said that he could help from the Cuban side, which is where I needed assistance. His consulting company, he said, with offices located in the Cayman Islands, and was actually representing a number of other U.S. companies currently doing business legally in Cuba.

Specifically, he represented shipping agencies and labs that did work for the Cuban government on

U.S. soil in conjunction with legal sales to the Cuban government. He further explained that he received commissions on the shipments made to Cuba under legally sanctioned sales made by large multinational companies such as Con-Agra and ADM. He actually showed me a spreadsheet indicating ships, products, tonnage, and value of shipments. There was a column showing some fairly modest commissions that were due him. The amount due was paid by shipping agencies in the states. I also saw various emails from these two shipping agencies and reports on ships underway between New Orleans and Havana. He explained that this representation gave him access to high-level government offices in Cuba.

I had the adventurous urge to do business in Cuba so I signed a contract with J.W. He explained that he still had people working for him in Cuba, but that his personal involvement now was practically nil. He made it clear that he would go to Cuba with me, but that his employees were more than capable of handling everything.

J.W. was living in Merida because he had purchased a well-known U.S. based hamburger franchise for all of Mexico and Merida would be the first market of entry for the franchise. He developed an upscale shopping center in the north part of town for the location of the first franchise restaurant. The second he placed downtown.

Both stores, he said, set records for the company in terms of initial sales. He formed a corporation with his two Mexican partners who he had known from previous ventures in Mexico. The two were brothers-in-law of one another. Alberto was really the more successful of the two since he owned a

Chrysler dealership. His brother-in-law Freddy was sort of tagging along on Alberto's coat tails as J.W. explained it. About fifteen years previously the three had a rent car agency with offices in Cancun and Merida. It had been successful and was sold, but the three partners had remained in contact.

J.W. explained that he had put the franchise deal together, including financing from the U.S. The three partners formed the Mexican corporation, Trifecta. After I got to know J.W., he levelled with me. His Mexican partners, Alberto and Fredy, screwed him. Each had 33% of the company and the two Mexicans, who had controlling interests between them, decided to transfer the assets of the franchise from Trifecta to another corporation owned only by them. J.W. was embarrassed that he had put himself in such a vulnerable position, but he had trusted them implicitly after years of doing business together and explained he had never expected anything like this.

He had instigated litigation against Alberto and Fredy. I know a couple of times associates of J.W. flew into Merida to meet with lawyers. I never met any of these associates, but according to J.W. one of the participants at the meetings was an individual named "Anthony" who J.W. said was his cousin. Anthony is a lawyer and ran what was left of J.W.'s grandfather's business investments.

J.W.'s grandfather, he said, was Vito Genovese, the infamous Mafia Don. He explained he wanted nothing to do with this business and that while he loved his family, he wanted no part of its business. His last name was Barnes because his father, of English descent, had married the daughter of Vito,

Mary, his mother. In New York, J.W.'s dad had been a fundraiser and not directly associated with the Mob, but had benefited from the family ties. I had always thought that the Mafia did not marry outside parties. At any rate, J.W. explained that Anthony was plenty mad at Alberto and Freddy and that he would eventually frighten them into settling the lawsuit.

By this time, I had been to Cuba and met a couple of Cuban nationals who worked for J.W. in Cuba. In turn, they had introduced me to a high level Cuban government official in the process of my pursuit of a chicken contract. Therefore, I concluded that the Cuban situation as he had represented it to me was real. And I had confirmed that his contacts were high-level and real.

Soon J.W. and I decided to go into business together in Merida. We enjoyed one another's sense of humor and had fun together in social settings. I respected his business acumen based on the stories he told about his own business successes. The business logic he expressed in explaining what he had done was impeccable. One particular cantina in Merida, The Bull, was very entertaining and had become sort of a meeting place. We decided to do a cantina ourselves; it would be a small investment and we would have a good time without much risk.

I explained, "J.W., I want to be clear on this. My involvement will be solely as a passive investor. I am not going to do this if you are not going to agree to be the operational partner, that is, the manager of the business."

He responded, "Don't worry, Gus. I am bored stiff and need something to do other than just hang around the pool all day. Look, my Cuban and Cayman offices are running on auto pilot. Through email or phone once or twice a day I can take care of my other businesses. Running a cantina will be a blast."

I put a limit on the amount I wanted to invest. J.W. said, "Fine, my friend Keith will want in as a partner, too."

"Great," I said, "the more the merrier. Who is Keith?"

"Keith," J.W. explained, "is a very successful psychiatrist and a really good friend in Georgia. He's making a fortune through his business that receiving Medicare funds for providing psychiatric and home care services. Hell, he would love a lark like this."

Keith came down to Merida, and we all formed a corporation. I suggested we give 1% to a Mexican friend, Gabriel, just to have a Mexican shareholder. They all thought it a good idea. However, J.W. said, "You know I can't really have my name listed as a stockholder until I get this thing with Trifecta cleared up. I don't want them knowing anything about my business."

I thought that made some sense and said I did not really care as long as all understood my investment was limited and passive. "No problem," J.W. explained, "I will actually pay Keith for my share and just put the stock in Keith's name."

We formed Operadora Coyote Feo (Coyote Ugly). The idea was to make the bar a type of Coyote Ugly cantina as nothing of the sort existed in Merida. We began looking for a place to remodel and negotiating with a brewery to handle their products.

However, it was at about this time in our relationship that I began to become disenchanted with J.W. and began to note discrepancies in some stories.

I also noticed that J.W. had a habit of speaking badly of mutual friends, but only behind their backs. Obviously, if he was speaking ill of them to me, he was likely saying very uncharitable things about me to them.

Furthermore, I had recently overheard him at social gatherings explaining his business in Cuba. At first, I thought I had not heard correctly. But I overheard the story again later. Basically, he was implying that the ships for which I knew he was simply receiving modest commissions for expediting paperwork going between the U.S. and Cuba were ships that he owned. I did not say anything as I was really eavesdropping on a conversation and not directly involved. I heard others repeat the story about J.W. and by then there were no longer insinuations. The general view was that J.W. was an Aristotle Onassis-type wheeler dealer in the free-for-all world of shipping and international trade. He had become a legend in Merida. Perhaps, wrongly I decided not to burst anyone's bubble about J.W.

I decided I needed to begin to distance myself, especially after hearing about all of his international shipping successes, which were myths. Besides, shortly thereafter J.W. essentially dropped the ball on negotiations with the brewery. I just assumed the deal was dead and quit asking about it. I didn't mind losing a small investment just to start a Mexican corporation that would be inactive. I did not realize how active it was to become.

꧁꧂

Port of Mariel, Cuba March 25, 1998

Construction on the development of the seaport at Mariel continued. Despite the Customs agents' warnings, John Bailey was determined to follow through on this project. The financial rewards would be too high. The Customs agents who had warned him not to follow through about six weeks ago were not lawyers but bureaucrats. John believed that bureaucrats lacked imagination. That, in his view, was why they were bureaucrats.

Bailey, on the other hand, was a creative entrepreneur who was going to be rich and famous. He was certain his loophole in the law would work for him if he was ever arrested. Besides, he was looking to get some heavy hitters involved. With these moguls on board, it would be too hot a topic for the bureaucrats. Furthermore, unknown to the Customs agents, he already had a top U.S. Department of Commerce official on board for the project. This individual's contacts in the U.S. government would be the strategy to get others on board. Once done, no bureaucrat was going to be able to stop this deal.

Accordingly, the project was going forth. On this day, an engineering firm was present in Mariel to make an inspection in accordance with the terms agreed upon in the contract. Bailey received a certificate of inspection indicating that the structural repairs and improvements of the docks at Mariel were sound and according to specs. The certificate also covered hydro-technical work being performed. Pictures supporting the conclusions of the engineering firm were provided to Bailey.

Around this time there was an official ceremony of the opening of the Free Trade Zone at Mariel as covered in the Letter of Intent. Pictures were taken including one of John with Carlos Lage, First Vice President and Economic Minister of Cuba.

These photos would give John more credibility with potential investors.

Bailey began to develop a prospectus to present to prospective investors. This was going to be a huge undertaking requiring millions of dollars.

Bailey had committed to invest in this venture at least one million dollars of his own money. The problem was that Bailey had suffered some financial setbacks. He could not let that fact get in the way of this deal – it had too much potential. He had a solution. He could "borrow" the money from his childrens' trust funds. He would be able to pay it back once the project got off the ground.

John was under a lot of financial pressure. He believed divorce was part of his future. He could not lose face on this project with the Cubans due to a lack of personal funds. Neither could he lose the opportunity to make millions. He needed sole control of his kids' money. That meant simply moving it offshore. He already had the Cayman corporation, and the Cayman Islands were well known for their banking secrecy.

Atlanta, Georgia November 3, 1998

Things continued to go downhill for John. There was no money coming in. He had moved all his money, including his children's money, offshore. For all intents and purposes, his marriage was over, although at this time neither party had filed for divorce. On the positive side, he felt he was ready to turn the corner and to finalize his plan to solve the problems with pressure about money.

He filed for bankruptcy. He did not want to have to pay child support or alimony. These added expenses would create too much of a problem for his plans to make millions in Cuba. Of course, he was not bankrupt. But *within the United States he was.* He had many more debts than assets *located within the U.S.* Therefore, by his own reasoning he was bankrupt within the U.S. and that is where he was filing for bankruptcy. And who would be the wiser? Certainly not his wife since she was uneducated about the ways of business and would not be able to keep up with his sophisticated manuverings.

Atlanta, Georgia December 4, 1998

A confidential source contacted U.S. Customs with regard to a transaction that was to take place in Cuba involving a John W. Bailey. The source was sure the transaction was illegal under U.S. law. According to this source, Bailey wanted to contract with him as a marine drilling and dredging consultant to assist Bailey in developing the seaport at Mariel, Cuba. The source went on to specify that once the dredging was complete that Bailey was planning a refuelling service for vessels crossing the Georgia straits at the Port of Mariel.

Agents in the Customs Service were somewhat sceptical. After all, it had been made abundantly clear to Bailey almost a year ago that his intended transactions in Cuba were illegal. Furthermore, Bailey, although using very specious reasoning, had appeared to back off from the transaction and claim that no deal had been consummated. Customs agents were sure that Bailey had the picture back in the February meeting with his lawyer and were sure his lawyer had made it clear that to pursue the deal he would be risking some serious legal trouble.

Nevertheless, the Customs agents felt it necessary to follow up on the source's information. A plan was developed by the agents to determine what was really in Bailey's mind.

Augusta, Georgia, December 8, 1998

U.S. Customs agents asked the confidential source to obtain a meeting with Bailey. This individual was surreptitiously wired for the purpose of recording the meeting. Bailey was under the impression that the confidential source was interested in investing with him and/or performing professional services in assisting with the port development.

Accordingly, an appointment was made, and the source met in Bailey's offices in Augusta. The conversation was monitored and recorded by two U.S. Customs agents, Michael Simpson and Alvaro Sanchez.

The meeting began at about 10 A.M. During the meeting, Bailey indicated what he had done to negotiate the deal. He was clearly pleased with his expertise in negotiating. The land, he explained, had been leased from Cuban nationals and described the deal in some detail including what the profitability would be. Included in the project were the plans for a Free Trade Zone, which would attract investment to the development, Bailey said.

John believed the source had the expertise and contacts needed to take the deal to the next phase.

He asked the source for help in development and financing of the project. He told the source that he had invested 920,000 dollars of his own money, but that he would need additional investors.

Bailey was selling the project as a once-in-a-lifetime opportunity. He felt the source could not go wrong if he invested with him. He provided a number of documents to this individual in an effort to sell the investment. These documents included a prospectus and signed copies of Letters of Intent in both Spanish and English. John was very enthusiastic and convincing.

During the meeting, Bailey was asked by the source what method of transportation he used to go to Cuba as he knew it was difficult to get to Cuba legally from the U.S. Bailey responded that it was not a problem. He would go one of two ways. If he flew commercially he would fly first to Cancun, Mexico and then board a flight to Havana. The other way was to fly to the Bahamas and then from the Bahamas to Cuba using private aircraft.

The source left the meeting without making a commitment except to consider participating. Later that day he met with the Customs agents who had been recording the conversation.

※

I had introduced J.W. to quite a few people, mostly ex-pats. One of those was Mike. Mike had come to Merida to develop a hostel. He called it The Nido. Mike was in his early sixties and had retired from advertising. He had his own agency as well as an advertising school, but sold them to move to Merida and semi-retire.

The Nido did fairly well at first. When it opened for business, there had only been one other hostel in Merida. Mike wanted to move to Cancun and start another hostel, The Cancun Nido. Mike's strategy was based on the synergy of two hostels – both would feed off the other; if the Merida guests had a good experience and if they were planning on visiting Cancun they would be inclined to stay at the Cancun Nido and vice versa. It was a strategy that made good business sense.

However, business began to drop off in Merida after Mike moved to Cancun to start The Cancun Nido. Mike was considering closing the Merida Nido and selling the property. J.W. told Mike that he could operate it and turn it around and wanted to do so really as a lark. Mike knew of J.W.'s entrepreneurial successes and agreed to basically give J.W. free reign.

J.W. took over operations of the Merida Nido around February of 2005. He made all kinds of management changes. According to J.W., the Nido turned around under his guidance. For the first time, he claimed, The Nido Merida was making money.

Besides that, J.W. was really enjoying himself as the entertaining host and owner of The Nido, as he described himself to the guests. I told J.W. that he had found his niche – he was fantastic at making people feel at home, and he ensured everyone had a good time. Clearly, he was also having a good time. He often had barbeques at the hostel for the guests. He was a great host. J.W. was very charming, with an engaging sense of humor; everyone had fun when J.W. was around.

As part of the entertainment he provided, he would sometimes bring guests over to my house.

While this was always a diversion, I noticed that J.W. was getting drunk at each of these occasions. There were a couple of instances when he left with guests so inebriated he was barely able to walk. I insisted the guests drive his car. This was obvious confirmation that J.W. was not at all a disciplined person.

He developed a plan to actually buy the building from Mike in which The Nido was operated. A contract was signed for the purchase, and J.W. was to operate the business through the corporation that we had established with Keith, Operadora Coyote Feo (OCF).

When I discovered this was his plan, I told J.W. that I had not been consulted on this as a stockholder of OCF and that I wanted J.W. or Keith to buy my 30%. I explained if they wanted to do this venture I wished them luck, but I would not participate and wanted no further legal interest in OCF. J.W. agreed that he or Keith would buy my stock.

It was when J.W. and Keith were buying Mike's property that J.W. paid back the loan I made him. He was five months late. J.W. seemed very humbled and appreciative of what I had done for him.

The manager of The Nido was J.W.'s live-in girlfriend, Lola. Lola did not speak much English. Lola had a daughter that was about 10 years old. J.W. was a good surrogate father to the daughter, Angela.

The relationship between Lola and J.W. was stormy to say the least. This also made for difficult times at The Nido and awkward moments in front of the guests.

I remember once J.W. called and wanted to borrow a padlock. I said sure and asked why. He indicated there had been another break-up with Lola, and he wanted to ensure she did not have entrance to the house that the two of them rented. He described an enraged Lola who was screaming at the top of her lungs and ran out of the house with Angela threatening to come back and destroy everything.

Actually, J.W. barely spoke Spanish so I really don't know how they communicated or how he would have understood threats that she supposedly made. He did understand how badly he had upset her on one occasion, however. He called wanting a place to stay saying that the police were at his house. Lola had called them, he said, claiming that he had hit her. The police had asked him to leave. While he never denied that he had been physical with Lola, I do not believe he would have hit her.

At any rate, J.W. and I went out that night with another acquaintance of mine, a fellow named Sam who was a partner of a very expensive boutique hotel. J.W. and Sam kept drinking after I went home, and Sam offered a free room for J.W. at the hotel instead of staying at my place. J.W. accepted, and I was more than happy with this solution.

J.W. always had his ear to the ground for business opportunities. However, I no longer introduced J.W. to friends, particularly those who were in business as I did not want other friends in Merida thinking that I was recommending or vouching for J.W. in any way. But in the case of Sam it was too late since I had already introduced the two.

Sam had been trying to put a deal together on the Caribbean Coast of the Yucatan near Mahajual as a companion project to the boutique hotel he and his partner had in Merida. He explained the project to J.W., and J.W. became interested. J.W. insinuated to Sam that he had deep pockets of his own.

Sam's partner, Frank, had plenty of capital. Frank lived in Los Angeles and was quite successful as the manager of well-known rock musicians. The concept of the project that Sam and Frank wanted to complete was an ultra exclusive hotel/villas that would rent for maybe a thousand dollars a night on the Caribbean Coast of Mexico. Sam indicated there were hotels in Cancun charging $750 a night, but this was in the middle of thousands of people; in Mahajual, there would be the added benefit of total seclusion.

I thought it a little extravagant, but I did not run with the Hollywood crowd and surely did not understand this market. They were looking for investors. J.W. with his family connections was the guy they needed, or at least this is the idea he sold them. J.W. wanted to do the project through OCF.

Frank was travelling fairly often to Merida from Los Angeles. He met J.W. and was charmed by his sense of humor and apparent business acumen. I knew they spent a good deal of time together, and J.W. mentioned that Frank agreed that J.W. should be the managing partner, not Sam.

J.W. had taken the Mahajual project and begun to run with it. To J.W.'s credit, he discovered that the land that Sam and Frank were going to buy was actually not owned by the "seller." The "seller" was a Mexican who was leading Sam around by the nose, according to J.W. J.W. found better land. By now, at least as he described it to me, he was in control of the project, as he described Sam as incompetent. He had made the same comment about Mike who had owned the Nido. Again, it was J.W.'s entrepreneurial expertise that had saved the Nido from assured demise.

J.W. went to a lawyer to get a contract written between OCF, now managed by him, Keith, and Frank. The contract was to formalize the legal agreement to purchase land and each partners' rights and obligations. Also, Frank was going to buy stock in OCF, which would be the entity to own and operate the hotel.

J.W. indicated things were progressing quite well with respect to finalizing the purchase of the land and the contract with Sam and Frank. They were all going to make a fortune, he said. Then one day J.W. received a call from Sam saying that Frank had decided not to invest in the project. I asked J.W. "why?" J.W. responded that they would not give a reason other than they had decided not to go forward at this time. This was totally out of the blue and unexpected by J.W. I had always had a feeling that the deal would go sour at some point, knowing J.W. I remember thinking they must have found out something about J.W. and decided against it. Later I discovered they did find out something, but it was not about J.W.

This rejection did not stop J.W. I have to give that to the man. He was focused on getting this deal done, one way or another. He kept after it. I remember he found two other guys who were going to help him. One was an older guy who I never met but had much experience in developing properties for hotels. But at some point J.W. stopped mentioning both guys, so I guess they disappeared off the radar scope as well.

At social gatherings I would hear J.W. describing his venture to others. Sometimes the story was that he had already bought the property. At other times, the contract was about to be signed. And still other times, the deposit was paid and the contract signed.

The deal, as he described it, was for land valued at either 5 million or 8 million USD; J.W. had given different values at different times for the same land. These various stories were being told in the early part of 2006.

⁕

West Palm Beach, Florida December 15, 1998

John Bailey landed from Nassau, Bahamas, at the Palm Beach International Airport in a private aircraft he had leased. He had a passenger with him identified as John Jones and another, unidentified passenger. As they cleared Customs, each man indicated that they arrived from a trip to Nassau.

Examination of Bailey's and the other passengers' passports revealed an "In-Transit" stamp from the Bahamian government. Such a stamp is placed in the passport of passengers arriving in one country from another country who are only in the arrival country in transit to another. That is, Bailey and his passengers did not remain in the Bahamas, but were only passing through, so to speak.

Initially, Bailey maintained to Customs agents in West Palm Beach that he had been only in Nassau. Ultimately, however, he admitted to having travelled to Cuba via the Bahamas.

There must have been information in Customs data bases about Bailey. At about midnight, Customs Agent Sanchez in Atlanta, who had monitored and taped the conversation between Bailey and the confidential source, was telephoned and advised that Bailey was being detained. Within the coming days, Agent Sanchez obtained a federal search warrant for the contents of Bailey's laptop computer and exercised it, although Bailey had been released by that time.

The contents of the computer were revealing. It was clear that Bailey continued his involvement with the Cuban project. His computer files indicated numerous trips to Cuba. These computer files also contained records of various bank wire transfers to Bailey's bank, Wells Fargo Bank, from foreign bank accounts in Panama and the Cayman Islands.

At this point, Customs may have not known that Bailey had filed for bankruptcy indicating that he had no assets and numerous debts. However, Bailey surely had to know that he was now running an incredible risk of having sworn to Federal Bankruptcy Court that he had no assets when, in fact, he was clearly controlling money from foreign bank accounts. No doubt his attorney had advised him how serious it was to perjure himself in federal bankruptcy filings.

Agent Sanchez decided to continue the investigation. Despite the obvious risks and personal warnings that John had received, he seemed determine to continue the project in Cuba, which was clearly contra to U.S. law.

Augusta, Georgia December, 1998 – January, 1999

Sanchez continued to use the confidential source as a means of gathering evidence. During this time, the source continued meeting with Bailey. Those conversations were recorded. John discussed the Cuba project with the source and his continuing involvement in the project. He also maintained his efforts to try to induce the source to invest and to assist in creating an operational plan to bring the project to fruition.

John was either willing to take enormous risks, was breathtakingly stupid, or both. Over the course of a year he had been caught by U.S. Customs twice for taking illegal trips to Cuba. He had been interviewed by Customs agents with his attorney present making it very clear that his signed Letter of Intent represented an illegal transaction and to pursue the transaction would be illegal. His computer had been searched revealing continued involvement despite all the warnings. Furthermore, his computer records revealed perjury to a federal court involving his bankruptcy filings. And, yet, he continued his pursuit of the Cuban port deal. Rather than simply walk away from the project when the outcome had to have become obvious at this point, he actually seemed to almost flaunt his involvement.

Santa Monica, California January 20, 1999

Cases of Trading with the Enemy where Cuba is involved are relatively rare. The U.S. government knew that the prohibition against commercial trade, except for specific trade that was legally sanctioned by the U.S. government, was being ignored in some instances. However, these instances involved relatively minor amounts and the government apparently did not believe litigation worthwhile in these instances. Agent Sanchez decided that this case was worthy of pursuit especially since Bailey seemed to be flagrant in his attitude about conforming to the law and the warnings given to him.

Due to the rarity of cases brought for this violation, Sanchez wanted to leave no stone unturned. Therefore, U.S. Customs Agent Michael Simpson was directed to pose as a potential investor to develop more evidence to use in the case. Simpson had been involved in the taping of the conversations with the confidential source and was, therefore, familiar with the case.

Simpson was particularly suited as an undercover agent in this case because he has a Masters Degree in Economics. He also had over twenty years experience with complex international finance cases in his capacity as a Customs agent. Furthermore, he was a smooth conversationalist, dressed well, and could talk the lingo.

Accordingly, Simpson obtained an appointment with Bailey, supposedly to learn about investment opportunities in the Cuban project. The two met in Santa Monica to discuss the possibility of Simpson's participation in the project. In his capacity as an undercover agent, Simpson had represented to Bailey that he could be a major investor in the project in Cuba through the auspices of John's company, Port Development International.

The meeting was tape recorded. Bailey was very forthcoming in his explanation of his negotiation of the Letter of Intent and the progress he had made on bringing the projects to their current status. This included his description of the money he personally had invested. He was somewhat braggadocios in his description of the negotiations and numerous business meetings and transactions that he had already completed in Cuba. These meetings and transactions involved Cuban nationals as well as Cuban government officials, including Cuba's Economic Minister. Bailey wanted to make it clear that his connections went to the highest levels within the Cuban government and that these connections would be essential to the viability of the projects.

As in the meeting with the confidential source, Bailey gave to the undercover agent numerous documents. Included in the documents were various contracts and the same business prospectus that had been provided to the confidential source. Bailey's preparations for the project had advanced beyond the meeting with the confidential informant; Bailey now had a private offering memorandum for the development of the Port of Mariel. John did a great job presenting the project; he was enthusiastic, charming, and convincing.

Bailey offered numerous and detailed investment opportunities to the undercover agent. He intimated he already had other investors and that there was growing interest in the project. He also indicated that there was a high level U.S. government official who had already committed to participate financially. Bailey also dropped the name of U.S. Congressman Sean Gibson from Georgia, and insinuated that Gibson was an investor. The meeting ended with Simpson showing significant interest and wanting time to analyze the prospectus and the private offering memorandum. Simpson committed to call Bailey after having studied the material.

By this time, Bailey had to be feeling fairly confident of raising the additional capital to complete the projects. He had what he felt were some pretty good prospects in various parts of the country, including a U.S. government official who he mentioned to Simpson.

He also had Simpson and the confidential informant. Of course, he did not know that he was being set up by both of the latter prospects.

Atlanta, Georgia/Havana, Cuba February 6, 1999

Undercover Agent Simpson phoned John Bailey. Bailey had given his schedule to Simpson and indicated that he would be in Havana on this date. Further, Bailey had provided the agent with his phone number in Cuba. The conversation was tape recorded.

Simpson led Bailey to believe that his interest in investing had grown. Additional financial details were discussed. To close the deal, Bailey offered an additional face-to-face meeting with Simpson and proposed to introduce him to other investors. To do this, Bailey suggested a meeting the next week in Annapolis, Maryland. Simpson accepted, and they scheduled the meeting.

Atlanta Georgia February 8, 1999

Agent Sanchez, the agent in charge of the investigation, wanted to confirm certain technical details of the investigation. Bailey had represented to Simpson that the phone number he gave for his office in Cuba, 011-53-7-243970, was, indeed, Bailey's office. GTE Telephone confirmed that this number in Havana, Cuba was listed to Port Development International Holding, Inc./Ltd, Bailey's Cayman Islands company.

Annapolis, Maryland February 11, 1999

After supposedly analyzing the investment, Agent Simpson in his capacity as the potential investor agreed with Bailey to invest 6.25 million dollars. Simpson explained that he was the representative of a group of U.S. investors that lived abroad. He told Bailey that he explained to his investment group what the deal was about and that they all agreed to buy in for their proportionate shares.

Simpson agreed to make one million dollars available to invest initially. The balance of the 6.25 million would be made available to Bailey as the port deal progressed in the form of progress payments.

A U.S. government undercover account had been established for this purpose. One million dollars of taxpayer money was deposited so that Bailey could verify the balance. Simpson gave Bailey the account data. On this same day, Bailey verified the balance in the bank account. A date was set for an additional meeting when Bailey would introduce another investor. Bailey was ecstatic. He now had the commitment for the capital needed to finish the project. Little did he know that he had been scammed by his own government.

Augusta Georgia February 22, 1999

Simpson met with Bailey again. At this meeting, Simpson was introduced to an individual, John C. Black, identified as a senior U.S. Department of Commerce official. Bailey said that John C. Black owned stock in his company Port Development International Holding, Ltd. Various financial matters were discussed and all involved echoed the feeling that the deal had enormous potential.

The next day Simpson and Bailey met with Bailey's accountant, John Bowden. Numerous offshore bank accounts had been established by Bailey. Accounts were established in Panama, Cuba, and the Cayman Islands to handle the financial transactions associated with the Mariel Port development. At least one account had also been established in the U.S. to facilitate transfers to the offshore accounts outside of Cuba. These offshore accounts provided a veil of secrecy under the banking laws of the respective countries. Therefore, Bailey and Bowden explained, once money entered those accounts, it was untraceable by the U.S. government. From these offshore accounts, the capital needed to finance the projects in Cuba could be transferred into Cuban banks, and U.S. authorities would never be the wiser.

Simpson agreed to transfer the money into the U.S. account set up by Bailey within a matter of days.

⁂

Washington D. C. February 24, 1999

The Office of Foreign Asset Control was asked to give a determination concerning the legality of Bailey's transactions involving his Mariel Port development. Accordingly, a Letter of Determination was issued by OFAC. OFAC asserted that Bailey had committed numerous violations of the Trading With The Enemy Act. Among other things, Bailey had engaged in unlawful dealing in property in which Cuba or Cuban nationals have an interest. Also, it was determined by OFAC that Bailey unlawfully provided services in which

Cuba had an interest. Furthermore, Bailey had unlawful travel-related transactions in Cuba.

Atlanta Georgia March 2, 1999

An arrest warrant was issued and Bailey turned himself in without incident. His attorney immediately requested release under bail. Since John was supposedly bankrupt, the only asset he had to put up for bail was his home. However, he was also still legally married, and the wife would need to sign a Forfeiture Agreement. The Forfeiture Agreement is needed in the case that John jumped bail and then the house would be taken by the government.

John and his wife Angela were in the midst of a divorce. Under the circumstances, Angela refused to sign. This presented a problem for John if he wanted to avoid jail while his case was adjudicated. Accordingly, his mother agreed to put up her house as collateral for bail. John was also required to surrender his passport. He did so. If, for any reason, John jumped bail, his mother would lose her home.

The local press had become quite interested in the case, and John became somewhat infamous over the next few days in the local community.

In late November 2005, my supplier of chicken called to tell me he had an oversupply and wanted to know if I could help him by selling chicken to Cuba. The hitch was that the chicken had to be sold and moved by the end of January as the Cuban government contract had certain stipulations about the time period between slaughter and shipment. This was a fairly short window. I knew if I went through normal channels I did not have enough time, and that I would need assistance from the Cuban side to make the sale work. From previous experience in dealing with J.W.'s former employees in Cuba, I knew that J.W., indeed, had contacts. With some hesitation I called him to see if he could help grease the skids in Cuba.

J.W. told me, "Look, I am very sure I can make the deal happen. But I am going to need a retainer paid to my Cayman office. I'll contact them and have them send an invoice." I received a bill via email from Angela in the Cayman office. It was for several months' services.

I called J.W. and asked, "J.W. why am I being charged a retainer for several months? The deal will be done or not done within thirty days."

He said, "The retainer is through the date that your export license expires as we will need to continue servicing your account through that period of time." He asked that I simply transfer the money to the OCF bank account so that it would not have to be wired from the Cayman Office back to him here in Mexico, which would also save time. I paid the bill in full by transfer to the OCF account in Merida.

J.W. was to fly to Cuba in two days. He was to visit personally with Alexander, who was in charge of Alimport operations, the "company" the Cuban government used to purchase all food stuffs. I had previously been introduced to Alexander by J.W.'s former employees. At that time, Alexander asked how John was doing and clearly knew him, further indication that J.W.'s contacts were real.

When J.W. returned from Cuba he had to immediately go to Mahajual for his project, which he claimed was in the final stages of closing. He did tell me the news from Cuba was not good: he implied that I had talked in negative terms about Castro while there on my last trip and that this had been reported to the government. About a week later he said he would have to return to Cuba to see if he could repair the damage that I had supposedly done and get the contract completed.

I always had problems at immigration in Cuba since my passport has a unique feature – it was issued while I was living out of the country through a U.S. Consulate and has imprinted on my photograph "Foreign Service." This always threw the immigration officials for a loop in Cuba. I was normally detained for as much as two hours while various officials met and discussed whether or not I was really a spy. J.W. knew of my problems and also knew that once I was detained with some Cuban nationals by the Cuban Police as I was being transported in a private vehicle, which in Cuba is against the law, although I had not known it at that time. The Cuban driver got into some trouble only because he was helping out a friend and me.

When J.W. came back from what was presumably the second trip to Cuba, he suggested a meeting. Over dinner at a restaurant he explained, "Gus, man, while I was in Alexander's office, he showed me a file on you. You have to remember," he said, "Cuba is a Police State. The file contained, among other things, comments by your supposed friends in Cuba claiming you are making negative comments about Castro and the Cuban government. Gus, you can imagine that they are not amused."

I knew where J.W. was going with this, but I let him continue. "Look, with time I can smooth the situation out. It's just that it is going to take several months because this is serious, man." He continued, "Your export license is expiring in a few months. You need to renew the license and in the meantime I will continue working on Alexander and repair the damage that either you or your supposed friends have done."

While he did not specifically say so, I knew this would require more funds to be paid. My response was, "J.W., you are painting a very grim picture. Based on what you say I don't see any way that this can be fixed. Just go ahead and refund the remaining part of my retainer less your expenses."

His face dropped. He told me, "Hey, man, don't worry I can fix it in time." But I was not wavering. Eventually he said that he would get the whole amount of my retainer refunded but he would have to talk to the Cayman Office.

I said, "Not to worry. I only want the balance as I know you have incurred expenses and time." We changed the subject and enjoyed the rest of the dinner. But I had decided I would no longer involve myself with J.W. once I got my refund. What J.W. did not know was that I tried to locate him after his last "trip" to Cuba. He told me he would be back on a Wednesday. When I had not heard from him, I called him on Friday morning at the hostel. Lola answered the phone. She said J.W. was not there, but would be back shortly. Nevertheless, she said, we are leaving for Mahajual in about an hour. I asked her when did he get back, meaning from Cuba. She responded "W*e* got back on Wednesday."

The use of the plural "we" instead of the singular "he" raised some questions for me. I knew J.W. would not have taken Lola to Cuba, as J.W. had a girlfriend in Cuba. Therefore, I asked her if they had been in Mahajual and she said yes. While I had suspected he had never actually gone to Cuba, she confirmed it unwittingly. I called J.W. on his cell. My first question was, "Hey, when did you get back into town?" I purposefully did not ask from where.

His response was, "*I am just now coming into town from Cuba.* But I am about to leave to go to Mahajual and will get back with you on Monday." He did not realize that Lola had inadvertently exposed him and confirmed my suspicions about his lies of having travelled to Cuba. I said great and we had the dinner discussed above where I told him I wanted my refund.

From that Monday night I remained friendly with J.W. for awhile. I assumed the refund would be forthcoming in a matter of days. When I next asked about it he indicated that he had to wait to get all his expenses, including long distance calls to Cuba, to turn into the Cayman Office. He expected that to take another two to three weeks.

At the end of that period I asked about the refund again – J.W. was never forthcoming with information about why he had not provided the refund. I was told that all expenses had been turned in to the Cayman office, and the refund would be arriving by wire transfer as soon as the expenses were "approved" in the Cayman Office. Days went by without J.W. returning phone calls. When he did return my call I asked him, "J.W., are you avoiding me?"

"Of course not," he claimed, "I've been busy and in meetings with lawyers about the Mahajual deal." The next day I got the following email from him: "This in this morning from Robert, forwarding to you" This was from J.W.'s email account and time stamped 7:51 AM. The forwarded email came from the email address of the "Cayman Office" and was time stamped 7:49 AM and signed by "Robert." What "Robert" said was that the expenses were received in good order and that "the sooner we settle this account the better." I couldn't help but sense J.W.'s sarcasm in that sentence, which was supposedly written by "Robert." one of his employees in the Cayman Office.

It was clear that J.W. had written the email from the "Cayman Office" email account to his personal email account at 7:49 and signed it "Robert." When it went through cyberspace and arrived at his personal email account he simply forwarded it on to me at 7:51. He wrote both emails from the same computer with two different email accounts and signed one from Robert. J.W. was getting sloppy.

Soon I received an invoice via email. It reflected an amount due me of about half what I had paid and showed expenses for airfare to Cuba, hotel, and meals. There was no backup for the expenses. It showed a number of hours of work done by "Account Representative," presumably "Robert," at 175 USD per hour. Secretarial was billed at 70 USD per hour. J.W. had charged a number of hours for his "work" to this job and had very generously waived his rate of 350 USD per hour.

The invoice was created in a Word document. Therefore I was able to check certain attributes of the invoice. Curiously, the "Properties" function of the Word software showed that the document was created and saved on a computer named "Angela," the daughter of Lola, J.W.'s girlfriend. It was emailed to me from the Cayman Office email address with a copy to J.W.'s email account. If there were any alternative explanations that could be used to explain that this was anything but a scam on J.W.'s part, they were just demolished by the facts of the Word document used to create the invoice which was supposedly created by "Robert" in the "Cayman Office." J.W. clearly prepared the invoice on his computer at home, which was Angela's, and then emailed it to me from the Cayman Office email account to continue the illusion that all was coming out of the Cayman Office, which most surely did not exist.

I was most affected by the fact that J.W., supposedly a trusted friend, lied to me. The money was of much less interest to me than the betrayal of our friendship and the abject abuse of trust. I had always responded to J.W. when he was in need. Soon after I first met him I had loaned him $10,000. He did pay me back, as explained previously, although late. I never charged him interest. I had loaned him small amounts on two other occasions. I got the money to him immediately because I considered him a friend in need.

At this point I began to press J.W. daily for the refund he admitted he owed me. He quit answering his phone, so I asked him by email, "Either you are not the friend you profess to be or you don't have the money, or both. Why don't you either send the money or drop the pretence?"

He responded by email apologizing that there was a system-wide failure in the bank and that I would soon have the money. He claimed for three days that the bank system was still failing. Clearly, this was not reasonable. Then he began complaining of chest pains and claimed he had spent the entire morning in the hospital. He explained the physician told him he was under too much pressure. I did not believe this and took it as J.W.'s attempt to gain sympathy from me so that he would not have to address the issue at hand.

After several days I called J.W. at home and Lola answered. I fully expected her to say he was not there, but she gave him the phone. "J.W., I need an update," I said.

His angry response was, "I don't want to talk to you about this any more."

I told him, "J.W., fraud is illegal in any country." He hung up on me and I never spoke to him again.

It was clear he did not have the money. It had been foolish on my part to lend him so much money in the past, but I had risked the loans out of friendship. He always had a similar story about why he needed the loans: a wire had not been made on time or the sale of property in Panama had been delayed for some reason. I suppose this time he no longer had the ability to produce a viable lie and did not want to lose face with me explaining that his whole story about being a wealthy entrepreneur had been a lie, and he was now broke. If he had, I suspect I may have helped him again. But he did not come clean with me. Looking back, I realized that pressure created desperation and bad decisions on J.W.'s part.

I called his friend and partner, Keith, in Georgia. Keith supposedly was both a psychiatrist and a wealthy businessman who had a reputation to look after. Keith sounded very happy to hear from me; we had always gotten along well. After the initial phases of the conversation, I asked him point blank if he knew J.W. was using Keith's Mexican corporation,

OCF, to scam people. He sounded disgusted and responded that he did not know that and said he had already decided he was sending no more money down to J.W. to operate the company. He further stated that despite the money he had sent to operate the hostel and finance the search for property in Mahajual, he at least had a mortgage on the building that had been bought for the hostel and, therefore, had an asset to show for all the money that he had spent.

I told him, "Hey, I could be mistaken but I think that the building still belongs to Mike because J.W. never complied with the contract by making the down payment that Mike was expecting."

Keith responded with confidence. "Gus, I know you are wrong. I've got signed documents. I have had three different lawyers look at this deal. I sent the money and J.W. paid Mike."

"Well, like I said Keith, I could be wrong, but last time I talked to Mike, he still owned the building that the Merida Nido is operating in. Look, just to make sure why not call Mike and confirm?" I asked. I gave him Mike's phone number.

Unfortunately for Keith, I was right. According to Keith, J.W. had taken some $60,000 from Keith and had never given the money to Mike for the down payment. Over the next few days I had several conversations with Keith. Keith believes that when J.W. paid me back the $10,000 that the funds came from the $60,000 that Keith had sent for the purchase of the building. Keith was also speaking to Mike. I finally asked Keith, "Who is J.W., really?"

Keith came clean with me. "His real name is John W. Bailey, and he is a federal fugitive. About six or seven years ago he was charged with Trading with the Enemy, but the government subsequently dropped the charges because a number of politicians had been involved in the deal that he was working on in Cuba. So, the charges were just too hot for the authorities to pursue." He continued. "Then he caught his wife in bed with a male stripper or something and got real pissed off at her. He decided that he was going to screw her by filing bankruptcy and sending all his money offshore where she could not get it."

I was surprised, but not surprised. I asked, "Well, why is he a federal fugitive if the charges against him were dropped?"

Keith replied, "The problem is, when he filed for bankruptcy he did not mention the money he had offshore; he lied under oath on his bankruptcy declaration, which is a federal offense, and so he was arrested again. Then, after his mom put up the money for his bail he fled to Cuba."

༄

SUMMARY OF PRESS STORIES ABOUT JOHN W. BAILEY FROM THE LOCAL NEWSPAPER

March 3, 1999

"The charge Bailey faces, Trading with the Enemy, nearly unheard of in Atlanta's federal courts, carries a maximum penalty of 10 years in prison and $1,000,000 fine.

After his release on bail, Bailey declined comment. Bailey had been detained in the Bahamas when found with a Letter of Intent to develop a seaport. He was not arrested at that time. About a year ago he was visited by Customs agents who reminded him his intended transactions were against the law. Yet federal agents learned he was lining up drilling and dredging plans. Bailey maintained an Augusta address with bank accounts in Cuba, Panama, and the Caymans.

"Meanwhile, Bailey was looking for investors and met a smooth-talking, well-dressed man who promised to invest 6.25 million, but who neglected to mention he was an undercover Customs agent."

March 4, 1999

"John W. Bailey entered into bankruptcy last week. His estranged wife says all available assets went toward his business in Cuba.

"The Augusta businessman arrested Tuesday on a charge of illegally trading with Cuba is a former Buick salesman beset with financial difficulties.

"Although 43 year-old John W. Bailey was negotiating to build a multi-million dollar airport and seaport in Mariel, he received a final decree of bankruptcy last week listing $530,000 in unsecured debt.

"Bailey's wife sued him for divorce last month, claiming he had a new home in Cuba with a paramour. He recently began acting strange and had threatened to leave Georgia with their three children.

"Bailey was helped by an unnamed senior employee of the U.S. Department of Commerce. Arrests under Trading With the Enemy Act are rare, but do occur.

"Bailey and his wife Angela moved to the county from New Hampshire about nine years ago. Bailey's previous Georgia business dealings had several reversals, according to interviews and public records. His former company, Southern Imports, set out exporting cars to foreign buyers, but was ultimately dissolved.

"Bailey owes a Swiss man $84,000 from one such deal gone bad. Bailey and another corporate entity of his, Southern Export Management, Inc., owe Sun Medical Inc. $202,000.

"Still, Bailey tried to live well. In 1994, he and his wife bought a three thousand square foot house on a cul-de-sac in an upscale neighborhood. He was working at Royal Buick in Atlanta.

"The bankruptcy petition that was filed last October made no mention of bank accounts in Cuba, Panama, and the Cayman Islands that a U.S. Customs report claims he had established.

"Cuba watchers say many people are eager to invest in Cuba before Castro's demise. "There are a significant number of U.S. businessmen who have this romantic idea of being a rum-runner," says a Miami lawyer who gives advice on Cuban investment and who has not met Bailey. "They tend to be fringe people. Most serious businessmen don't openly flout the law because there is no cost benefit to it."

March 5, 1999

"The Augusta businessman accused this week of trading with Cuba made an appearance Thursday in federal court, but shed no new light on the senior U.S. official who supposedly had been helping him in his dealings.

Asked by a reporter Thursday for the commerce employee's identity, Bailey said, "I don't know who it is" and then strode away.

"Bailey, 43, seems an unlikely candidate to be a major port developer. Despite his multimillion dollar project, he is a former car salesman and drives a 1984 Lincoln with 300,000 miles on it."

September 1, 1999

"Charges were dropped without prejudice against John W. Bailey, meaning that the case can be reopened later. Lawyers claim that the arrest was made in a sting to get Sean Gibson, who was a U.S. congressman from Atlanta with a sterling reputation.

"Gibson, who retired from Congress in 1996, was more forthcoming on Tuesday. Not only had he not done anything with Bailey, Gibson said, he barely knew the man from a Washington social event:" as much as you can know anybody from a two-minute conversation in a party with 400 people." Gibson said he had no idea why anyone might invoke his name."

May 26, 2000

"Former Augusta businessman John W. Bailey's legal journey took another turn this week when he was indicted on charges of fraud and perjury. Bailey failed to appear before the Magistrate.

"Bailey is believed to be in Cuba where he has a residence and a girlfriend. Agents from the F.B.I. and U.S. Customs showed up at a child support hearing for Bailey earlier this month, but Bailey failed to appear.

September 27, 2002

"The opening of the first U.S. food and agribusiness exhibition in Cuba in more than 50 years attracted quite a cast: Fidel Castro and his older brother Ramon, Minnesota Gov. Jesse Ventura, and even a former Augusta businessman turned fugitive. Meanwhile, one participant wasn't eager to chat. John W. Bailey, 47, wore a name tag that read "Juan Torres" and sat at a booth leased by three Louisiana companies:

Med USA Inc., the Baker Marine Group, and Port Agencies Inc.

"He's known in the Atlanta area for his May 2000 indictment on federal charges of bankruptcy fraud and perjury. He disappeared shortly thereafter.

"Bailey acknowledged his identity to a reporter and said he was 'just taking care of business.'"

NOTE: SEE ANOTHER ARTICLE IN EPILOGUE

◦❖◦

Keith was also baring his soul and J.W.'s real story to Mike. Mike and I were talking. At some point Mike sent an email to many people indicating that J.W. was wanted by the FBI and giving email addresses of those folks who could be helpful to those of us having problems with J.W.. Mike's intention was to inform and ensure that no one else was hurt.

Many of us who had known J.W. well began talking. I spoke to Gabriel, the other stockholder in OCF. Gabriel was very upset with J.W. as he had loaned money to J.W., and J.W. had still not paid him back. He was particularly upset because J.W. took weekend trips to the Caribbean with Lola and spent more in a weekend using Gabriel's loan than Gabriel was earning every two weeks.

Apparently, J.W. was playing the wealthy entrepreneur along the Caribbean coast, looking for beach property on which to build his development. He had to appear to be wealthy; he was appearing that way using other people's money.

Gabriel said he always knew there was a problem. He had met J.W. through another American, Kyle, who told him that not only Kyle, but also J.W.

were on the run from the law in the States. More on Kyle later.

At this point I became worried that my name was associated with J.W. as a business partner and called the attorney, Alvaro, who J.W. had told me was handling the stock sale from me to Keith. I wanted to ensure I was no longer associated with OCF. He told me that the stock transfer had not been finalized because J.W. had given him a hot check on the OCF account for 9,000 pesos for other work and, therefore, would not do any work for J.W. without payment up front.

Alvaro said he had done quite a bit of work for J.W. in writing a contract for the purchase of land in Mahajual. He accepted J.W.'s proposal not to charge for the work until after the sale was consummated. J.W. had told him not to worry about payment and that in the interim J.W. would send his private jet to pick him up, take him to Cabo San Lucas, where J.W. owned a hotel, put Alvaro up for free and send him on fishing expeditions. Alvaro, a pretty tough lawyer, bought the story until he tried to cash the check. In explaining his foolish behaviour with J.W., Alvaro indicated that J.W. had an incredibly convincing manner. I had to agree since the same had happened to me.

Gabriel and I were looking for ways to get our money back. Mike was looking to get J.W. out of the building that J.W. kept promising he was going to buy. Eventually, J.W. agreed to leave the premises on good terms. Mike said J.W. never asked why Mike wanted him out. But they both understood what was going on.

Gabriel and I asked Keith to come down and assist with legally obtaining the car that J.W. used as a way to get some of our money back. The car was registered in the name of the company, OCF. Under Mexican law one cannot really enter into any kind of legal business transactions without the signature of the "Legal Representative" of the corporation, which was Keith. Faxed signatures did not work. The physical presence of the Legal Representative was required, presumably due to the prolific fraud that occurs in Mexico. Keith adamantly refused, saying he was afraid of being arrested once he landed on Mexican soil. I thought this a strange response as I knew of nothing that Keith had done that was illegal.

I asked Keith to simply send an email giving us permission to take possession of the car. Keith responded in an email that he did not think it was proper to get the car. He believed that this would make J.W. "a desperate man even more desperate." He also said, "J.W., and I cannot say more, will probably be extradited for trial here in the USA. His path of destruction has to stop... Fairness will prevail, I will see to it. This mail MUST stay between us...Understood? If and when I make a trip, I will not be 'alone'. I feel I am betraying, but too many have been hurt. His kids and wife included"

Keith's promise that "fairness will prevail" notwithstanding, Gabriel and I wanted our money back. We began strategizing. Up until now, J.W.'s status in the country as an illegal had always worked in his favor. He was able to do business through entities established by others. In actuality, he had no risk for these businesses as he appeared nowhere as a stockholder; he could not since he had no legal presence in the country as J.W. Barnes. This had worked well for him in the past.

Keith, as legal representative of OCF, had given J.W. the internet access codes to the bank account so that J.W. could control the money of the corporation. Under Mexican law only the Legal Representative could change the bank access privileges. Gabriel, as a stockholder, had been assigned check-signing privileges by Keith. Of course, J.W. could not sign checks since he had no legal presence, so someone other than J.W. had to be listed as signatory authority. However, J.W. had the check book and had simply brought checks for Gabriel to sign. Gabriel had trustingly signed blank checks in the past.

Gabriel's privileges did not really matter as there was no money in the OCF account. Or at least that was what we thought.

While we were weighing our options, J.W., began following up on his attempts to buy and sell property in Mahajual. He did not yet know that Gabriel had reached the end of the rope with him. J.W. asked Gabriel, as a stockholder in OCF, for a bio; he explained that this would be part of a private placement offering to sell stock or bonds to raise money to buy the Mahajual property. J.W. sent Keith's bio as an example for Gabriel.

Keith's bio was quite impressive. According to the Offering, Keith had been the owner or partner in about nine very successful businesses. Most of them were medically related service businesses and one was described as the largest full-service health and wellness outpatient clinic in the nation.

The Offering also described the history of OCF as follows: "In December of 2004, Keith, after deciding to enter into the hospitality business, with the ultimate goal of creating or co-creating an ultra-exclusive, high end villa-type resort in the Costa Maya. Operadora Coyote Feo, S.A. de C.V., a Mexican Corporation, was founded in 2005 as the company that would own and develop this and other projects in Mexico."

The project outlined in the Offer required a total initial investment to be raised from investors of 8 million USD. The strategy outlined in the private placement offer was quite impressive. J.W. actually had a good idea and was trying to put it into play. In the building and revenues section, the project reflected total projected revenues of almost $80,000,000. The only problem was the same problem J.W. always made for himself: the offering document was not truthful.

First, the investors were being asked to make their financial contributions to OCF, which according to the Offer had cash and equivalents in the amount of $2,360,000. In fact, that company had a bank balance of about 50 pesos and numerous hot checks outstanding. Second, the description of the formation of the corporation was totally false. This corporation was formed by Keith, Gabriel, and I to operate a cantina, but the Offer indicated that it was formed by Keith after a vacation he spent on the Maya Riviera and developed this vision for the company and the project as a result of his vacation. Third, numerous statements about Keith in his bio were untrue, as I was soon to discover.

Meanwhile, J.W. indicated he had found a buyer for Gabriel's stock. He provided Alvaro, the lawyer, and Gabriel with the name, address and passport number of the buyer, one Ronald Lankston. Gabriel was quite happy about this development.

A short time later, I received a call from Gabriel informing me that J.W. had come by to pay him back the money he owed to Gabriel. He also wanted Gabriel to sign some checks on the OCF account. Gabriel did sign a check for money he had lent J.W. personally that J.W. was proposing to repay with OCF funds. J.W. then told Gabriel to sign additional checks that were blank. Gabriel said he no longer felt comfortable doing that since there were a number of hot checks floating around with Gabriel's signature on them, including one to a lawyer. J.W. became infuriated and left very unhappy.

After Gabriel related the story to me, I suggested that we check the bank balance. Obviously money was now in the account despite what Keith had said about not sending any more money. We went to the bank and obtained a bank statement indicating that some $5000 had entered the account and most had been quickly removed through internet transfers except for about 12,000 pesos. Gabriel had his money and the remaining balance was far short of what J.W. owed me. Gabriel suggested calling Alvaro, the lawyer, to tell him he should deposit his hot check quickly.

Gabriel's point was that he was living and always would be in Merida. Alvaro was with a prestigious local law firm. Gabriel was a businessman trying to make an honest living and felt badly that he had unknowingly signed a hot check to Alvaro.

I agreed that was the best thing to do. Alvaro was called and was very appreciative. He collected on the check. Unsurprisingly, J.W. went ballistic next time he checked the corporate bank balance and sent an unpleasant email to Gabriel demanding that Gabriel replace the money because it was J.W.'s money. We found it curious that J.W. was referring to money that belonged to someone else as his and was indignant that Gabriel, an actual stockholder in OCF, which was the owner of the funds, had told Alvaro, to whom it was actually owed, that he could now collect what was owed him.

Out of curiosity Gabriel checked the bank balance again in a few days. To his surprise he found another deposit of about $5,000. He immediately called me. We both went to the bank together to discover what actions we could take to conserve the money; that is, to keep J.W. from taking it out of the bank. We knew we had to act quickly, and we had to explain something fairly serious without fabricating a story.

Fortunately, J.W. had opened the OCF account at my bank and the executives knew me. We used J.W.'s illegal status to our benefit. We explained to the bank executive that he was in Mexico illegally and had no legal status in the corporation. Additionally, the Legal Representative was refusing to come to the country to settle the problem. Furthermore, we explained, there was money entering this account from unknown sources, and the money entering the account was not being used for operational purposes since the hostel was closed.

The banker believed us and said the only thing he could advise us to do and to help us do was cancel the internet access, which Gabriel as signatory authority had the power to do. This we did immediately. To obtain control of the funds we would need the check book and Gabriel could write checks. However, the check book was in the possession of J.W., and he obviously would not give it up. The banker explained that he could ask for another check book but that it would be coming from Mexico City and would take several days to arrive.

We knew that a cat-and-mouse game would now ensue. We knew there was no way J.W. would give up control of this money very easily. In the meantime we had to wait for the check book to work its way through the Mexican bank beauracracy.

It did not take long for J.W. to discover he could not transfer funds via internet. He immediately called the bank, and someone at the bank told him that Gabriel had been in and cancelled the internet access. J.W. called Gabriel, who told a made-up story that the bank had requested him to do so suspecting money laundering and were asking for a temporary suspension of activities. I am sure J.W. did not buy the story but his only question to Gabriel was: "Was Gus with you at the bank?" Gabriel's response was, "Why don't you ask Gus if you want to know that?" J.W. never asked me.

Meanwhile, Gabriel began trying to get Keith, the Legal Representative, to play ball with us as this was the only sure, quick, and legal way to get things under control. Besides, J.W. had caused another set of other problems by failing to file payroll taxes.

Under Mexican law the corporate accountant, Gabriel and the Legal Representative were responsible. Therefore, a plea was made to Keith to assist with settling all corporate matters in a legal manner. Keith's response was via email and brief. The response in its totality: "I believe I have made my very last trip to Mexico. Good luck to you."

Finally the check book arrived. We checked the balance and now another $25,000 had been deposited in the bank account.

We were immediately concerned about the source of these funds. Keith claimed he was no longer sending any money. In Keith's emails and conversations before he quit responding it was clear he was completely disgusted with J.W. and wanted nothing further to do with this. I believe this was one of the few times that Keith was telling the truth. However, since that conversation some 35,000 USD had been transferred into the account.

We requested the bank to trace the source of the funds. In the meantime, Gabriel opened an account in his own name and transferred the balance after debts to this personal account to secure the money for the rightful owners.

Gabriel paid directly out of the company account all debts that he knew of. This included the debt to me. We had checked with the company accountant and the money I had deposited in the account supposedly for J.W.'s professional services that were never provided had been accounted for as a loan to the company by me on J.W.'s instructions; this covered Gabriel from a legal standpoint in case there was ever a question.

Shortly thereafter, I received a call from Keith. He told me he had received a desperate call from Lola telling him that J.W. had disappeared. My initial thought was that someone had finally had enough and done something to him. After all, J.W.'s throat had already been slashed once, and he was lucky to be alive.

Keith mentioned something about the possibility that he had been arrested. I remembered his email about having J.W. extradited. Then Keith essentially began a soliloquy that seemed to have the purpose of distancing himself from J.W. He said, "Listen, J.W. told me that all charges of any kind had been dropped.

He also said that the statute of limitations had run out and that he no longer had any legal problems in the States. Look, I relied on J.W.'s representations and therefore I was doing business with him." He sounded as if he was trying to convince me.

All of this rang hollow to me as I was listening. However, it really was not relevant as far as I was concerned. When he finally quit talking I began to question him. "Keith, how about coming down to straighten things out and take Gabriel and others off potential legal hooks? I mean, really, it's the right thing to do – these people did not know who J.W. was, and they are basically innocent bystanders."

He responded, "Look, Gus, I don't want to come down there and get arrested. I'm a legit businessman here in Georgia with two kids."

"Keith," I said, "that is ridiculous. What do you think you would be arrested for?" He was vague except for the mention of all the hot checks and un-filed tax returns and other government paperwork that had been left undone. "Look, if that were the case," I said, "three-fourths of the citizens of Mexico would be in jail if the police went after such petty crimes." I also said, "You know, it is curious that you are un-localizable on the internet." However", I explained, "when you quit responding to phone calls and emails that I had sent you I began to research you and I learned quite a bit about you through other sources."

He became very quiet. I was later to learn why. Basically, my knowledge of him came through J.W.'s private placement offer, naming all the businesses that Keith ran including one that was represented in the offer as the largest of its kind in the nation. I had done research through a Georgia state government web site and found that most of these businesses were inactive. This was only part of why he was quiet.

I asked him, "Did you participate in making a private placement offer on the property in Mahajual?"

His response seemed genuine. "I don't know anything about that. Look, as far as I know the Mahajual deal had been over months ago; I threw in the towel and I thought J.W. had too. If J.W. is doing something like that I want no part of it. Furthermore, that's just another reason not to come down there."

Again, I told him that was ridiculous; if he had done nothing wrong he should not worry, and it was important for innocent people who had been adversely impacted by J.W.'s actions that he come and help them out. He said he had his family to think about and had to put them first.

I agreed, "Keith, that's exactly what you should do and, in fact, all of us are doing the same thing ourselves and putting ourselves first. However, your coming down is not putting you or your family at risk – to the contrary. You are the Legal Representative of OCF and by not trying to solve the problem you run the risk of creating a bad impression for yourself with Mexican authorities." I did not go into all the money in the account that we were now trying to get access to.

"By the way," I asked, "Have you sent any more money to the OCF account?"

"Absolutely not," he responded. "And I am not going to."

In the meantime, the bank came through with the trace on the approximately $30,000 that came into the account – the money came from the Ronald Lankston Trust. Ronald Lankston is the individual who J.W. had told Alvaro would buy the stock from Gabriel in

OCF. J.W. had convinced Mr. Lankston to pay $30,000 USD for Gabriel's 1% interest in a corporation that had a negative net worth. No one will ever be able to question J.W.'s ability to sell.

Meanwhile, it appeared that J.W. must have actually been arrested. I received a call from a mutual friend, Brian, asking what I knew about J.W.'s disappearance. I told him all I knew. He told me that Lola had called other friends who had rushed over to her house. In the meantime Lola had received a call from someone representing herself to be a federal agent, a woman who spoke Spanish. This woman told Lola that J.W. was in custody in Houston and that he wanted Lola to know that he was OK. Lola was to receive more calls and was given an email address through which to contact J.W.

Lola explained to Brian that J.W. had taken the daughter to school by car that very morning. He never returned. However, Lola found the car parked in front of the house on the street with the keys in it and also J.W.'s cell phone was in the front seat.

Hearing Lola's story of the disappearance, there were those that thought J.W. staged his own disappearance. That is, that J.W. ran off on his own and set it all up through Lola to make it appear as though he was out of the picture. Presumably, this would take the heat off him from those looking to get re-paid or those who may have been looking to do him harm as had happened in the throat slashing. However, over time the theory of his staged disappearance lost credibility.

While J.W. was around, Lola and he had always come up with some money somehow. Now Lola was without J.W. and without financial support. She had been a waitress in a cantina when she met J.W. The Nido was now closed. She really had no prospects and no real preparation for employment except as a waitress.

She had apparently come up with the idea of taking possession of the car and selling it for money; she did not know how to drive. However, Gabriel had been trying to get the car to help pay the debts of the corporation that J.W. had incurred.

J.W. had been trying to get the car's factura (invoice/title under Mexican law) so that the car could be sold. J.W. had spoken to Alvaro about how to do this since he could not find the factura. J.W. told Alvaro that the car was in the name of OCF.

Gabriel ultimately found the factura at some point prior to J.W.'s disappearance but did not tell him. The factura was, indeed, endorsed first to Michael Harrison from Trifecta, the ill-fated corporation that had the Checkers franchise, and later Harrison endorsed it to OCF; this was the document supporting the chain of title as J.W. had described it to Alvaro and to Gabriel. Therefore, Gabriel was within his rights and the law to obtain possession of the car. Lola did not want to give it up.

In the midst of this controversy Lola was desperate for money and wrote a very contrite email to me. She said she is sorry to bother me but one day she woke up and she did not have her boyfriend and was out of money. She explained that OCF owed her severance pay. She asked me to persuade Gabriel to pay her the money since he had access to the account.

She continued that neither her nor her daughter were at fault for what happened between J.W. and me and that she knew that I was not a bad person. She was requesting 4,500 pesos as severance even though the legal amount was 17,500. Mexican law stipulates what is the amount to be paid based on various conditions. Regardless, it is common practice to negotiate a lower settlement than what is strictly formulated by law. It seemed ironic to me that while J.W. was running the company and had access to the bank account, he did not obtain for Lola her full severance.

Gabriel verified with the accountant that Lola had not received her severance. Gabriel further stated that he would provide her the full legal settlement despite her desire to only receive 4,500 pesos on the condition that she turn over possession of the car to the attorney for the corporation. Lola agreed to the condition.

Lola went to the attorney's office to pick up her check, but refused to turn over the car. Gabriel said, "Fine let her have the car. We don't care as long as we report it as stolen to the Police so that the corporation has no liabilities if something happens in the future involving the car."

However, this was not the end of the car story. Out of the blue, Gabriel started receiving emails from Mike Harrison, who was the only American stockholder in the ill-fated Trifecta. At some point, Harrison apparently came in contact with J.W.. As a result he sent the following email in the typically demanding manner of J.W.:

"Gabriel, I have been instructed by J.W. to instruct you to please give the invoice (factura/title) of the car to Lola." Gabriel ignored the request. The "instructions" J.W. was issuing went contrary to the best interests of the corporation and the stockholders.

Soon Keith came into the picture again. Harrison denied endorsing the title. We certainly did not know the facts about whether the factura was really endorsed by Harrison or not. But J.W. had told Alvaro and Gabriel that he did want to sell the car. He had also given the factura to Gabriel some months earlier already endorsed by Harrison. But we also knew that J.W. was capable of forging Harrison's name. It was clear that regardless of the actual facts that Lola, J.W., and Harrison now wanted the car. Harrison threatened Gabriel that he was going to report all of this to "the authorities," and Gabriel encouraged him to do so. Within the next few days the car disappeared from Lola's garage, Lola moved to an unknown location, and Harrison stopped emailing (for the time being).

Epilogue I

After J.W.'s disappearance, I began to learn more about him. Emilio, the owner of the company that managed the security at the plant, had been introduced to me by J.W.. I asked him after J.W. disappeared how he met J.W. since this had never been made very clear. Emilio had met him through Kyle. This was the same Kyle at the scene where J.W.'s throat was cut.

It turns out Emilio was with Kyle the night J.W.'s throat was slashed. J.W. was arguing, he said, with a young woman who was Kyle's girlfriend's sister. The argument became more intense and the young woman left in a hurry. There were two other men inside with J.W. Emilio heard Kyle come down the stairs and some commotion. Emilio walked back inside to see J.W.'s throat cut and in a complete panic, as any of us would be. Emilio said Kyle took control of the situation and wrapped towels around J.W.'s neck, rushed him to the car, and took him to the hospital. One of the two men inside accompanied Kyle and J.W. to the hospital and the other, saying something to the effect he wanted no trouble, left alone. Emilio left as well.

Another friend, Nick, to whom J.W. had introduced me was at the hospital that night. Nick later told me the throat slashing was due to a drug deal that went bad and over some money that J.W. owed some "Mexican Mafia."

Nicks's partner, Hank, was also at the hospital that night. On another occasion, Hank referred to the events of that night. Hank had called one of his friends, a Mexican Police Commandante. Hank told me that if the Comandante had not been there that night to prevent the normal procedure of reporting this type of problem to the Consulate, J.W. would have had some serious problems. Hank said J.W. was exceedingly lucky. I now know why, and I guess Hank always did – J.W. was not J.W., but a federal fugitive.

Emilio says that the relationship between Kyle and J.W. deteriorated quickly after the slashing. Eventually, Kyle left Merida for Cancun. Emilio had heard that Kyle had been stabbed in Cancun. Next time Emilio saw J.W. there was a comment from J.W. that led Emilio to believe that J.W. was taking credit for having Kyle stabbed. He implied to Emilio that he had sent some thugs to rough Kyle up. I suspect that no one will ever know if J.W. was responsible for Kyle's stabbing or not.

Then there was Bill, a Canadian married to a Mexican National. Bill is an expert in designing, building, and operating natural gas pipelines. J.W. had said that his "people" in his Cayman Office had obtained a consulting engagement for Bill in the Middle East. J.W. maintained that he was very disappointed in Bill because Bill had only stayed on the job about two months in the Middle East because he was "homesick." He painted a pretty sorry picture of Bill. I had met Bill through J.W. and was surprised to hear that Bill was the type to get homesick. Certainly, I never asked Bill about that to save him the embarrassment.

By coincidence I ran into Bill one day after J.W. disappeared. We talked about J.W. Bill indicated that J.W. never got him any consulting assignments. He explained that he was a consultant and obtained his own work through his own efforts and reputation. He said their relationship soured because J.W. owed him quite a bit of money.

Bill told me that J.W. had come to him approximately two years before about investing in an Italian company that was installing telephone lines in Cuba. I recall that J.W. had mentioned something about this project. While it sounded interesting, I knew that this type of project for an American was illegal.

However, Bill, a Canadian, could invest in Cuba legally. The investment Bill made through J.W. was several thousand dollars. He claimed to have ultimately received about what they had invested. No additional money came in despite J.W.'s claims of high and quick returns that would continue over a period of years. Apparently J.W. never explained why the investment no longer paid dividends, and the subject just sort of died. I doubt there were ever any telephone lines installed as a result of their "investment" with J.W.. Looking back on the time frame, I think Bill's return of investment came about the same time I made the loan to J.W..

Since J.W. had told me the name of the other Mexican stockholders in the hamburger franchise, I called the majority stockholder, Alberto, and obtained an appointment to see him after J.W.'s disappearance. Alberto could not have been nicer. He opened up completely and told me the story.

It turns out J.W. really had nothing to do with the franchise deal except to have promised financing. J.W. did not put the deal together nor build the shopping center in which the franchise was located, as he had told all of us. J.W. was to be admitted as a partner for a capital contribution. J.W. asked that the stock of the newly formed corporation, Trifecta, be issued in the name of Mike Harrison. As much as a million dollars had been promised, and Alberto proceeded forward on this promise.

Expenses began growing and were unpaid as the promised capital did not arrive. J.W. always had an excuse as to why. Finally, small amounts began to arrive, but not anywhere near the amounts needed. These amounts came from Michael Harrison and were sent direct to J.W.. Alberto says that much of this money was used by J.W. for his own living expenses, and the rest was used to pay overdue bills of Trifecta. But equipment needed to be acquired. Alberto told J.W., "Look, if you can't get the money here in sufficient quantities and on time, I have no alternative but to look for other investors." J.W. could not comply, and Alberto, as the franchise owner, obtained other investors and began another corporation.

This, of course, infuriated J.W.. He and Harrison filed a criminal lawsuit that was quickly thrown out. Then a civil suit was found to have no merit. Emails forwarded to me that J.W. sent to others indicated he told Harrison another story and gave hope to Harrison that eventually he would recoup his investment. Alberto explained to me that he had attempted to meet alone with Harrison to describe the actual situation and work directly with Harrison to avoid misunderstandings. However, Harrison refused to meet without J.W.

We had all been told by J.W. that he and Alberto had owned a successful car rental agency years ago and had sold it. According to Alberto, J.W. had absolutely no ownership in the car rental agency Alberto owned. He told me he first met J.W. in 1992 in New Orleans. J.W. was trying to sell his Fun Cruisers to rental car agencies. Alberto gave him a down payment and a letter of credit for 20 Fun Cruisers. He never got them.

Alberto did visit J.W.'s "factory" in Georgia where discarded postal jeeps were being transformed into Fun Cruisers. The factory was described as a sort of small storage warehouse where two jeeps were being worked on. J.W. had indicated to all of us that it was a big operation, and he was under contract to buy every postal jeep that the U.S. Post Office took out of service, which would have been thousands. Alberto had the impression that the 20 he ordered, and did not receive, was the biggest order J.W. ever had.

One day I received a call from Sam, the owner of the hotel in Merida who was presumably forming a partnership with J.W. for the property in Mahajual. We began comparing notes about J.W.. I asked him what had stalled the Mahajual deal. He indicated that because Frank, his partner in the hotel, was considering investing almost five million dollars with J.W. and Keith, they had hired a private investigator to check the two out. The PI, of course, found nothing on J.W.. However, they had more success in discovering facts about Keith in Georgia.

It seems Keith was employed in the medical field as a male nurse working in a psychiatric ward of a local hospital in Atlanta and was not the wheeling, dealing entrepreneur in creating medical service companies, but instead of living in a mansion that he had described to Sam, Keith lived in a rented apartment.

Before becoming a male nurse, Keith had a criminal history, according to the P.I.'s report. In 1981, he was arrested for two counts of burglary, two counts of dealing in stolen property, and grand theft in the first degree. In 1982, he was sentenced to ten years probation. It also seems that in recent years, Keith has had a proclivity for litigation, either as a defendant or plaintiff. Six separate lawsuits were listed from 2001 to 2005.

After reading the PI's report, obviously Sam and Frank thought better of investing with J.W. and Keith. And, of course, they could not tell J.W. why they decided not to invest in the Mahajual deal.

Reflections on J.W.

J.W. is a guy who has a great sense of humor and can be very charming. At the same time, he seemed to be a very angry person. Sometimes he veritably seethed with anger and resentment toward supposed friends, Mexico, and everything else in general. There was one friend in particular for whom J.W. reserved his most vitriolic comments.

This particular friend spoke often in a fairly authoritative manner on how things are in Mexico. This truly enraged J.W., but never to the friend's face. Looking back, I believe what upset J.W. about this friend more than anything was that J.W. sort of "lost the floor," so to speak, and lost, at least in his mind, some authority as the famous entrepreneur.

If true, as reported, that J.W. stole his children's trust funds, he literally robbed their future so that he could continue his illegal deal in Cuba. I should not have been surprised that J.W. would rob from me or Keith or anyone else if he would rob from his own children.

I also think that J.W., as the alter ego of John W. Bailey, was making an effort to be the person that John never was. Judging from the news reports in the papers, John was never a successful entrepreneur and businessman. At least at the beginning of their relationship, J.W. was the perfect gentleman with Lola. He would open her car door and made a heroic effort at being the real gentleman.

By all accounts J.W. was a good surrogate father to Angela. He often bragged on Angela's intelligence and other characteristics. Near Christmas one year he even asked me to call Angela and tell her I was Santa Claus. I did and she loved it.

I think J.W. had a knack for causing disasters. Wherever he went he left a wake of destruction behind him. The Cuba project, while reflecting a great business strategy, certainly became a mess in the end. Before that, J.W. seemed to have a number of deals gone bad as reflected in the press stories. While he claimed he turned The Nido around, Mike indicated that The Nido had done no better under J.W.'s guidance. Apparently, J.W. continued operating The Nido by receiving money from Keith which Keith thought he was sending for other purposes. And it seems the Mahajual deal, while driven by a good strategy, was ultimately screwed up from various angles.

J.W. seemed to not react well under pressure. When the going got tough with the Cuba project, he made some bad decisions. The worst was to rob his childrens' trust funds, send the money overseas, and then file for bankruptcy and commit perjury in the process. While under pressure in Merida and looking for money, he began to get sloppy with his emails from the "Cayman Office," which gave me confirmation of the scam.

His business logic always seemed excellent. However, his business judgement in application of the logic was usually suspect and often illegal.

There is no question that J.W. had enormous potential, but perhaps he enjoyed operating outside the law, thinking it is easier or preferring to live on the edge. His potential has most likely evaporated as of now.

Reflections on me

I realize that I was too trusting, to say the least. What would I have done differently? First, I now recognize I probably make friends too easily, or at least, too innocently. Second, once I have identified someone as a friend, I know I will always prefer to risk money and emotions on a friend than to be so suspicious as to not give reasonable assistance to a friend who I believe needs help.

However, I have learned a great deal about forming business relationships with people I know only on a social basis. In the future when considering a business relationship with a friend, I will be far more cautious about accepting a friend's comments about his own business prowess at face value; I will perform the necessary due diligence as I would with any proposed business relationship.

Admittedly, it felt good to sort of reverse scam J.W. by preventing his access to the bank account. It was also rewarding to retrieve the money that he had stolen from me.

Epilogue II[5]

From J.W.'s local newspaper on August 18, 2006:

"For six years, former Buick salesman, Augusta businessman and father of three John W. Bailey eluded federal authorities.

"In 2000, he disappeared after he was indicted on three counts: two perjury charges and one charge of concealing assets. Since then, Bailey's been a fugitive. No longer.

---

5   The information about John W. Bailey came through news stories, Keith, court documents and a sworn affidavit by U.S. Customs.

"Bailey, 51, was booked into the County jail Wednesday and held without bail after pleading guilty Aug. 2 to one count of perjury, according to federal court records.

"Bailey is scheduled to be sentenced at the end of this month, said a spokeswoman for the FBI's Atlanta office. He was arrested May 9 by Mexican authorities after he was detained at a port, Hall said. He was then deported to the United States.

"More details on his arrest were unavailable Thursday, Hall said.

"On an arrest report, Bailey listed his address as Bosques Del Poniente, Mexico.

"Bailey got into legal trouble in 1999, when authorities said he negotiated the development of a multimillion-dollar seaport, airport and free trade zone in Mariel, Cuba. He was arrested under the Trading with the Enemy Act.

"Those charges were dropped, and in 1999, a federal judge ordered that Bailey's passport be returned.

"Bailey vanished in 2000, when he was charged with bankruptcy fraud and perjury after authorities said he concealed his interest in a company, Port Development International Holding Co.

"He was accused of using the company to develop the Mariel project.

"A federal arrest warrant was issued in May 2000, but he had disappeared by then, according to court records. His former wife, Angela Bailey, was among those trying to find him. She had won a substantial divorce settlement, but not before he allegedly took money from the children's trust accounts and lost their home in Countryside. She could not be reached for comment on Thursday.

"It's unclear whether Bailey was employed while he was a fugitive or exactly where he lived.

"In 2002, he was spotted at a trade show in Havana, Cuba, wearing a name tag that read, "Juan Torres."

"He was wearing a shirt with the logo of Port Agencies Inc., a bulk cargo handler in Louisiana, and declined to talk to reporters."

"Apparently, John plea bargained after initially entering a plea of not guilty. It appears as such because court records reflect that on November 27, 2006 John Bailey was sentenced to time served and three years of supervised release as a result of pleading guilty to one count of perjury. Court records reflect an original plea of not guilty. He was also fined $3,000.

"His supervised release included a number of conditions. These conditions required Bailey to remit reports on his activities each month, to look for gainful employment, to support his dependents, to not leave the jurisdiction without permission, to advise any third parties of his criminal history, to not associate with known felons, to not engage in excessive drinking, among other conditions. It did not take J.W. long before he began to ignore the conditions of parole.

"On December 2, 2006, three days after he was released from jail, Bailey sent the following email to Gabriel:

CONFIDENTIAL

Gabriel:

I will be returning to Merida within the next 30 days or as soon as I have completed my work here. In the meantime, I believe that we should talk, kindly forward me an appropriate telephone number for you and I will be in touch after Monday. I will also be driving another vehicle there on my

trip and would like to arrange insurance from the frontier on. Please advise as to what information will be required.
Respectfully
John W. Bailey

Bailey emailed from his old email account used by J.W. Barnes. Interestingly, he signed the email using his real name. He also, apparently, wants the information kept confidential. Since one of his conditions of probation is not to leave the jurisdiction without permission, and it is doubtful that the government would give permission for him to return to Mexico where he had been hiding as a fugitive, clearly he wanted the information confidential. Gabriel ignored the email. Subsequently, Gabriel received a phone call from Bailey, which indicates that he had Gabriel's phone number all along. Bailey wanted information on the OCF funds and wanted the title to the car. When Gabriel was evasive, Bailey became aggressive and implied unpleasant consequences for lack of cooperation. The last thing he told Gabriel was that he and Keith would soon be in Merida and would see him face to face. Since Keith is a convicted felon himself, J.W. was again ignoring one of his conditions of release.

On December 7, Gabriel received an email from Keith wanting to know about the funds in OCF and the whereabouts of the car and the title to the car. Also, Keith implied the same unpleasant consequences that J.W. had already mentioned if Gabriel did not cooperate with him, J.W. and, Harrison: "...it could get messy for all of us, even you, and I do not want that."

Shortly, Harrison was emailing Gabriel again demanding to know about the title and threatening some sort of action. Harrison began accusing Gabriel of forging the document and made several comments that are easily proven wrong but with the apparent purpose of deflecting suspicion from J.W. for a forgery.

Finally, Keith responded on 12 December, basically withdrawing from the situation. He also mentioned in the email that he had been scheduled as a witness for the FBI against J.W. had the case gone to trial.

J.W. continued to email former friends in the Yucatan, except Gabriel and me, indicating he would be back down shortly and wanted to continue his efforts at selling the Mahajual property. He even emailed Frank, who had hired the PI, acting as if nothing had happened.

Keith did not stay silent long. He began emailing that Ronald Lankston, who had sent the funds to OCF, was under the impression that Gabriel and I had stolen his money and was going to sue us. I suggested to Keith that Ronald sue Bailey who had induced him to send the money. As far as I knew, Gabriel had spent the money properly to pay debts of OCF, for which J.W. was responsible. Gabriel eventually sent a list of all OCF expenditures to Keith. Interestingly, Keith would never provide the contact information for Ronald Lankston.

Shortly, Gabriel received a visit from an ugly looking brute who said he was sent by Bailey. The message was simple: Deposit the money in an account that Bailey was to provide by the end of the week or "something bad will happen to you, your sister and your family."

Within an hour, Keith sent an email to Gabriel with an account number to which the money was to be deposited. The account was for a company named Mahajual Consultants Ltd in Georgia. Clearly, Keith and J.W. were working together again.

Gabriel was frightened and contacted me. We both began contacting police and consular officials. Presumably, someone made it clear to both J.W. and Keith that they had gone too far. To date, neither Gabriel nor I have heard from either of them. But I doubt that J.W. understands the concept of "going too far," so I suspect that the story has not ended.

Epilogue III

In March, 2008 I received a phone call from my friend Lyman. "Hey Gus, I ran into J.W. last night in Pancho's. He was with some friends and was drunk. I just want you to know that he is saying that you and Gabriel stole $25,000 from him."

I was surprised, to say the least, that he would have come back to Merida, as everyone by now knew who he really was. I was not surprised that he was saying I had stolen money from him. J.W. simply has a severe problem with the truth.

Lyman continued. "He says he is working in Cozumel developing a marina project."

Again, I was surprised. I could not imagine that someone would give him a job, especially in Mexico, given his history. I had to respect J.W.'s sales ability once again. He was always very convincing. Then it occurred to me that he may have skipped the country again. After all, I could not imagine that the government would allow him to come back to Mexico. My thought was that he must have had his parole lifted.

Lyman said, "He is also saying that he has multiple sclerosis. He told me that is why he has been gone all this time – he was receiving treatments for the disease, and finally his doctors just told him that he could receive his medication here as well as in the States, so he came back. But he only has five years to live."

I told Lyman, "Well, I hope it is not true that he has a fatal disease. I really doubt that it is true – this is his cover for being in jail."

Lyman had another bit of interesting news. "J.W. says that Lola stole his car and ran off with an Argentinian."

I responded, "I'm not surprised, but it was not his car to steal. The owner of that car was OCF, but it really makes no difference."

A few days later I received a phone call from Sam, the partner of the boutique hotel with whom J.W. had tried to scam. Prior to investing millions with J.W. in the property in Mahajual, Sam and his partner had hired the PI who discovered Keith's real identity. He began with an incredulous tone, "Gus, you are not going to believe who called me over the weekend – our old friend J.W.." Sam began laughing and went on, "He was acting as if nothing had ever happened or changed. He told me, 'Let's get together for a beer sometime soon.' I just said, Yeah, sure." He told Sam of his new venture in Cozumel as well.

By coincidence, the next day I received an email from a friend in Atlanta who is a retired lawyer. I asked him if he would do me a favour and check with the parole office in Atlanta to see if John Bailey had been released from parole. My friend emailed back the next day saying that Bailey had not been released and that the parole officer, Courtney Cole, wanted to know why he wanted to know. My friend told me to have Gabriel call Courtney since it was Gabriel's life that had been threatened by a man who said he was sent by Bailey.

My first thought was that Bailey had skipped the country. It never occurred to me that the government would knowingly let him come to Mexico under the circumstances. To save time, I called Courtney Cole. She was not in so I left a message, but she never returned my call. I called again in a few days and left a detailed message wondering if she understood the threats on Gabriel's life and the complete Bailey story. Again, she never called me back.

A few days later Bailey called Gabriel. Bailey left a message simply saying, "Gabriel, call me." He left no number. Gabriel had no intention of calling Bailey. We assumed that Courtney Cole did speak with Bailey. I assumed that Bailey had charmed her into believing he was a really sweet guy who has been the unfortunate victim of circumstances and bad faith on the part of others. I am disappointed that a federal employee would not take the time to return my phone calls. It almost appears that she is more interested in assisting convicted felons than in honest taxpayers. I did not know what else I could or should do.

It was not long before I received an email from Mike, the owner of The Nido. He forwarded an email to him from J.W.. In the email J.W. was inviting Mike to his birthday party at the marina where he was developing a project. He told Mike that he had multiple sclerosis and had looked forward to returning to Merida, marrying Lola, and "slowly losing all bodily functions." J.W. was keeping his famous sense of humor if, indeed, he really did have multiple sclerosis. However, he related that Lola had stolen his car, all his personal possessions, and run off with another guy. He also said Gabriel and I had stolen $25,000 from him.

I thanked Mike for the email and said I did not understand why he had not sued us if we had really stolen his money. In reality, J.W. had no money to steal. We both lamented the fact that J.W. was such an entertaining fellow and a shame that things could not have worked out better for him and our friendships.

To date, neither Gabriel nor I have heard directly from J.W.. However, boarding a plane in Houston to come to Merida, I ran into J.W.'s old friend who had accompanied him to the hospital the night his throat was slashed. He told me, "Hey, your friend J.W. is back in town."

"That's what I hear," I responded.

"Yeah, Gus," he said, "his situation is really a shame. He had been looking for me through friends for several days and I told them, 'Don't give him my phone number.' I really don't want anything to do with this guy. But one day I am driving into my drive way and there he is. He wanted me to find someone to kill his ex-girlfriend."

I was only slightly taken aback, given J.W.'s pattern of sending thugs around to kill or threaten to kill. I had no way of knowing if it was really true, but it did parallel the experience that Gabriel had. J.W.'s old friend was known as someone who worked the system in Mexico. He had done well, and as far as I knew, never did anything illegal, but knew how to use Mexican business connections to his favor, shall we say.

He continued, "He told me that she had stolen his car. So I asked him, 'Is the car yours?' J.W. told me that it wasn't. I told him, 'Look I'm not a gangster – I don't do that sort of thing. My advice to you is to just forget about it and go on about your life.'"

I was surprised that J.W. admitted that the car was not his. I guess it was no longer important to him.

He said J.W. had multiple sclerosis. He postulated, "You know, bad things happen to you when you go around stealing from everyone you know."

"I do believe there is something to the idea that we create our own karma," I responded.

I did not know how serious J.W. was about having Lola killed. Talking about it was one thing, but actually causing it to happen was another. Was Lola really in danger? I contemplated calling Courtney

Cole again at the Atlanta Federal Parole Office. However, Courtney seemed more interested in J.W. than in others, so I did not believe this would accomplish much.

I decided to wait. I believed that J.W. will be unable to live an honest life in Cozumel and will run afoul of the law in some fashion. J.W. seems genetically incapable of doing the right thing.

He also had very unrealistic perceptions. After all, he committed a crime and was discovered. You can't commit a crime and then not expect it to become public. Nevertheless, he returned to Mexico and apparently wants to start all over again as if nothing had happened, claiming to have been gone for treatments for multiple sclerosis. I would think a smarter move would be to start over somewhere else where he could take advantage of anonymity.

I know that will not happen and the story will continue. But I suspect J.W.'s story is nearing the end.[6]

---

[6] In March 2009, I found a reference to J. W. (using his real name) on a web site with pictures of his wedding. On this web site viewers could add comments. Apparently some of J. W.'s female cousins did add some unflattering comments about J. W. and advised his new bride to hide her money and run for the hills, as well as admonishing J. W. for leaving his children. At some point that web site removed the comments and the ability to add other comments, but left the photos. Subsequently a web site using J. W.'s real name in the URL appeared with his police blotter and mug shot. One of the charges was "ESPIO" which may have been the federal court's abbreviation for espionage.

CHAPTER FIVE
A Contextual Reference

In some ways, Mexican culture and mores are almost surrealistic, at least by U.S. cultural standards. That, of course, does not mean that our standards are better—it only means that that things are often vastly different south of the Border. This was one of the things that surprised me most about living and working in Mexico. While working in Mexico had always been a dream of mine, and I had visited Mexico often, the culture shock that I experienced living in Mexico was not expected. Besides traveling extensively throughout Mexico as a tourist, I had grown up in Texas and thought I understood Mexico. My mistake.

On the surface, everything appears similar to the culture in which I grew up. But scratch that surface and there is an enormous difference in the substructure holding up the cultural edifice.

My perceptions of Mexico are mine, and were formed by my previous life experiences. I have done my best to filter my experiences in Mexico through the lens of objectivity, but realize that my perceptions cannot be sterilized of all bias. Attempting to tell the story with objectivity also means that I tell the story with warts and all. I want to give anyone who is thinking of moving to Mexico or of doing business in Mexico the benefit of my experiences so they can know what they are getting into and so that they can know both the risks and the rewards involved.

I have had no anthropological training, but I do have a theory about why the cultural differences between the U.S. and Mexico are so great. In a nutshell, Mexico was *conquered* and the United States was *settled*. The Spaniards, who were the first conquerors from Europe, came to conquer and enslave. All opposition was squashed without mercy. The purpose of The Conquest was to expropriate and extract resources, which this creates a short-term outlook by the conquerors and the conquered. The whole concept of *conquest*, in my opinion, has had eternal and pervasive effects on Mexican culture.

The highly respected Georgetown University historian Carroll Quigley, in his monumental *Tragedy And Hope, A History of The World In Our Time*, ascribed this attitude to the long Arab/Muslim occupation of Iberia. He pointed out that the ethos of exploitation and corruption that prevails wherever the Spanish and Portuguese have colonized is not European in character, but is an exact mirror of how society has been organized in the Muslim world for centuries. He called this nexus the "Pakistani-Peruvian Axis," and noted that it was one of the main impediments to the application of modern Western values in both the Mideast and Latin America. In short, Quigley believed that corruption and force are the main cultural and political determinants all along this axis, and that it would be very difficult to replace them with notions of equity and justice.

Famed Beat Generation novelist William Burroughs, who himself spent several years south of the

Border, put it more bluntly: "Temperamentally, Mexico is an Oriental country."

In contrast, the United States was settled by those fleeing England and Europe with a purpose of gaining a better life for themselves, their family, and their future. They wanted to *colonize*. They brought with them the Protestant work ethic. These settlers wanted to *produce*, not extract and expropriate. This, in my view, creates a long-term outlook.

WORKING AND LIVING IN PARADISE

Hopefully, nothing that I have to relate will be interpreted in any way as negative toward Mexicans in general. I have nothing but respect for the vast majority of Mexicans, and especially Mexican workers. These are very noble people who give their utmost and will respond and go the extra mile when you ask, despite the hardships they face.

One example of these hardships is the difficulty of even getting to work. Since most of my employees do not have their own transportation, they rely on public transport. Of about five hundred employees, only slightly more than a dozen have autos. In our case, we contracted with private bus lines to pick up our workers in the downtown area and transport them from downtown at our cost. For those who live in outlying areas we send our hired buses to pick them up in their pueblos. Nevertheless, most workers spend well over an hour getting to work and another hour or more getting home. I have one supervisor who lives in Halacho who must wake up at 4:30 A.M., catch a taxi from there to Maxcanu where our hired buses retrieve about a hundred other workers. When this supervisor is asked to put in overtime, she never refuses even though this means she would miss our private buses and must take public transport home which takes much longer, as public buses are constantly stopping en route for disembarking and embarking passengers. If she works overtime, she arrives at her home between 11:00 and 12:00 PM and will still be back at work the next morning, after waking before 5:00 A.M. This is an extraordinary commitment to work, but it is not at all uncommon in the Yucatan.

I often see Mexicans sleeping on buses in transit from one place to another. When I first noticed this, my initial impression was that this is another example of the stereotypical view of Mexicans as lazy. But I have learned that most of those people are simply exhausted, not lazy.

The knack that many Mexicans have for entrepreneurship is astounding. On very little capital they will start businesses out of their home. Little stores are constantly springing up in neighborhoods; the living room of their residence is sometimes converted into the store. The most common are *tienditas* that sell mostly bread, soft drinks and snacks. Many have small copiers in the store as the government bureaucracy is constantly requiring copies of paperwork for the most innocuous of bureaucratic requirements. Since the government offices do not make copies for their citizens, a market for small copy stores has emerged. The most interesting combination of sales and services that I have seen in these tiny entrepreneurial ventures run out of one's home was a beauty shop that also advertised services for copies, faxes and the internet.

The majority of Mexicans live in an economic state that those of us from developed countries would characterize as well below the poverty line. Many do not have flushing toilets. In fact, a question on the questionnaire that national census takers ask is: "Do you have indoor bathroom facilities?". There are those in the States and other developed countries who will say that poverty in Mexico exists as a result of individual irresponsibility. I have to confess that before I moved to Mexico, my thoughts were tinged with this misconception about native Mexicans. Now I believe without any doubt that the economic problems that exist in Mexico exist not because of individual irresponsibility but due to the Mexican government's fecklessness, lack of compassion for its citizens, and government employees and politicians who place their own personal self interest above all else.

It is incomprehensible to me that a country with the fifth largest oil and gas reserves in the world still has such poverty. The root cause, I believe, has to do with The Conquest, which has left a heritage of corruption and the belief that if a power discrepancy exists it should be used to the advantage of he who wields that power at all times and without mercy. Government officials in Mexico yield enormous power, even at the clerical level.

Mexicans are abandoning their country in droves because there is little opportunity in Mexico for the average Mexican. The economic problems that exist in Mexico, as many have written about, are not due to lack of resources nor to lack of desire to work by the average Mexican. The problems are political. The Mexican political culture is dominated by the elite, regardless of political affiliation. There appears to be no political will nor strong political leadership focused on true change that will provide opportunity and a use of the national wealth to actually develop the country's potential.

One reason the economic status quo can be maintained in Mexico is the porous border with the United States, which acts as a natural safety valve. Speaking about economic problems faced by the masses in Mexico, Norman Bailey, a former Reagan official involved in international affairs, reportedly has said, "Most countries either collapse or do the necessary thing. Mexico has never been in the position of being forced to do the necessary thing".

With each immigrant to the United States from Mexico, the Mexican government is relieved of a burden. I have heard that the Mexican government actually prints pamphlets that it distributes near the border that educates its citizens leaving the country for the U.S. on how to make the illegal crossing successfully. Furthermore, payments from Mexicans working in the States, either by legal or illegal immigrants, to their relatives in Mexico produce an enormous cash inflow to Mexico. Therefore, not only is the burden of unemployment reduced, but cash inflow to the country is increased.

In the States we openly debate all sides of this issue, including listening to ridiculous arguments in public opinion. However, I was struck by the Mexican perception of the illegal immigration dispute in the U.S. As a result, I have a new appreciation for why the American press should act more responsibly in reporting political disputes. Mexicans are convinced that the entire issue is driven by racism. The Mexican press focuses on news that reports the most exaggerated claims made in the U.S. press as if this is the American norm and mainstream belief.

For example, one day during the well-reported Minute Man vigilance of the border, I was having lunch with the Mexican partner in charge of the financial audit of my company. He is a partner of one of the four largest multi-national accounting firms in the world. Obviously, he is well-educated. He reflected deep concern over what had been reported in the Mexican press as a well-established fact: The Minute Men were armed and actually hunting to kill, like deer, illegal aliens crossing the border.

I was flabbergasted. The illegal immigration issue, I explained, was about *illegal* immigration. I continued that I did not doubt that there were racists in the United States, as there are in Mexico, that may be against *all* immigration, but that no one was "hunting" Mexicans. I pointed out that if my immigration papers were not in perfect order in Mexico, I would be subject to deportation. Mexican rules for work visas are much more stringent, in my opinion, than those in the U.S. And, while I might complain about the rules, I would never complain about Mexico's right to set whatever rules, however ridiculous they may be, that it decides to set. If I wish to live legally in Mexico as a foreigner, I must abide by those rules.

The illegal immigration issue is very simple. In my view, the U.S. press is out of control and exacerbating our political problems around the world by irresponsibly reporting ridiculous accusations. Many reporters appear to be as selfish and power hungry as Mexican politicians. I don't recall seeing reported in the U.S. press the core reason that Mexicans are fleeing their country, but I wish I would.

Illegal immigration to the United States is only going to worsen. The root cause is the deplorable state of the Mexican economy. Compounding the problem is the birth rate in Mexico. The only real solution lies within Mexico and the Mexican government shows no will to solve it.

The Mexican government provides no welfare payment to the unemployed. Those cross border payments from Mexicans working in the U.S. obviously ease the Mexican government's economic plight and assist Mexicans receiving the payments. However, these payments really only serve to keep the recipients in a subsistence state and promotes a reliance on this type of private welfare that could not have beneficial social consequences.

A quick example to illustrate the Mexican government's lack of regard for its citizens, especially the poor and powerless. Water in Mexico, as we all know, is not fit to drink. How can that possibly be in a country so incredibly rich in natural resources? How difficult would it be for the government to create infrastructure to make the potable water drinkable? These are rhetorical questions, as it would not be difficult at all in the 21st century to provide drinkable water to all citizens if the government had the will to do so.

However, it actually could be that Mexicans are better off without drinkable water than with drinkable water provided by the government. The reason is corruption. Take the example of The *Comision Federal de Electricidad* (CFE – Federal Electric Commission) which provides electricity through the Federal government throughout the country. The cost to the consumer is incredibly high, for two reasons. In the first place, these revenues help to fund the government. The underground economy in Mexico is huge; therefore, the government replaces lost income taxes through other types of revenues. It is reported in several studies that between 40% and 70% of all taxpayers either cheat or pay no taxes at all. Secondly, corruption is rampant. So much so that the CFE has placed it's slogan on every vehicle, invoice and other printed material to combat the obvious: *Comprometido con la honestidad*—"Committed to honesty." However, the CFE is no more committed to honesty than any other institution in Mexico. I am told it is easy to have a CFE employee connect you illegally to your neighbor's meter for a small bribe paid direct to the employee.

As far as honesty in government, it is clear to any sane person that many Mexican laws are actually designed to encourage corruption. Some examples will be related later. In general, there are so many complicated requirements placed on simple matters that most Mexicans just pay a bribe to go around all the hurdles placed in their way.

Official corruption has been notorious in Mexico. Former presidents and high government officials reportedly stashed hundreds of millions of dollars in overseas accounts. Supposedly these amounts were robbed mainly from PEMEX, the government owned oil company. According to the Mexican press, it is almost a certainty that Carlos Salinas, President of Mexico from 1988 to 1994, stole hundreds of millions. President Salinas moved to Ireland after leaving the Presidency and his brother Raul spent time in a Mexican prison.

What astonishes me is that nearly everyone believes that Salinas lined his pockets while president, as did all his predecessors. Nevertheless, there has been no real investigation of Salinas by any governmental agency, despite the change in political power from the PRI to the PAN. Government corruption and theft seems to be tolerated as a respected tradition. In the U.S. we seem to go to the other extreme, investigating the slightest hint of malfeasance. It would be prudent for both countries to find a proper balance between the extremes, but I don't have much hope for either country.

Returning to the theme of God's favor to Mexico by blessing it with a plethora of natural resources and also his curse of allowing PEMEX to administer the resources. In order to protect PEMEX, Mexico prohibits foreign investment in oil and gas exploration. The only other country in the world to adopt this policy is North Korea. Even Cuba and Venezuela allow foreign investment in their oil and gas exploration programs. As a result of this policy, and possibly due to theft of revenues, PEMEX is going broke, despite high oil prices and enormous reserves in the country.

PEMEX is not the only government owned business in Mexico. There were many others until the government began a privatizing effort under President Zedillo who was elected after Salinas left office. Prior to Zedillo, all the seaports and airports were government owned. The telephone company, Telmex, was government owned. No doubt there was much corruption present in the privatizing process. For example, Carlos Slim, the richest man in Mexico and recently elevated to the richest in the world, became the controlling owner of Telmex, now a publicly traded company. Carlos Slim was personally very close to President Salinas.

A recent newspaper article reported that 12% of the GNP of Mexico is lost due to official corruption. The article reported that Mexicans begin to practice bribery on average as early as age twelve when they begin paying their teachers for grades. A study reported that 57% of all Mexicans by age thirty have paid at least one bribe. I would not be surprised if these estimates are far too modest.

Another recent article reported on a survey of Mexicans done by Transparency International. The results of the survey indicate that the most corrupt area of Mexico is the Police, followed closely by the political parties, the legislative branch, the judicial system and public services.

The good news is that things do seem to be changing for the better in terms of corruption. In 2000, the PRI, the political party that had control of the presidency for seventy years lost the election. Vicente Fox from the *PAN* political party took over. In 2006, *PAN* won again with Felipe Calderon, as president. This, I believe, represents at least a subtle signal that the populace wants change. It is not that the *PAN* has ethical superiority over the *PRI*. Corruption and scandals continue. However, things do seem to be changing, but it is the equivalent of turning a ship that was headed at full steam to the north and now needs to go south. The ship may be now headed northwest, but has a long turning radius to make a southern heading.

An example of the progress with official corruption was illustrated in a recent news article in the *Diario de Yucatan*. Various mayors and local officials had been caught in financial scandals. While this is not news, the news is that higher government officials are taking action. Reportedly a total of over $1,000,000 was missing from various pueblitos scattered through the Yucatan. This is a stunningly high number for an economically depressed region. Mayors and other government functionaries were responsible. While only about $50,000 had actually been collected from the perpetrators, the Mexican IRS equivalent was beginning to attach the property of the officials involved. The good news is that there are now consequences to official corruption.

After living and working in Mexico, I realize that Mexico is really a socialist country masquerading as capitalist. The most glaring example is the labor law, which is essentially the same law originally passed about eighty years ago. Specific examples of the repressive effects on both employees and employers of this law are related later. In general, it is very difficult to fire a worker, even with cause, without paying three month's severance. The law contemplates a mandatory minimum of 10% profit sharing with all employees. There is a minimum mandatory Christmas bonus of at least two weeks salary.

The law, coupled with rampant corruption in its application, creates a situation that rewards non-productivity and makes Mexico less competitive in the world market. Furthermore, the rich and powerful are always able to defeat the law's intentions to protect the worker. Often the worker actually ends up worse off under these laws.

While I often marvel at how hard many Mexicans work, there is a part of the society that tries to play the game using the labor laws to their advantage. In actuality, they are often the ones who get played. Nevertheless, they continue to be duped by the system set up by the government that leads them to believe there is a free lunch. This segment of the labor force looks for ways to get fired, and sometimes these people even dare the employer to fire them so that they can collect their severance.

A Mexican friend who recently returned to Mexico to live after living twenty-five years in California once asked me why the work ethic for "wetbacks" in the States so different from many of their brothers who stay in Mexico. I had noted also that illegal and legal immigrants to the United States from Mexico have a strong work ethic. I believe the reason for the difference is the culture and the laws set by the two countries.

In the U.S. almost anyone can get ahead through hard work. And most immigrants soon learn the hard lesson that if you do not work hard you will be fired and another will be there to take your place. Furthermore, upon firing, there will be no severance pay. Since the purpose of these immigrants is to make money, a system with real consequences to those who are not productive will force the vast majority to become productive. That is, the system in the U.S. works for those who want to better themselves economically.

The most astonishing example of the creation of unrealistic expectations in the work force by the Mexican government is a lawsuit filed against us by a former employee. It seems that when we moved our factory to another location she was not in agreement with the move. So she quit coming to work. On the first pay day since the move she showed up and asked for her paycheck. She claimed that we had "renounced our address" and that if we had stayed she would continue to work for us. But because we had decided to move to a larger factory and she was not in agreement with our decision, we should have to continue to pay her!

Another example of the effects of socialistic concepts is the health care system that is administered under the Mexican social security system. First, to be included in the system, workers must be currently registered as being employed by a business that is paying social security to the government on their behalf. Due to the large underground economy and the efforts to reduce costs, many employers do not register their employees with social security, nor do they pay their social security taxes. Therefore these employees have no right to treatment in the social security health system, nor can they afford private medical care.

For those who are legally registered and treated under the social security health system, the treatment is atrocious. To my knowledge, there is no concept of medical, or any other type, malpractice in Mexico. The pay for doctors in the social security medical system is very low. Many doctors work in the social security system part time and have their own private practices on the side. It appears that if patients are being treated in the social security system, the theory is to look for the easiest and quickest short term solution, which often results in only treating symptoms without providing quality health care. For example, workers with accidents who have had, say, a thumb cut badly and are undergoing treatment at a social security hospital, may find that the doctor will simply amputate rather than attempting to make the thumb usable for the future.

This is often fine with the worker as, astonishingly, the government has set prices for appendages that are lost in the course of their work. They will receive a one time payment from their employer. For Mexicans, many of whom literally live day to day, a payment of several thousand pesos for a lost thumb is a godsend. Little thought is given to the future implications of not having the thumb. In fact little consideration is given to planning or thought about the future. I think the main reason for this is the hand-to-mouth existence that many Mexicans live. They don't have the luxury of planning.

As mentioned earlier, there are no government payments for unemployment. Although employers have a higher tax rate under social security than we do in the United States, none of the higher taxes translate to unemployment benefits. There is no unemployment welfare in Mexico.

The Mexican government has demonstrated to me in numerous ways that compassion it lacks compassion for its citizens, the foregoing being some examples. There are others. Fraud is rampant in all walks of life in Mexico, and the government appears to have little interest in enforcing the laws against it. Citizens in Mexico understand that there is little chance of punishment for penalty breaking the law, whether their actions involve fraud or simple driving regulations. This situation forces every citizen to maintain a constant defensive posture in order to keep from being defrauded. Nor does the government assume an aggressive stance to prosecute those who commit serious crimes.

The lackadaisical approach generates innumerable dysfunctional behaviors compared to what is considered the norm in most modern societies. A serious and alarming result of this recently caught my attention in a U.S. news story about Mexico. The report indicates that Mexico ranks number two in the world, only behind Iraq, in the number of journalists murdered. Sometimes I believe that Mexico is barely held together by very thin threads that could break at any moment.

To compound a fairly difficult situation exhibited by a lack of appropriate legal structure and order, it appears that the government is in a state of denial about the realities of the global economy. NAFTA was a great boon to the Mexican economy. When it was passed in 1994, it was really the first free trade treaty of it's kind and gave a competitive advantage to goods made in Mexico. Mexico had a sort of monopoly on free trade with the U. S.

However, free trade treaties are proliferating and Mexico no longer has a favored position. Worse for Mexico, China was admitted to the World Trade Organization and factories that flourished in the 1990's in Mexico are now closing and moving to China.

Thomas L. Friedman poses some interesting questions that relate to China versus Mexico in *The World is Flat: A Brief History of the Twenty-First Century*. Why, he asks. with all the geographical advantages and plentiful natural resources that Mexico enjoys, is China eating Mexico's lunch? What enables one country to do all the things necessary in a sustained manner to develop a strong economy, while another country can't?

He believes the answer lies in China's ability to pull together as a society and sacrifice for the sake of a common future. He also notes the presence of strong leaders in China, leaders who have a vision of what needs to be done and the will to do it. Mexico lacks all these things. One pervasive theme that I note in Mexican society in general is an unwillingness to sacrifice in the short run in order to have a better future. In one sense, it is very understandable. The vast majority live literally from day to day. This fact makes sacrifice much more difficult than the kind of sacrifice that those of us from developed countries make in order to get ahead financially.

Mexico lacks strong political leaders that have the capacity to sell a vision of sacrifice for a better future. When Fox came into office, he recognized the need for reforms in labor laws, tax collection, and remedies for corruption, among other reforms. All of these reforms stalled in the Mexican Congress, which was divided between various political parties, none of which wanted any other party to get credit for anything good that might happen. There are no real statesmen in Mexico, apparently. Nor am I convinced that there are any in the U.S., Canada or the rest of the world either. While I believe Fox could have been a good leader, he appeared to have run out of political energy after losing a number of tough battles in his first two years.

So Mexico continues its search for visionary leaders who are willing to make tough decisions and sell the citizens and their political adversaries on their vision. The jury is still out on Calderon, although his war against the drug cartels is admirable and promising in terms of showing leadership qualities. In the meantime, the Mexican government continues to place onerous and unreasonable burdens on its citizens and investors. Customs regulations, despite NAFTA, are a nightmare and create additional non-value-added costs.

The government has created a business climate that makes things in general much more difficult than they should be. As an example, the World Bank found that on average it takes fifty-eight days to start a business in Mexico compared to five in the U.S. and compared to twenty-seven in Chile. For medium sized companies, which is precisely the level of investment Mexico desperately needs, there is a higher corporate income tax rate than prevails in the U.S. Adding insult to injury, there is a national value added tax of 15% on nearly everything.

Tax evasion in Mexico is rampant, but the government seems determined to solve the problem by increasing taxes on those who are actually paying them rather than going after the law breakers who are avoiding them. This is one of many examples where the government is simply looking for the easy way out by treating the symptom rather than the illness.

One final example concerning the government's seeming lack of economic interest in its citizens. NAFTA has made goods cheaper in the U.S. by removing tariffs. However, the Mexican government does not seem to apply NAFTA within Mexican borders. My last reading of the NAFTA treaty indicated that all tariffs would be removed by the year 2006 on automobiles. Nevertheless, U.S.-made autos are still more expensive in Mexico than in the U.S. because apparently import tariffs are still charged on foreign vehicles sold in Mexico.

If the government would truly embrace capitalism, I believe the country's economic plight would improve immensely. In spite of the legal and economic limitations placed on its citizens by their government, Mexicans are finding ways to overcome. Nevertheless, embracing capitalism coupled with a crackdown on corruption would create an environment where the natural resources, including human resources, would be released and directed in such a powerful economic stream that the country would come crashing into the First World like a meteorite. I hope this will happen soon, but it will take a strong leader with the vision of what needs to be done coupled with the will and the ability to make his case against centuries of bad habits and entrenched interests.

CHAPTER SIX

Operadora Ganso Azul S. A. De C. V.

I started my company in 1998 for the purpose of doing what many people want to do when they move to Merida: owning and operating a bed and breakfast. Happily, I came to my senses when another opportunity presented itself before I could move to Merida and start my B & B. That is why my company has such a whimsical name. Once we saw we would be doing serious business, we thought about changing the name, but ultimately decided against it.

Ganso Azul is translated as Blue Goose. The name came about for two reasons. First, my name, Gus, is pronounced in Spanish as "Goose," due to the fact that there is no "uh" sound in Spanish. Secondly, I was married at the time to a Mexican lady, Claudia, whose nickname as a baby was "Azul," which of course means Blue. She had this nickname because the family already had two girls and one boy and was absolutely sure she was going to be a boy. Her room was painted blue as a result and, hence, the nickname.

The story of those who make up the management team at the business is going to be the most entertaining to write and, at the same time, the most difficult. I am writing with some anticipated melancholy, since I am planning to return to the States within the next year and remove myself from day-to-day operations of the business. As I write this, no one in the company knows my return is imminent. I have extreme angst about the anticipated move. The company has become in many ways my family since my biological family is physically many miles away and culturally on another planet. Many of us in OGA, we refer to the company by it's initials, have bonded through the very tough and the very fun times and we have shed together blood, sweat, and tears figuratively and literally.

Most of my family and friends back in the States thought I was nuts to move to Mexico at age 50 and start a business in a risky industry that I knew nothing about. Besides that, I gave up a tenured, full professor's job that paid much more than it should and more than I would be making for years to come even if things in Mexico went well. As a tenured professor I was working without risk. You may have heard the old saying, "If you are a tenured professor, the only way they can fire you is if you are caught in bed with a live boy or a dead girl." Since neither of those two conditions was contemplated, I was exchanging a no-risk deal for one that had nothing *but* risk. I guess I was nuts. But many people have said and written in different ways what Don Juan said in Carlos Casteñeda's books of the 1960s and 1970s, "You have to take the road with heart." I was at a position in my life where I was not willing to deal with the petty politics of higher education and self-important professors and administrators, regardless of pay.

I have been living my dream. Since I was a kid, I was enamored with Mexico. Previously, I had traveled throughout Mexico as a tourist. My Grandfather went to Mexico in 1910 to roughneck. A roughneck is the vernacular for workers on oil rigs. I asked him why he did it. He said, "The pay was much better. I received a dollar a day." My Grandfather moved to Mexico from Arp, Texas, a small town in East Texas.

He left Mexico after the Revolution began. Mexico has had a number of revolutions, so I am not sure why this one is The Revolution, but that is the way it is known. He worked on an oil rig located about sixty miles from Tampico in the middle of the jungle. He and his co-workers had to hunt for their own food. Once the Revolution got into full swing, Pancho Villa's men would come by their camp about once a month to collect "taxes" from them. Those taxes were usually paid in the form of deer meat that roughnecks hunted, killed and butchered for their own consumption. My Grandfather said that over time he and his co-workers could predict when Villa's men were coming and would hide the "taxes". Villa's men were satisfied to take part of whatever they found and, apparently, never questioned that there might have been something hidden.

My Grandfather worked for Gulf Oil, whose properties were expropriated once the Revolution ended. At some point in 1912, Gulf ordered its employees out of Mexico. On the way out, my Granddad got caught up in a battle. He was only a spectator, but at the end of the battle, he did take pictures of some captured *Federales*, who Villa hung from a tree.

For me, Mexico has always had a romantic appeal. As mentioned, my dream had always been to live and work in Mexico. While there were certainly times when I thought the dream I was living with OGA was going to turn into a nightmare, we, as a team, overcame the obstacles and the dream survived.

Our quality problems mentioned earlier were solved and quality standards were initially met through the hard work of Claudia and Mary Solis, our head supervisor who eventually became our Quality Manager. Ultimately, we were able to create a culture of quality with the sewers. We learned the hard way the old maxim that quality is a culture and cannot be inspected into a product. That is, it is not cost-effective to find errors through inspection. Quality must be built into the product during the production of the product, although inspection is an important control. The quality culture was created through the dedicated work of a lot of people over time.

I look back with pride and pleasure thinking about the members of our team who made OGA what it is today. Our first employee, Delia, was our first supervisor and stayed with us over five years. She was a young widow whose husband, a professional boxer, was run over and killed by a car. After she was initially hired by us and waiting on equipment to arrive so that production could begin, she basically acted as a janitor every day washing floors, sweeping, and cleaning in the tiny factory we originally rented. Not once did she complain about having to do such menial labor. I will always appreciate her efforts and her attitude. She resigned once she married again.

The first production engineer we hired who really made a difference was Francisco. He was with us about a year and a half. We lost him due to marriage also. Francisco married a Gringa and moved to the U.S. Parting was difficult for both of us and emotionally charged. We stay in touch from time to time.

He has bought into the American Dream and is very happy with his mortgage and his job as a production manager in the U.S.

Before Francisco, we were like an airplane moving down the runway and gaining just a bit of speed but not enough to take off. He caused us to get into the air and start flying before the runway ran out.

After Francisco had been with us several months, I had my first bad experience with Mexican workers. We had a work stoppage. As will be more than clear later, Mexican labor laws are stacked against the employer. Mary Solis and Wendy, our accountant, came into the office to give me the bad news and to tell me that their demand was to speak to me. Instinctively, I told Mary and Wendy to inform the workers that I would gladly talk to them about their complaints but not until they went back to work and, if they did return to their machines, at their morning break we would talk as a group. This was a strategy to establish control and assert authority by placing the condition that they return to work before I would speak with them. Thankfully, they accepted the condition. In the meantime, we attempted to contact our labor lawyer for advice. He could not be reached before the break time, so I was on my own. Claudia was out of town that day.

At this time we had about sixty-five employees. We all met in the back of our tiny factory, about 7000 square feet. There I was literally with my back against the wall of the factory and unhappy workers surrounding me. After about thirty minutes of sparring around, it became clear that they wanted me to fire Mary and Francisco. I asked if that was true, and they finally openly confirmed it.

I made it clear that both Mary and Francisco had really done a great job for the company and that, as a result, I had complete faith in them. Several employees commented that the operators were going to quit unless I fired Mary and Francisco. Basically, they wanted me to choose between Mary and Francisco or them.

This worried me. I did not know how we could replace and train sixty-five workers quickly. We were just beginning to hit a production rhythm. If they walked off the job, I was not sure the company would survive. Instinctively, I said, with my best poker face and a large knot in my stomach, that I would not be firing Mary or Francisco and that those who wanted to stay must return to work and those who did not could resign.

Finally, the silent majority began to speak up. They said they had nothing against Mary or Francisco and that really things were not bad. I breathed a sigh of relief. This had not been a comfortable situation for me, but I learned a valuable lesson that day: follow your instincts and do not give in to intimidation. We lost about four sewers, but our two key employees stayed on and kept moving the company ahead. Incidentally, within about three months, two of the four employees who resigned returned and asked for their jobs back.

I happened to be on sabbatical and still employed at a university for the first year of operations of the factory. I completed a book while on sabbatical and had to return to the States. At that time, I felt as though the company could grow to perhaps 100 employees, and I would continue traveling back and forth for awhile. I had a commitment to complete one more year at the university after my sabbatical.

Claudia and Mary nursed the momentum that Francisco had started, and the company continued to grow. The customer soon asked us to expand to another facility to increase our capacity. We rented a 35,000 square-foot facility and began to produce shirts as well as pants.

At about this time a local factory owned by a Canadian company was closing, and the General Manager of this factory was looking for a job. Claudia liked him and once I interviewed him, I knew we were not only going to be good friends, but that he could help us immensely.

Joe Toste was originally from Portugal, and moved to Canada with his family at age fifteen. He began his career as a mechanic at a sewing factory in Canada and worked his way into management. He came to Mexico about eleven years earlier and eventually ran a factory of about four hundred people.

I knew Joe could take us to the next level. I hired him and he did. We needed to convert ourselves from a small-factory mentality to a medium-sized, serious business mentality. Joe took us there. In the process, we expanded our second factory building, which had become known as OGA II, from 35,000 to 50,000 square feet. When we hired Joe we had grown to about a hundred and fifty employees. I knew that I could not be an absentee owner at this point. Claudia and I were having marital problems. We decided to separate, and I decided to move to Mexico on a full-time basis, as my commitment after the sabbatical was now completed.

Joe took us to about three hundred employees and jumped production and efficiencies significantly. In the process, he enabled us to hire a number of his former key employees and supervisors. Unfortunately, Joe could not stay with us over about a year and a half. We were a growing company with enormous capital needs, and Joe had a family and two kids. I made a deal with him at a low salary, both of us hoping that the financial situation of the company would improve and give us more flexibility in the near future. Unfortunately, that flexibility was about a year late in coming. Joe had to take another job in Campeche where he stayed another year before moving back to Canada.

Like Francisco, Joe left an enduring legacy at OGA. First, while Francisco had lifted us off the runway, Joe took us to and altitude where we could fly with the big boys. We had become a professional factory under Joe's production leadership. Joe left us with had another legacy. He had mentored Sergio Can and Santiago Peet at his other factory. These were young Mexicans who we hired on Joe's recommendation, and Joe continued mentoring them until he left OGA. Both of these men are an integral key to OGA's continued success. Joe also brought in the best supervisors that we have, all of whom had worked for him before: Mirna Hu, Rosy Castillo, Miriam Aragon, and Gloria Canul.

When Joe left, as when Francisco left, it was difficult for me. I knew both had left enduring legacies. Francisco was young enough to be my son, and I almost thought of him as a son. Joe was close to my age, more like a brother. Joe is an incredibly ethical man for whom I have and will always have enormous respect. We still stay in touch.

Joe was a treasure of knowledge for us. He'd had eleven years working under the Mexican legal and cultural system and taught us the tricks of how to manage under some conditions that were very strange by U.S. norms. Joe tells me he also learned from us about a different style of managing that is, perhaps, more humanistic than the norm in Mexico.

CHAPTER SEVEN
My First Car Accident

There are many rules and regulations in Mexico. Cultural studies show that Mexicans like rules to remove as much ambiguity from life as possible. However, the culture also allows for much flexibility. There are rules, but that does not necessarily mean they have to be followed in practice. Driving is a perfect example.

I believe that driving *mores* indicate much about the culture in which you are driving. Most of my experience is in the U.S. and Mexico, although I have driven in Europe, the Caribbean and South America. I was expecting European and South American driving to be closer to that of Mexico than the U.S. I was wrong. Driving in Merida is the closest representation of barely controlled chaos that I have seen in practice.

With such "flexible" driving customs, one might suspect that accidents would be rather prevalent. Actually, this is not so. There are relatively few. But I follow normal driving mores and I have had accidents. I was judged wrong in all cases. I had not been living in Merida long when the first accident occurred as I was returning from the marina in Progreso, about 20 miles from Merida after an outing on the boat I had bought from Lee. I had always taken the same route, because it was the quickest. The road leading from the marina to a main artery was straight and without stop signs at the intersections en route until it reached the main artery. I had travelled that road many times without incident. In Merida, as in Progeso, the tradition is to build houses to the edge of the sidewalk or street. This makes it very hard to see around corners, obviously. However, there were no stop signs on this route so I had no need to overly concern myself with traffic at the intersections as I had noted that there were stop signs on intersecting streets for autos entering the intersections from the cross streets. I should have concerned myself.

Entering an intersection, I was plowed into by a combi, which is a van that carries passengers and takes given route. The collision was the passenger side of my new truck, which had only 125 miles showing on the odometer. The collision knocked the truck into a telephone pole on the other side of the street. My arms went through the steering wheel, and I remember being struck by the fact that the air bag did not deploy – I was happy for that.

Within seconds, I was surrounded by screaming neighbours. I recall thinking, uh oh, they are going to want to sue me. They will see me as the rich Gringo despite the fact that I knew I was in the right since there was no stop sign on my side of the intersection.

The combi driver was a woman who got out limping. I thought I saw dollar signs in her eyes. She claimed she was in the right. I checked her side of the intersection –no stop sign either.

Police came quickly since the Progreso Police sub station was only two blocks away. The combi driver was taken to the hospital for "observation." I was taken to the police station along with my truck. No one was hurt other than the combi driver who I felt was making a big deal of her knee which she claimed was badly injured.

Friends and my insurance agent arrived, who happened to also be the agent for the company who owned the combi. This was a Friday and by now it was night. It was explained to me that if the other driver did not sign a release then I was going to jail because the judge was gone for the weekend and could not let me off the hook despite the fact I had insurance that was sufficient to cover any eventuality. This was my first experience with the Mexican legal system. It was incomprehensible to me.

Also incomprehensible was why I was being held at fault. At first, it was explained to me that the other street had "traffic preference." I asked the police how that was determined and his response was, "Everyone in Progreso knows the other street has preference." I explained the obvious: I was not from Progreso.

The insurance agent and I went to the intersection. After inspection, we found a metal post cut off about 1 inch above the sidewalk on my side of the intersection. The police who accompanied us then said, "Oh, that's right. About a year ago, we put a sidewalk on this street and we had to take down the stop signs to do it." He laughed and continued, "We just forgot to put them back." I did not find it very humorous. The stop signs are still not in place years later.

The insurance agent was able to convince the combi driver that she should sign the release form that would enable me to leave police custody at about 11 P.M. The accident had occurred at about 3 P.M. I was at last a free man.

CHAPTER EIGHT
Wayne Trotter

Wayne is a legend in Merida. All the local ex pats know who he is even if they don't know him personally. He came here over thirty years ago from Canada as a young man in his twenties and started a tiny bar called Pancho's. Over the years, Pancho's kept expanding, and Wayne did exceedingly well.

I met Wayne soon after I moved to Merida. He seemed a bit stand-offish, even aloof. As I got to know him better, I realized that he is not in the least aloof, but because of his past experiences in Mexico, he is careful about making friends. Over the years, we have become closer and socialized together. I have the utmost respect for what he has accomplished in Mexico and also for him as a man.

Pancho's is the obligatory tourist trap though Wayne cringes at that description. Located one block from the main square, it is the prime destination for whole busloads of vacationing Europeans. But it is not really a tourist trap because all the ex pats living in Merida frequent Pancho's. I have never taken anyone to Pancho's who did not enjoy the experience. It's got *jene se quois*. It is an open-air restaurant bar where all the waiters wear white outfits with leather bandoliers that have wine corks in the bullet holders of the bandoliers. They know how to have a good time, and they ensure that the patrons do as well.

In the late 1980s, Wayne started another restaurant, an Italian place called La Tratto. Located out in the northern part of town and mostly frequented by locals and ex pats living in Merida, it is not a tourist hangout. La Tratto is also an outdoor experience with only a small part of the restaurant under roof.

The third restaurant that the Trotter family owns is just around the corner from La Tratto and is called Trotter's. Wayne converted a home located on a thoroughfare into a restaurant with incredible atmosphere. One would never expect an ambience such as Trotter's in Merida. Perhaps in Miami, but not in Merida. While there is an outdoor dining area, the main part of the restaurant is indoor.

There were ventures into Cancun and Playa del Carmen, as well. These did not turn out to be as successful.

Wayne made his first trip to Mexico when he was about eighteen years old. He was working in Canada at an advertising agency, and all of his friends decided to go to Acapulco and invited him along. Unfortunately, Wayne's mom did not think it a good idea and did not give permission. He was disheartened and did not have enough of his own money to go, so his friends left without him.

He related his sad situation to an older co-worker at the ad agency, Henry, who told him that he could go to the bank and get a loan. In fact, if Wayne did this, Henry said, he would agree to go with him. Wayne did not hesitate and soon the two were on their way to Acapulco to meet their friends.

Wayne is one of those guys who has the good luck of attracting interesting experiences that normally turn out humorous and where no one gets hurt. The trip to Acapulco spawned a number of such mini adventures. These are best told by Wayne over a tequila in Pancho's.

Once arriving in Acapulco, he had the good luck of meeting a beautiful young Mexican woman named Auris at the pool. She was on vacation with her family from Merida. He had only three days left in Acapulco adventure, but he spent them with her. They both reluctantly parted at the end of those three days, but vowed to stay in touch. They wrote to each other over the next nine months and further developed their friendship.

Wayne's travel experience to Mexico left him bitten by the travel bug. He booked a trip to Jamaica. After a few days in Jamaica, he decided he did not like it but noted the proximity to the Yucatan Peninsula where Auris was living. Soon he found himself booking a flight to Merida.

Auris was happy to see him. Soon he realized he was in love and proposed to her. They set the date in the next few days. Then panic set in. Wayne was staying in a hotel near the airport and had his bags packed to fly out after questioning just what the hell he was doing. After all, he had only been in Merida two weeks. Somehow he fought the urge to flee and went through with the marriage. Now he says, "It's the smartest thing I ever did."

After the wedding, the plan was to return to Canada where Wayne had a job. It was winter and when they left Merida, the weather was perfect. Stepping off the plane in Canada, they were greeted to temperatures well below freezing coupled with a strong northerly wind. It was an incredible shock, especially for Auris. Wayne said to me, "I don't know how she stayed there in that climate, but she did."

After a couple of years in Canada, they moved back to Mexico. The real stimulus for the move was the death of Wayne's father-in-law. Through the contacts of his in-laws, Wayne got a job teaching English in Mexico City. That job lasted about two years, and Wayne lived it up in Mexico City; his prize possession was a red convertible in which he whizzed about town.

They returned to Canada for another seven years before making the ultimate move to Mexico. It is at this point that Wayne had the idea for Pancho's. The year was 1972. Pancho's began life with the name Pancho Villas Follies, but was changed to Pancho's as a result of an incident in Cancun several years later. He began the business on $5,000 his aunt had given him. At this point, Pancho's occupied a small space no bigger than a small store on Calle 59 downtown.

As with any business, the first three years were very difficult. In this particular case, the difficulties were compounded by the political situation in Merida. There was a struggle for power between the governor of the state and the mayor of Merida. This was during the time in Mexico when students would get involved in politics and sometimes become riotous. So there were constant political demonstrations with students and others, and Wayne got caught in the political crossfire.

His business problems were further compounded by the the trouble he had in obtaining a liquor license. Without the liquor license he could only sell beer, but he needed the sale of liquor to make the restaurant-bar combination work. But being a foreigner, he had been unsuccessful in obtaining the license.

In the midst of all this, students would come in and demand free beer. If he did not give the beer, trouble ensued. If he did give them the beer, he knew he would be forever held hostage to them and their demands for free beer, and he was just barely making enough to keep the doors open as it was. He decided to get a bouncer to throw the students out, because each time they were getting more and more demanding and threatening.

The presence of the bouncer finally brought things to a head. The incident began with shouts and insults between a number of students and the big bouncer. Then the shoving started. It was not long before real fisticuffs began between the students and the bouncer. Wayne was watching and preparing for his own defense and/or offense as warranted. The bouncer was holding his own when Wayne saw a chair going up in the air and arcing toward the bouncer. At the apex of the arc it seemed to stop briefly and then came down hard on the bouncer's head. The bouncer slumped to the floor unconscious.

No matter. Wayne was prepared. He had previously purchased a can of mace for just such an eventuality. Wielding the can, he sprinted to the front of the bar where the students were admiring their handiwork above the limp, unconscious body of the bouncer. The students were caught by surprise and looked up just in time as Wayne began spraying the mace. Unfortunately, at this very moment, one of those cool tropical breezes that everyone in the tropics loves came out of nowhere, and all of the mace was redirected by Mother Nature back into Wayne's eyes. He was left temporarily semi-blinded, with his eyes burning as if they were on fire. Amazingly, in a rare show of compassion for the momentarily disabled Gringo, the students left without further incident.

One night during this same period, Wayne decided to go to another bar to relax and have a drink. He sat down at the bar and looked around after ordering his rum and coke. He noticed a group of students sitting at a table in the bar at about the same time they noticed him. He knew instantly that his coming to the bar was not a good idea. After he was served, a couple of the students walked over to him. No words were exchanged, but one of the students picked up his drink and poured it over Wayne's head. Wayne knew the difference between discretion and valour. He asked for his bill, paid and left the bar.

Wayne was naturally becoming very frustrated with his situation. He was barely eking out a living, and the political situation seemed bleak. He began to question the wisdom of his move to Mexico and accordingly took a short trip back to Canada to visit friends and family. In the back of his mind hung the dreary possibility of returning to Canada. Arriving back home and visiting friends, he noted that nothing had really changed during his absence. His friends all had the same girlfriends, and they all went to the same places as they had two years before. This was boring and depressing for Wayne, so he decided that he did not want to stay in Canada, Come what might, his home was now in Merida where he felt his life was more interesting and dynamic than it could ever be in Canada.

Meanwhile, the political situation in Merida did not improve. At some point a student was killed in a political rally, and finally troops were sent in to calm the situation. During this interim, Wayne went to the office responsible for issuing liquor licenses where the bureaucrats were apparently in a rare state of bliss as a result of the relative peace. He obtained the license in about ten minutes, a record time in the bureaucratic world of Mexico. From that moment on, Pancho's flourished.

No doubt one of the reasons that the three restaurants have been so successful is the innovation that Wayne applies to the business. One of the first innovative ideas was the Dance Room. Back in those days in Merida, single girls could not go out on dates without chaperones. So when young men brought their dates to Pancho's, they were accompanied by chaperones. Obviously, this sort of throws a wet blanket on romance. The first expansion to Pancho's had been made by building the Dance Room at the back of the patio/terrace. Wayne had brought the first professional stereo equipment to Merida from Canada. He set it up in the Dance Room.

Since chaperones would not accompany the girls to the dance floor, the Dance Room served as a chaperone filter. Because the dance floor at Pancho's was a room, there was privacy, at least from chaperones. The Dance Room was a great success. Wayne believes that quite a few local couples who married in the 1970s owe their matrimonial bliss to the Dance Room at Pancho's.

Wayne continued to meld into the Merida business and social scene making friends and having fun while doing it. One of his new friends was Luis Reyes. Luis' father was very influential, and the family was involved in a huge irrigation project in the Yucatecan jungle that was being converted to agricultural land. The project was fairly remote, and they would have to fly in to visit.

The Yucatan is littered with Mayan ruins, and the area where Luis' irrigation project was being developed was no exception. Unfortunately for the Reyes family, when Señor Reyes, the father, got involved in a political dispute, the son was charged with robbing Mayan antiquities from the area of the irrigation project.

Everyone knew the charges were trumped up and that this was the penalty to pay for the father's erroneous political decision. Luis went to prison. But because Luis was who he was, he was kept in the "privileged" part of the prison. He had a special room to himself on the second floor and could receive visitors. Besides Wayne's social visits, Luis was allowed conjugal visitation, among other privileges not enjoyed by the rest of the prison population.

One day as Wayne was approaching the prison for a visit with Luis, he noted an immigration officer in a heated dispute with some foreigners. This particular immigration officer had given Wayne a hard time over the years. Wayne decided to come to the foreigners' aid and asked what was going on.

The intervention on Wayne's part enraged the immigration official. He drew a pistol and placed it on Wayne's head asking what the hell business was it of his? He then dragged Wayne into the prison and was attempting to arrest him. One of the janitors was cleaning the area and recognized Wayne as one of Luis' friends. The janitor immediately sent word through some of the inmates to advise Luis. In a short time, assistance arrived, and Wayne was released.

While Wayne was in "custody," he was kept in a room that had a rope hanging from one of the rafters. He asked his guard the purpose of this rope. He was told it was used by some prisoners who preferred to use the rope (the insinuation being suicide) to avoid being questioned in the next room. The guard grinned bizarrely and pointed toward a closed door on the far side of the room. Wayne was very thankful for his friendship with Luis.

In the mid to late 1970s, just as Pancho's was beginning to take off financially, many of the tourists and ex pats in Merida were Viet Nam vets. Many of these vets were into marijuana, and they wanted to do their drug deals in Pancho's. Wayne had made a pledge to himself after an incident that landed him in jail in Canada that he would never put himself into a position that could create that risk again. He would not allow any such dealing to go on within Pancho's premises.

The Canadian jail visit was a result of some unpaid traffic fines. He was stopped by Canadian Police for a traffic violation, and they ran a check on him and discovered he had several unpaid fines. The choice was to pay or go to jail for a night; he took the latter option as he was saving money for his impending move to Mexico.

He says now, "I am glad it happened to me because it taught me I needed to avoid jail at all costs, but at the time I was scared to death. First they made us all strip down. Then everyone is talking to one another as if they were all old friends, and I realized these guys were nearly all repeat offenders. They stuck me in some tiny little cell with a tiny metal cot and a miniature bathroom exposed to whomever was walking by. It had quite an effect on me. I felt as if I had absolutely no liberty. I did not sleep a wink that night. When they let me go in the morning, I remember running from the jail back to my home where I passed the zoo and thought what a great feeling it was to be running free and those poor animals living in the zoo were all trapped inside. I vowed I would never let that happen again."

Destiny did not allow him to live up to his vow, but it was not his fault. A frequent Customer at Pancho's during this period was an American named Joe Dusablon. Joe was an odd little guy who carried a notebook around with him constantly. From time to time, Joe would make notes in his notebook. Once he asked Wayne for a small loan. Wayne was reluctant, but lent the money despite his misgivings. Within a few days Joe returned the money. This happened several times. Then Joe was heading back to the States for a short trip, and Wayne asked him to buy a car for him and bring it back. The car was to have cost four or five thousand dollars. Joe agreed.

Wayne gave Joe the money, and Joe eventually returned with the car. But Joe now wanted Wayne to pay seven thousand for the car. Wayne said, "No, that's ridiculous, Joe. The car is only worth the money I gave you. If you don't want to transfer the title to the car to me, just give me my money back."

Joe said, "Okay, I'll give you a check right now."

When Wayne went to the bank to cash the check, there were insufficient funds, so Wayne and a buddy found Joe and said, "Fork over the car or the money."

Joe responded, "Wayne, there is some kind of a mistake at the bank. Let me fix it."

"Fine", Wayne said, "In the meantime, I will take possession of the car." Joe turned the keys over to him.

Wayne hid the car at a friend's house waiting for Joe to come up with the money. A couple of day later Wayne was leaving Pancho's with a friend when two cops grabbed him and threw him into a police car mumbling something about being part of a stolen car ring. Somehow, Joe had convinced a judge that Wayne had stolen his car and under Mexican law Wayne was to be thrown in the penitentiary while the Mexican wheels of justice began to grind.

He was left in a courtyard that had one small window along with about 200 other inmates. He began to talk to his fellow inmates about what they were there for. One responded, "Oh, I killed my sister." After several similar responses, Wayne quit asking and started worrying.

Then someone yelled out, "Hey, Gringo, they want you over at the window." Thinking help had arrived, he quickly strode over. Once he looked in he saw about a dozen other inmates who seemed to be insane; they were saying and doing exceedingly disagreeable things.

Finally someone recognized him. "Hey, you are Trotter aren't you?" After the last incident, he felt some trepidation in owning up to whom he was, but he did. The inmate said, "Come up here." There was a group in their own area with serapes hanging from ropes that closed in the area. He was invited in and given a warm reception.

"Would you like a smoke, something to drink?" This was another privileged area of the penitentiary, although not nearly as privileged as where Luis had been. Wayne was made to feel welcome and relatively safe there. He asked about Joe and one of the inmates said, "Yeah, we know him. His brother was in here and just got out. He has been coming here every day for several months to see his brother." Wayne had a better picture of who Joe really was now.

After a bit Wayne was released once the picture became clear for the authorities. However, by this time Joe had fled with his brother, supposedly to Chetumal, the capital of Quintana Roo. As others in Merida began talking, it was obvious that Joe had taken a large number of people for quite a bit of money. Wayne was actually one of the lucky ones, except for his stint in the jail.

Despite this little personal setback, the success of Pancho's continued. An additional expansion was made beyond the famous Dance Room where another patio was set up to accommodate more Customers. This proved not to be sufficient space and still another expansion was undertaken to bring Pancho's to its current size. At some point the Dance Room was taken out and that area became the lower bar. In the last part of the expansion the upper bar was built.

Since Pancho's was such a success, Wayne decided to move into the Cancun market in the early 1980s. He set up the same Pancho's theme in the

Hotel District and used the same name, which at this time was Pancho Villas Follies.

The Cancun Pancho's took off faster than the Merida version and began to do well. However, it seemed that the authorities were coming around every few weeks to shut them down in Cancun on some trumped-up charge. Wayne would open the next day, but the cycle would start again. One day one of the bureaucrats involved in the shut down pulled Wayne to the side. He said, "Look, I can't tell you this officially, but you are a good guy, and I want you to know something. General X (Wayne does not remember the name) drives by your place every day, and he is offended by the name. Pancho Villa is a great hero of Mexico to him, and he calls us and has us go through all this. Why don't you just change the name?"

That seemed like a great solution. Wayne asked, "What about just Pancho's?" The bureaucrat thought that would work. Since that point in time, Pancho's Cancun continued in operation without further run-ins with the authorities.

Nevertheless, after about five years as things were really taking off, Wayne's landlord wanted to negotiate new terms. In Wayne's opinion the terms were disastrous, so he refused to sign the contract. Within a few days, officials were removing the contents of Pancho's Cancun, and Wayne was closed for good in Cancun.

The landlord's son planned to run a restaurant in the building that Pancho's had occupied. Within about two months, Hurricane Gilbert came through and wiped the restaurant out; they never recovered. Wayne views this, and I agree, as poetic justice.

Wayne renewed his focus in Merida where Pancho's continued to do well. But he wanted another restaurant and decided to open a barbeque restaurant in the north part of town. This did not do well because Wayne was unable to control the quality of the Mexican meat he was receiving. He decided to change the restaurant to an Italian menu and changed the name to La Tratto. It has been successful ever since.

At about the time of the opening of La Tratto, Wayne's son, Paul, entered the business. Paul had studied in the United States and had been to gourmet cooking schools.

La Tratto had been operating about ten years when Wayne decided that Playa Del Carmen could be a good market. He leased a building and started a Pancho's Restaurant/bar in Playa, as Playa del Carmen is known, in the early 1990s and it went well. He decided after a time to build a hotel on the premises. In the mid 1990s Playa began to increase its tourist trade dramatically. Wayne's timing was perfect.

Except for the travel that Wayne had to endure between Merida and Playa, things could not have been better. Then history repeated itself. Wayne's landlord decided Wayne had it too good. The landlord wanted more rent, despite the fact that the rent contract had not yet expired. Wayne wanted the landlord to respect the contract and re-negotiate at the end of the contract. After several disagreements about the timing of the re-negotiation, the Federales showed up with weapons and shut down Pancho's, the restaurant and the hotel. In the process, Wayne and his staff were evicted.

Wayne had an enormous investment in leasehold improvements. Unfortunately, under Mexican law and traditional protocols, he really had no recourse. Again, poetic justice struck: the landlord died within a couple of years of a heart attack while on a commercial airplane flight.

Wayne re-grouped and now says, "Business-wise it was the best thing that ever happened to me. I would never have started Trotter's if Pancho's Playa was still in operation. I was getting really tired of travelling anyway." After the Cancun and Playa experiences, both located in the state of Quintana Roo, he adds, "I will never have another business in Quintana Roo."

Wayne, I believe, is a microcosm in the study of entrepreneurship. He persevered with his dream, despite various setbacks. His thought processes about his businesses are very dynamic. Despite being successful, he continues to change the menu, the atmosphere, and other characteristics of his business so that he stays ahead of the curve. His philosophy is captured by the new business axiom of "If it ain't broke, break it." It has obviously worked well for him.

CHAPTER NINE
BILL SIMPSON

Lee Richards' story would not really be complete without relating the story of the boat that I bought from him. After the purchase, I immediately took the boat to dry dock to have the hull cleaned and repaired. The boat was also painted.

I knew the boat needed a good bit of work. I had asked Lee if he knew anyone around who might be a good mechanic to check out the boat, as Lee was about to leave for Chicago. Lee told me that there was a guy that had recently arrived in Progreso named Bill Simpson and that Bill was a good mechanic who had been around boats all his life. By coincidence, we saw Bill in Progreso that same day.

Bill was about my age, which was fifty at that time. He was thin, but not a wiry thin, a muscular thin. He had red hair and freckles and stood about five feet eight or nine inches. And he knew what he was talking about when it came to boats.

Bill had motored his own boat from San Francisco to the Pacific coast of Mexico. Unfortunately, one night in a storm, he was blown over some shoals and lost his boat. I was initially concerned about this since losing your boat to shoals is not good form. I did not want him taking care of my boat in similar fashion. However, in talking to Bill it was clear he knew his business. I eventually came to understand that even the best of sailors have had this kind of accident in weather. After sinking his boat on the Pacific coast of Mexico, somehow he managed to navigate overland to Merida on the Gulf coast.

While my craft was in dry dock, I met Jorge. Jorge, who was from Progreso, was knowledgeable about boats as well, but he did not have the experience nor the advanced mechanical knowledge that Bill did. I liked both of them. Jorge was leaving for a job in the States in a few months. I was leaving to go back to the States as well. At this point I was travelling back and forth about every month and only staying in Merida a week or so at a time. It soon became clear that the boat was in worse shape than we thought, but since it had cost only $5000, I still had a bargain.

I agreed that Bill would live on the boat and put it in good mechanical order in my absence. In a few months I would be moving to Merida full time and wanted the boat ready to use. And, besides, Bill was sort of down on his luck and needed a place to stay.

I was with Bill and Jorge the day we took the boat out of dry dock and motored over to the marina. It was a bright and beautiful day. Those engines sounded incredible as we moved slowly through the bay from the dry dock to the marina. It was the equivalent of watching a powerful horse just walk along. You can see the muscles rippling and ready to break into a gallop at any point. Everything was right with the world. We docked at the fuel dock to gas up.

And that was when the trouble started. Bill and Jorge got into an argument about boat handling. It was true that Bill, who was piloting at the time, blew the horn rather aggressively at the Police Shore Patrol boat, which had crossed in front of us in the bay. They obviously did not like it. However, they did not do anything but stare ominously at us.

Nevertheless, Jorge wanted to make his point. Jorge was about thirty and Bill about fifty. I felt Bill's maturity would prevail and, since it takes two to tango, I ignored the argument at the beginning.

Then their voices began pitching higher. Guys on the docks were beginning to come over to enjoy the show. Finally Bill was repeating in a daring tone, "Jorge, you want to dance? I'll dance with you." I was back in the cockpit deck, and they were up on the bow now screaming at each other. My thoughts about maturity prevailing soon evaporated.

Surprised at my nimbleness and quickness, I bounced up to the bow just as the blows were about to start and jumped in between them. I explained this was my boat and if they wanted to fight to take it somewhere else. They slowly calmed down, and eventually the two of them became good friends. However, this did alert me to Bill's quick temper, which I was to see again.

Bill continued to take care of the many problems we encountered on the boat while he was living on it. Within a few months I was back in Merida living full time. By the time I arrived, the boat was in condition to take out, and we began going out for short day trips on the weekends.

One day Bill said, "Gus, you know something strange was happening while you were gone. Jorge kept coming over and visiting and would begin to search throughout the boat. He would pull up hatches on the deck and go below decks and spend a lot of time down there. At first he just told me he was checking things out to ensure all was in good working order. Later he levelled with me and said he believes there are gold coins on board. It has become an obsession with him to find the gold."

I knew that Jorge had known Lee. I also know that when Lee wanted payment for the boat, one of the options he gave me other than cash was gold coins. I had spoken with Lee about how he managed so much money in cash from his quasi-legal gambling establishment. He told me he kept some in cash and most in gold coins in safety deposit boxes in various locations. He also led me to believe he had some coins stored in a safety deposit box in Merida.

So, this must have been what was behind Jorge's treasure hunts. As far as I know Jorge never struck gold. I doubt that he would have told either Bill or me if he did. But I also doubt that Lee would have been that unorganized to have left gold coins on the boat.

Bill's mechanical abilities were amazing. He could fix anything, and he could do so under any conditions. In Mexico, it is especially difficult to get replacement parts that have not been fabricated within the country. The Chrysler engines for this boat and been built in the U.S. Everything I needed I had to import from the States even though there was a Chrysler dealer in Merida. Importing is costly because the Mexican government imposes high tariffs on anything brought in from outside the country.

Bill truly understood that necessity is the mother of invention. He actually made a head gasket from some material he found in Progreso that worked great. He also somehow straightened a bent push rod with common tools while on board the boat and made it work properly.

He was also incredibly intelligent and fairly well informed. Since he barely spoke Spanish, I really don't know how he stayed that way. The only problem was that except for the boat's mechanical problems, Bill could speak intelligently on any subject for no more than about three minutes. After that, his logic simply got used up. Or perhaps his brain cells went to sleep. I am supposing this condition had to do with substantial drug use in the past. Whatever the cause, this condition, of course, made it difficult to stay in a focused conversation with him about anything other than the boat.

I remember one weekend I went out to the boat, by now renamed *Ganso Azul* with her new, blue paint job, and Bill and I worked for awhile. I invited him for lunch. He began talking about the construction of nuclear reactors over our delicious fresh fish. He obviously had studied something about nuclear physics. I was amazed. However, after the traditional three minutes we could really go no further as he was unable to speak in a way that made sense. The conversation soon evolved into a bizarre fantasy about the Russians radiating us from outer space.

This was all very frustrating. Each cycle of each new subject could almost be timed at three minutes in length and was really good only for those first three minutes.

While on the boat, Bill's conversations were lucid if they were about the boat. We were unable to go out as much as I liked. It seemed as soon as one thing was repaired, another would break. Finally, we seemed to get everything repaired and I felt the boat was trustworthy enough for a long day trip to include friends. We left the marina around nine that morning with a group of about twenty friends on board. Some of them brought food and there was plenty of beer. Bill was on his best behaviour and so was the *Blue Goose*. Late that afternoon I brought the boat in with a perfect docking manoeuvre in the tight spot that had been assigned me in the marina. A good time was had by all. Unfortunately, there was only one other trip made out of the marina with company other than Bill.

At some point Bill, who was almost destitute, bought a softball and two gloves. I arrived one Saturday morning, and he showed them to me. Each time I went to Progreso after that we would play catch after we finished working on the boat. He insisted that I take one of the gloves back with me to Merida, which was really touching Bill had no money and was offering this glove to me. I think he viewed our playing catch as a way of bonding.

It was clear Bill thought of me as a friend. He really did not have many. I came to realize that he had a very aggressive attitude with everyone just like he had with Jorge. I was the exception, maybe because he was working for me. He was to exhibit a very genuine loyalty to me within the next few months.

The boat was becoming too much of a burden. I was spending almost all of every weekend at the marina working with Bill on the boat. Boat parts were costing me a small fortune. The old saying that the happiest days of a boat owner are the day he buys the boat and the day he sells it. Having owned two sailboats before buying this boat, I had five very happy days as a boat owner. I was now looking for the sixth.

I ran an ad in the paper. In Mexico, many people react emotionally about these kinds of purchases and never really consider the reality of paying for the purchase until the negotiations are complete. After several false starts with buyers who supposedly had the money but in fact did not, I finally found a real buyer. I never met him face to face. I was off on a business trip when he came to see the boat. Bill took him out and he told Bill he wanted it and was in love with it just like I *had* been. A week went by and he never called. I thought, "Another one."

Then I received a phone call from him at the office one day and he claimed he did want to buy the boat. He was a very nice guy who happened to be the Director of the Port of Campeche, the next state to the west of Yucatan. We agreed on a price of the equivalent of $12,000. I was actually going to make a profit on a boat, which was certainly a different experience than I had with my other boats. He said he would send his accountant over with the money.

A few days later a pleasant young man arrived with half the money, cash of course. We had agreed the other half would be paid once the boat was delivered. I would have preferred that the buyer use his own captain to move the boat from Progreso to Campeche, but the buyer said he had seen Bill handling the boat and wanted Bill to go with his own captain since his own captain was unfamiliar with the boat. I agreed that Bill would do so. I should have known that this was a recipe for disaster, but I guess I was so ecstatic to unload the boat and at a profit, that I was not thinking.

However, there was one last problem before the boat could sail. Lee, the previous owner, had never bothered to get the boat registered as Mexican. I had not done so either and, in fact, had it documented with the U.S. Coast Guard. As such it was still a foreign boat. In Mexico, foreign boats or cars cannot be sold without having them imported and paying duties and taxes.

Fortunately, for all of us, the buyer, as I mentioned, was the Director of the Port of Campeche and had quite a few connections. That old saying: "It's not *what* you know but *who* you know" is more applicable in Mexico than anywhere. As a result, we got the paperwork done and duties paid in about two days – a record by Mexican standards as this usually takes two months or more.

We gassed up at the fuel dock in Progreso. I happily paid, not worried about the several hundred dollars just spent on fuel that I would not be enjoying. I still remember them motoring off toward Campeche. Bill, the new skipper, and his mate never looked back; they were all in their element. I was on the dock thinking, "What a relief – I will never buy another boat." Then I remembered I thought the same thing after my last boat.

I still needed to collect the other $6,000 for the *Blue Goose*. They should be in Campeche in about 24 hours travelling all day and night. Upon delivery of the boat the money was to be brought back to Merida by the young accountant.

However, the boat did not arrive as scheduled, and they were unable to reach the boat by radio. Knowing that the boat was not in tip-top shape, to say the least, we did not become overly worried. The boat did arrive about a day late.

It seems that there were mechanical problems on the boat en route. I was not surprised to learn that during the repair of the problem Bill and the other captain had a disagreement. Apparently, the disagreement resulted in fisticuffs, and while there was not a clear cut winner of the fight, bad feelings hung over the crew for the rest of the trip.

Upon arrival, I was notified. During the call, the new buyer told me of the fight between Bill and his captain. He also told me that Bill had announced that he would not give up the keys to the boat until he had spoken to me and I had given him permission since he wanted to ensure I had the money. The new owner said, "Don't worry, I am sending Guillermo (the young accountant) over to Merida right now with the cash. He should be there within two hours. We will not attempt to take the keys from Bill until you call him and tell him it is OK. However," he continued, "will you please talk to Bill and ask him to calm down?"

I agreed. I told Bill first that I appreciated his loyalty to me by assuring that I would get my money before he gave up the keys. He made it clear to me and all who were listening that no one was getting the keys until he knew for sure I had the money. I also asked him to calm down, and he agreed as long as they did not "hassle him." I told him that I seriously doubted that they would, given what had already transpired.

Guillermo arrived with the money and I made the call to Campeche. The new owner agreed to let Bill sleep on the boat that night as he did not have a hotel and would be returning to Merida the next day. I thanked him. All resolved. I thought.

The next morning I got a call from the new owner. He told me, "Look, Bill has hidden the keys to the boat and will not tell us where they are. On top of that, we were filling the boat with gas and he pulled the nozzle and hose out of the gas tank and gas went everywhere. Now he is threatening to strike a match. Will you please talk to Bill if we can get him over here?"

"Yes, of course. I am sorry. Tell him I want to talk to him." I could see there were still hard feelings, to say the least, about the fight en route to Campeche. Bill was not handling this very well, although I was very proud of his loyalty to me.

About a half hour later I got the call from Bill. The first words out of his mouth were, "Gus, you won't believe this, man, but I saw a sword fight on the docks last night." He seemed to be on another channel.

"Really?" I asked, astonished on several levels.

"Yeah. Two drunk guys got into it, and they both had machetes. They got cut up pretty bad."

Obviously, I felt I needed to get to the point at hand. "Bill," I said, "why don't you give them the keys to the boat. I have my money."

He acted somewhat hurt and surprised and said, "Gus, I did! They lost them. These guys are a bunch of incompetents. This captain doesn't know what he's doing. He was filling the boat with gas, and I had to go over and yank the hose out before there was an explosion." He gave me some explanation that the gas vapors were building up in the boat making for a dangerous situation.

I told him, "Bill, just give them the keys and come on back here to Merida and let's finish this."

"OK," he said, "I've got another set of keys I will give them since they lost the one I had given them." I knew there had not been two sets of keys.

"Great, please do so, take the bus to Merida and come by the factory when you get here." He agreed to that and showed up late that afternoon in Merida.

When Bill arrived I really could not thank him enough for being so concerned that I would get my money. I told him so. I was going to take him to his boarding house downtown where he had rented a room since he would not have the *Ganso Azul* for accommodations anymore. As we walked toward my car, one of our employees was leaving the factory. I spoke to her and thought it would be good manners to introduce Bill to her. In Mexico, it is often Customary to peck a woman on the cheek upon greeting her. This is usually done once you have known the woman, and it is usually done with some finesse. This employee, Delia, was an attractive woman of about thirty. Bill kissed her and kissed her good, without the slightest finesse. Her eyes registered amazement and fear, but Bill meant no harm and thought he was doing the right thing. I apologized to her later and made the mental note that I should always follow different modalities with Bill.

Once Bill was ensconced in his room downtown, I did not see too much of him anymore. Occasionally he would call or come out to the factory. The business was growing, and I really did not have a lot of spare time to sit around and chat as we had out at the boat. Once or twice I ran into him on a weekend downtown. He showed me his room, which really was not as nice as his stateroom on the boat.

Over time I lost touch with him. He did not have a phone and the few times I had called him at the boarding house they could never locate him. Also, the business grew sufficiently that we changed factories, and I doubt he was able to locate me.

Then one day out of the blue I got a call from the United States Vice Consul in Merida. He said to me, "I don't know if I have the right person, but there is a fellow in the jail who is a U.S. citizen, and he is using your name as someone to contact as a reference." Immediately I thought of Bill.

I asked, "Is his name Bill Simpson?"

"Yes it is", he responded with a tone of some amazement. He immediately asked, "Does Bill need some medication that maybe he has not been able to get?" Before I could answer he continued, "The reason I ask is that he seems pretty disoriented and seems to be fantasizing about some pretty wild stuff. For one thing, he told me that he was working on a peace plan in the Middle East with Hillary Clinton and G. Gordon Liddy!"

I answered, "Look, I don't know about Bill's medication. What I do know is that he is fairly intelligent but has a real hard time focusing for any length of time on a particular subject and continuing to make sense on that subject. I just always thought it was the residual effect of too many drugs."

The Vice Consul laughed and said, "I know what you mean. He does seem to be able to talk intelligently for awhile and then he loses it. I felt like he was probably on some kind of medication and ran out and can't get any more now that he is here in Mexico."

"What was he arrested for?" I had a feeling that Bill's temper had got the best of him and maybe had committed a serious crime.

"He got caught with some drugs; I think marijuana, in Progreso. Because he says he is a U.S. citizen they called the Consulate. I went out to see him. The problem is, here in Mexico, if you are in jail you have to pay for your food, for your toilet paper – everything. Do you know if he has any money? Does he have money in the States or family up there?"

I said, "About money, I don't know but I doubt it. With regard to family, I know his mom is still living, but I don't know where she is, and that he has a brother living in Japan. Look, if he needs money, I can help, but I really don't want him to know that it came from me."

He laughed and said, "I understand. Don't worry, I'll tell him G. Gordon Liddy sent it." We both laughed at that. Then he said, "If I need some money I will call you. Our government will support him long enough to get him deported if he has no funds. He is not in the country legally. The problem is he says he does not want to be deported because he is wanted for something in the United States. Let me see if we can get some help from his family if I can locate them and what other solutions might be available. I will get back to you."

About a week later I got another call from the Vice Consul informing me that they had somehow located a savings account that Bill had in the States with a balance of about $2,500. They were entitled to use this money to get him out of jail, but the Mexican government was going to deport him. The Vice Consul said that in the States he will be able to receive the medical help he needs so that he can get better.

I felt a lot of sympathy for Bill. He was a good person who had fallen on hard times. I imagine most of this bad luck was a consequence of his own decisions, but I still felt sympathy for him. I also believed in the long run this was a good solution for Bill.

I thought this was the end of the story. However, it was not to be. A few days later I received a call from Bill. I have no idea how he got my phone number. He was being detained in Mexico City. He had with him a Mexican friend from Mexico City and, presumably, the Mexican authorities there had given him permission to call me.

After initial greetings where he was almost hysterical, the conversation went something like this: "Gus," Bill said, "They tricked me in Merida. They told me I was getting out of jail and they were sending me to Mexico City so I could get my Mexican papers and as soon as I got off the plane they arrested me. They are going to deport me. What should I do, I don't know what to do?"

"Bill," I told him, "Look, you are in the country illegally. You have no money. They have let you out of jail. The best thing is not to fight this but let them fly you back to the States and with time you can get your papers in order, and come back if that is what you want to do. At that point you will be in the country legally, and they won't hassle you any more."

"But I don't want to go back," he said. "I have some problems in the States. George Tennant (CIA Director at this time) is a friend of mine. George told me if I ever needed anything to call him and he would help me. He has a ranch just north of Guadalajara. I can call him. They know where I am anyway because they implanted a chip in me. I am tracked by a satellite all the time."

It was clear that Bill had deteriorated beyond where he was as Captain of the *Ganso Azul*. I responded, "I don't think that will do you any good at the moment, Bill. It is best to let them take you out of the country. Call George when you get to the States, and he can help you there." I was trying to be the calm voice of reason.

"But, Gus," he continued in a rather high-pitched voice, "They are looking for me because I know who killed Nicole Simpson. Actually, *I* killed Nicole, not O. J."

He continued in this vein for awhile and also brought up Hillary and G. Gordon Liddy. I asked if his friend who was with him was nearby, and he said yes. Bill had once told me about this Mexican friend in more lucid times. He was supposedly an owner of a large factory in Mexico City. Bill put him on the line. We spoke Spanish, as I did not want Bill knowing what we were saying, and I asked him if he understood English. He replied that he did, and so I asked if he had heard what Bill was saying. Again he replied in the affirmative. We agreed it was best for Bill to leave without further resistance. It turns out the guy really was the owner of a large factory. I have no idea how he originally met Bill.

He gave Bill the phone again. I convinced Bill to accept what was being offered. The conversation left me with some depressing thoughts. I had some good memories of times with Bill on the boat. I will always have a touching memory of his purchase of the ball gloves and softball so that we could play catch out on the docks and then his gift to me of the ball glove. I still have it.

I never heard from Bill again. But I imagine he is in an institution somewhere in the States, hopefully receiving some kind of treatment. It would be nice if he could beg better and live on a coast somewhere so that he could be near or on boats. It would be nice to play catch with him one more time just so that I know that he is okay. Hope springs eternal.

CHAPTER TEN

OGA After Joe

With Joe Toste's departure from OGA, I took on the responsibility of managing the production floor. Claudia was in charge of Quality, with Mary as her right-hand man. I recognized that I had a near un-surmountable challenge running the production floor, since I had very little knowledge of engineering and even less knowledge of sewing. I was running the floor because both Sergio and Santiago wanted Joe's job, and I did not believe either ready for it. There had to be only one person responsible for making final decisions. I had to make those decisions based on input primarily for Sergio and Santiago, who both wanted the responsibility of making those final decisions. We limped along.

As Claudia and I worked our way through separation into divorce, the situation was taking its toll on us, the employees, and the business. I did not want to fire her because she had done a good job bringing the company to where it was. Besides, she was a charismatic woman with enormous potential. She also had a very good relationship with our customer. We walked an emotional tight rope for awhile and had a power struggle within the company. Even though I owned 95% of the stock at that time, she felt she had been the one at the company on a day-to-day basis and that she should be the power within the company. My feeling was that the company leader needed to understand both business models—the U.S. and the Mexican. I felt too that the leader should also be the one with more business experience because of the size and future growth that the company clearly would have.

At some point I managed to convince her that struggling against me was counter-productive to the company objectives and that pulling with me would be more satisfying to all of us. While I had been within a hair of giving up on her, I am glad that I did not. Once again, my instincts were correct, despite emotions and advice of everyone else that Claudia and I should divorce professionally, as well, for the best interests of the business. She now owns 40% of the stock and has earned her ownership through hard work helping to make OGA a successful company.

During this period of struggle with Claudia, I had been on a flight with a man who knew our situation, knew the industry, and had much experience in managing people. He told me, "Sooner or later you are going to have to move her out of the company and you know it. It is best to do it sooner rather than later, because later may be too late."

While I told him, "You re probably right," I continued to hold on to hope that things would change. I knew it went against all logic, but I felt that Claudia and I could make it work. We both sort of looked at OGA as our child and that we had to do our best to put ego and emotions aside and be mature "parents."

This same individual visited us later after we had moved to OGA III and told me how impressed he was that we made it work when all logic said it would not. I know it is odd to be business partners and work with your ex-wife, to say the least, but we are without any romantic interest and much better friends than ever.

After we moved to OGA II, our customer asked us to obtain ISO 9000 certification. The International Standards Organization sets quality norms that are recognized world-wide. This organization qualifies certain companies to act as external auditors to certify your organization as maintaining the ISO norms. Some federal law enforcement agencies will not buy products that are not made in ISO 9000 certified factories. Very few sewing factories need this certification, but to satisfy our customer we began the process. It was long and arduous. As always, our team bought into the idea that it would be beneficial to the company and increase the probability of long-term success. Everyone worked very long hours to complete the process, which finally ended in our certification in record time.

I cannot tell the story of OGA without mentioning Charles Rosen. Charles was hired by our customer to basically manage all of the customer's production from his own factories as well as all sub contractors. Charles and I took an immediate liking to one another, although I came to realize that Charles sometimes exaggerated certain events in his past.

Charles set his age at different times at either seventy-one or eighty-one during the first year he was coming to Merida. He was short and round, with his hair cut to the length of stubble. The operators in the factory had a nickname for him; they called him "Humpty Dumpty." He claimed to have been married six times and on good terms with all his exes. His current wife was in her late 30s. He described himself to us as a practicing Muslim, although he led people in his office to believe he was Jewish. I really don't know which was correct.

While there were a number of contradictions in Charles' life, there were certain things never in doubt. First, Charles was highly intelligent and extremely well-read. Second, he had been in clothing factories since he was in his teens and was a repository of knowledge. And thirdly, he could not have been more supportive of OGA in terms of helping us to be successful.

I always picked him up at the airport when he came to visit. On his last trip, I waited and waited. He did not arrive. I went to the counter and was told he did not board as a result of a "medical problem." I immediately called my customer and left a message. Everyone was shocked to learn that Charles had died in the airport from a massive heart attack waiting to board the plane to come see us.

Charles is one of those who will forever form a part of the soul of OGA. His first visit was in OGA I and his last was in OGA II. We improved after each of his visits due to the suggestions that he always made. He once gave our engineers a clipboard with three different stop watches on it. It was his personal clipboard and a type that is no longer made. We placed a notation on it in Spanish, "In Memory of Charles Rosen," and it now hangs in my office. I will be forever grateful to Charles.

CHAPTER ELEVEN
Graeme Woods

Graeme is a Scotsman married to a Yucatecan woman. He is in his early 40's, blond and short of stature with a slight build. He claims to be an electrical engineer. Graeme came to the Yucatan eight or nine years ago to work on the new, modern electric generating plant. Many foreigners were contracted for this project because there was not sufficient technical know-how among local Yucatecan engineers. Most of the work was subcontracted by the Mexican government to foreign companies.

After Graeme's contract expired, he moved to Playa del Carmen and operated a bar with a partner. However, things did not go well between Graeme and his partner so Graeme returned to Merida where his wife's family lived. The couple moved in with the in-laws while Graeme looked for work.

I first met Graeme at Pancho's while he still had the bar in Playa and was visiting his in-laws in Merida. We struck up an easy friendship. I enjoyed listening to his Scottish brogue, a unique sound in the Yucatan.

After the ill-fated bar in Playa del Carmen, Graeme eventually found work teaching English and seemed to be doing well except for the normal family problems. When I would run into him around town, he complained constantly about his wife and his in-laws. He always ended the conversation leading me to believe that divorce was imminent. Despite these problems, he stayed with his wife and continued teaching, although he said he was experiencing financial difficulties.

As time went on, a number of my employees asked me about the possibility of taking English lessons. I reasoned that this would be a win-win if I could get Graeme to provide lessons before and after work hours. He needed the extra money and agreed.

After each lesson in the mornings before production began, he would hang around the office and chat with some of us. Our friendship deepened, and he made other friends at my office. He told me he had an offer to go to Iraq and practice his trade as an electrical engineer. The pay, he said, was stunningly high, but he was correctly concerned about the risk. I knew his financial situation was somewhat desperate and encouraged him to go; it would be an adventure as well as a solution to his dire finances. However, he ultimately turned the offer down and stayed in Merida in his unhappy marriage.

Graeme is one of those unfortunate souls who seem to have bad karma following him. He came in one day about two hours late for his English lessons. He looked like he had been run over by a bus. I asked what happened and he said, "I was run over by a bus."

The only mode of transportation he owned was a bicycle. Bicycles are very common in Merida. Bus drivers are notorious bullies who make their own driving rules as they go. A friend described to me once an accident where a motor scooter with rider was completely obliterated by a bus driver who continued on as if he had simply swatted a fly. The motor scooter driver was killed, but this was apparently of no import to the bus driver who continued on after watching the devastation through his rear view mirror.

While Graeme was spared death and serious injury, his bike was destroyed. He described his rage at the driver who in this case did stop. He said the police arrived at the scene, but claimed that nothing was done to the driver, who was soon on his way.

Nevertheless, this was typical of Graeme's luck, which continued on a downhill slide. One Saturday I received a phone call at home from Graeme's wife, whom I had never met. She knew of me through Graeme and somehow had my cell phone number. She was beside herself with anxiety. Graeme had disappeared and had been gone about 48 hours. I asked her if this had ever happened before (suspecting that it had) and she said yes, but that he had always come home within 24 hours maximum.

She said she did not know who else to call but me. The idea of the police helping to find missing persons in the Yucatan is not a well-developed concept. I told her if he did not come back by Monday to call me again. She did and those of us at the office began a campaign of sending pictures of Graeme and flyers to local bars and places that ex pats frequented. We did contact friends at the police, but did not hold much hope for results through this medium.

No word was forthcoming for about ten days and we all feared the worst. Then out of the blue I got a call from Graeme. He was at home with his wife and very appreciative of our efforts. I asked, "Graeme, where were you and what happened?"

He responded, "I don't know, Gus. I've been depressed. One day I just started walking and didn't stop." His voice was quiet, and the words dripped with desperation.

I did my best to console him while also counselling him that what he had done was very selfish and scared his wife and friends. He said he knew that and was sorry for it. He claimed to have his head on straight now and was going to put things in his life back together.

Shortly thereafter he moved to Cancun. He called me from time to time just to say hello. I remember one day I got a call during one of the Carnaval parades in Merida. There was, of course, no way to understand a word he was saying over a cell phone in the midst of blaring live music and shouting, drunken spectators. I somehow got the message across to call me the next day.

When I got the call I discovered he was asking for a loan of about $300 to pay for expenses to get his tour guide license. He claimed to have found work with one of the local hotel chains and needed the license to comply with their requirements. I asked why his employers would not lend him the money, and he responded that they had already lent him the maximum they were willing to go. He promised, "Gus, I can pay you back within a month and with interest."

I told him, "Graeme, don't worry about the interest, just get the money back within the time frame you have promised."

Of course, Graeme was late in paying me back, but promised by email to make good. A month or so later he emailed saying he would be in Merida over the weekend with the money. I never heard from him again and don't know where he is.

While we had been desperately looking for him in his first disappearance, my secretary did a little internet research on Graeme Woods. It turns out there had been a certain Graeme Woods from Scotland who had left a young mother with their child in England about the time he said he arrived in Merida. She had posted inquiries around the internet hoping to find out where he was. I suspect it is our Graeme Woods, recently from the Yucatan. History is probably getting ready to repeat itself somewhere else.

CHAPTER TWELVE

Bob Gow[7]

---
[7] I believe Bob's autobiography is obtainable at Amazon.com: *You Can't Direct the Wind, You can Only Reset the Sails.*

I remember being seated in Bob's office, literally in the middle of the Yucatecan jungle, when Bob received a phone call from the New York Times in 2000. I only heard Bob's side of the conversation, but the reporter was clearly looking for dirt on George W. Bush during the early stages of the presidential election campaign. Bob was unable to assist.

Bob claims to be the only man, and I am sure he is correct, who worked for George H. W. Bush and later had George W. Bush working for him. This occurred at Zapata Corporation in Houston, Texas. At one time, the first President Bush was president of Zapata Corporation, and Bob was an executive. Later Bob became president of Zapata Corporation. After Bob started his own business, the second President Bush came to work for Bob. Bob became president of Zapata at age thirty-six. Under his leadership Zapata became one of the fastest growing companies on the New York Stock Exchange.

I have known two men whom I consider business geniuses, each in his own way. They have taught me much more than I ever learned in a classroom. Bob is one of those men. He has a strategic mind that is unparalleled and logic that is impeccable. These characteristics, coupled with an enormous drive and limitless energy, have made him a very successful man.

I met Bob through a mutual friend. Bob was looking for someone to assist him in the accounting and operations of his bamboo plantation and factory located in the Yucatan. I had not yet begun my business and, therefore, had time to work with Bob.

His plan was to grow bamboo and use the bamboo as the raw material in such products as furniture, fencing, and flooring to be exported to the U.S. The common name for the type of bamboo he chose "iron wood bamboo," and it is not indigenous to the Yucatan. However, this bamboo is very strong, is not hollow and grows in round clumps. He wanted to lessen poverty in the region and thought that this commodity could potentially bring wealth back to the region as henequen had once done.[8]

The plantation is located on Bob's hacienda, called Xixim, south of Merida between the relatively large pueblito of Muna (population about 2,000) and the tiny community of Opichen. He had bought the hacienda in the late 1980s. He has pictures of jungle vines growing through the ruins of the main house which he ultimately reclaimed from the jungle and restored. The hacienda had been an architectural study site for the University of Texas, which has placed the age of the site at around four hundred years.

---

[8] Henequen is the plant from which sisal, or hemp, is extracted to make rope fibers. Until 1930, when nylon was invented, the Yucatan was the world's biggest hemp supplier and many hacienda owners made huge fortunes as a result.

Nearly everyone who visits the hacienda agrees that it is certainly an interesting place and leaves one with a special feeling. There are thousands of bamboo plants and when entering the plantation there is a noticeable drop in temperature caused by the canopy of foliage. During the rainy season the bamboo shoots grow as much as a foot in height a day.

Xixim is in a somewhat isolated location. There was no phone service, but there was electricity. The workers come from the small villages nearby. Many of the workers do not speak Spanish. They can only communicate in Maya. Since neither Bob nor I speak Maya, those workers who also spoke Spanish would translate for us.

Xixim was not Bob's first venture into agribusiness. He left Zapata Corporation and founded a company, Stratford of Texas, which owned feed lots for cattle and a chicken farm.

Before going with Zapata, Bob had been an industrial engineer in a large factory and was trained to think in terms of always trying to improve efficiencies. With his characteristic scientific and methodical approach, he had enormous success with Stratford of Texas. The cattle that went to his feedlots put on more weight than in other feedlots. Besides that, Stratford's feedlots were less costly to operate than the normal feed lot.

In the early 1970s, Stratford was part of a group that began growing chickens in the Yucatan. This business was to become very successful and still exists today, although Bob has no remaining financial interest in it.

Around this same time, Bob took advantage of the high demand for indoor, non-blooming plants. Under the same umbrella of Stratford of Texas,

Bob bought into a series of greenhouses and plant farms in Guatemala, called Green Thumb. Again, Bob applied his scientific methods to improve efficiencies and exploit markets to develop a successful subsidiary.

During this period, Bob related that there was a mini civil war in Guatemala, and guerrilla warfare was on the rise. Bob had a bodyguard who was armed with an Uzi and had hand grenades hanging from his chest. At one point, one of their plant farms was attacked, and some of the workers were killed.

During this same time, the guerrillas sent a note indicating that Bob's manager of the operation would be kidnapped and killed if $500 was not left in a hollow tree on a periodic basis. Bob knew that if the extortion was paid it would only be the first in a series of payments. He also knew that if it was paid and the Guatemalan government discovered the payment, it was quite likely that the government would kick them out of the country and confiscate their property for supporting the rebels. On the other hand, Bob did not want his key employee killed.

A decision was finally made to secretly inform the Guatemalan government and set up an ambush. This was done and when the rebels came to get their extortion money, all of them were killed by Guatemalan soldiers. There was, fortunately, no retaliation from other rebels for this incident.

Soon the CIA contacted Bob and asked for his assistance in gathering information that might be helpful. Bob cooperated and made numerous reports to the CIA about what he knew and came to know through his numerous trips to Guatemala.

Stratford's success became legendary. An article even appeared in *Time* magazine on Bob and Stratford of Texas in 1973. Bob was also interviewed by Art Linkletter for a TV series entitled "America, The Men Who Made Her Great." Furthermore, Stratford of Texas became the subject of three cases used in the Harvard Business School.

Stratford had become one of the largest feed lot operations in the world. Green Thumb was the largest tropical indoor blooming plant business in the world. Green Thumb had grown from just over $1,000,000 in sales in 1970 to over $40,000,000 in 1975.

However, two decisions made by the Federal government doomed Stratford. First, price controls were instituted in the 1970s to combat inflation. These price controls constrained the price of beef, but unfortunately, not the price of feed. Stratford's core business was having its profit margin squeezed. Second, the government decided to sell grain to Russia. This created a shortage of grain and prices of Stratford's raw materials surged even more.

Bob, personally, and Stratford were ruined financially. But that did not keep Bob down. He was soon working diligently with bees and honey. He made this a family business. Bob learned how to keep bees and extract honey from their hives. The family set up their own brand of honey and even sold it on street corners.

Later Bob found work with a large company and slowly got back on his feet financially. Eventually, he paid each and every one of his creditors back.

Over the next few years Bob was involved in several successful projects and businesses. He also taught entrepreneurship at Rice University. There he met some professors and helped them raise capital for a project that produced a significant nest egg for him.

Bob soon began thinking of the Yucatan again. He had enjoyed Mexico and the Yucatan during his visits to the chicken business he helped found. He, therefore, looked for a hacienda to buy, found Xixim and bought it. Although Bob was financially able to retire, his active and agile mind would not let him. He started another business that took advantage of the Yucatan's geographic proximity to the U.S. and the manual dexterity of the small hands of the indigenous Mayas. This was a business that made dental crowns that could be fabricated and shipped back to the States within one day. He ultimately sold that business once he was struck with the idea of growing bamboo.

Now in his seventies, Bob decided on another venture in the Yucatan utilizing part of the land at Xixim that is not planted in bamboo. He began growing tilapia, a fast-growing fish that is now in much demand in restaurants and super markets in the States. As he did with bamboo, Bob has extensively researched the science of growing tilapia and the market for tilapia. He has been successful in raising capital and in raising tilapia at the hacienda.

Bob has a great sense of humor and immediately impresses his guests with his intellect. He is a gracious host and a joy to be around. He adds enormously in all respects to the quality of the characters in this part of paradise.

One of the things that make Bob a good businessman, I believe, is his ability to be objective; he always is. His most important business characteristic is his capacity to think strategically. He has taught me more than he will ever know and I am grateful for the opportunity to have known him and learn from him.

CHAPTER THIRTEEN
The Mean Streets of Merida

Driving in Mexico is barely controlled chaos. If you are a tourist, the experience will be much less emotionally charged and probably less expensive in the long run if you simply pay taxis. If you are not a tourist and absolutely must drive your own car, the first thing you must do is forget all you know about driving. Never attempt to apply driving logic from your home country. It simply won't work.

The best way to learn is to find a friend from your home culture who has been living in Mexico for awhile and has been acculturated. Ask this friend to take you places and pay close attention to how he manages in traffic. As you ask questions, try not to be shocked by the answers. For example, if you note your driver friend only slows for stop signs instead of completely stopping, don't be surprised if the answer is "If I come to a stop, I may be hit from behind."

In Merida, you will immediately see that the painted traffic lanes are treated as mere suggestions by many drivers. Other drivers apparently believe the white paint marking the lanes are really meant to mark where they should place the center of their auto. As might be expected, the result is chaos.

At some intersections there are more lanes on one side of the intersection than on the other. To illustrate, I've seen three painted lanes on one side of the intersection and only two lanes once I cross through the intersection, even though none of the lanes are turn-only lanes. I've also seen the opposite: three lanes on one side with a turn-only lane and two lanes on the other side, but with drivers in the turn-only lane who insist on going straight, forcing the law-abiding drivers going straight to get out of their way. Obviously, this makes for some interesting driving acrobatics, especially when you are not expecting these unforeseen changes. Driving in Merida is something akin to a Chinese fire drill.

The only time Meridians get in a hurry is when they are behind the wheel of a car, and this is especially true when a red light changes to green. Everyone behind the lead car at the stop light begins honking within a nanosecond of the change; you would think you were in Manhattan.

The stop lights are not synchronized, so, the honking cycle begins again at each new stop light. Several months ago the city government reported in the local papers that it was beginning the process of synchronization of stop lights. The report quoted city government officials who were talking as if this was as complicated as a moon landing with incredibly sophisticated software packages controlling stop light changes.

It's a good thing it was not a moon landing. The day the synchronization took place, all worked well for about thirty minutes. After that the lights went back to a random change. Apparently, the sophisticated traffic software has a glitch in that it has begun to control the stop lights in a reverse synchronized fashion. That is, the lights are set in a way as if to assure that you cannot make more than two green lights without encountering a red light on the same street.

After such fanfare about the "sophisticated" system that was to be installed, there has not been a public peep out of anyone complaining that the traffic flow is worse despite the supposed synchronization. There is one characteristic that I hope will change in Mexico: citizens are often too passive. Except when they get behind the wheel of a car!

The importance of synchronized traffic lights is lost in this country anyway. To many Mexicans time is relative. Why would you worry if you cannot move smoothly and quickly through traffic? After all, most Mexicans are not concerned about being punctual. This is what makes the immediate honking at the change of stop lights even more difficult to comprehend.

The lack of smooth traffic flow has hidden costs. This is a country where the majority of those driving are living in adverse economic conditions. Gasoline is expensive, especially in relation to per capita income. Constant stopping and starting uses gas and hurts those who can least afford it.

Actually, even if the traffic lights were synchronized, the situation might not improve substantially. The main reason for this is public transportation. There are a very few official bus stops. Yet buses will stop on any corner to pick up passengers. The streets are often narrow with heavy traffic. If you are behind a bus you never know when it will stop. This constant stopping obviously creates traffic flow problems, and even with perfectly synchronized traffic lights, the flow would only improve marginally.

Another impediment is the horse-drawn carriage. Since Merida is a tourist destination, romantic horse drawn carriages are available all over the city to take tourists around town. Obviously these carriages impede traffic flow as they move slowly down the street. Besides these ornate carriages, there are mule-drawn carriages that are packed with bags of topsoil that the drivers take through the city to sell door to door. I remember when I was coming to Merida as a tourist, before I began my business and moved my residence, how enamoured I was of these quaint horse and mule-drawn carriages. As a resident, I have come to hate them. You can't see them because big buses are trucks are obstructing your view. Then you get trapped behind them and the traffic in the other lane is bumper to bumper and a mile long. At times it seems like hours before you can get.

I was also initially enamoured with the huge number of bicycle riders. I thought this quaint also. Then I began driving on a daily basis and found the bicycle riders to be a terrible impediment to traffic flow. They don't make the slightest effort to move to the side or get out of your way. In fact, it seems they do the opposite, especially the young ones. The number of aged bike riders is astonishing, but they do seem to realize that it is better to get out of the way of automobiles.

But most distressing are the bus drivers. The normal bus outweighs the average car by several tons. Bus drivers know this and use it to their advantage. I am from Texas where bumper stickers abound with the slogan: "Drive Friendly". In Merida, bus drivers do the opposite of driving friendly. I have a friend that says that in order to get a job as a bus driver, you have to have been diagnosed as criminally insane. That is a distinct possibility.

Despite the fact that bus drivers ignore every traffic law ever passed, I have never seen one pulled over for a traffic infraction unless there has been an accident. This lack of police involvement in traffic in Merida is highly unusual, as I will explain later. My assumption is that the police have no interest in bus drivers, as they have little ability to pay a bribe to escape one of the many potential infractions they make in just about every block on their route.

Buses are omnipresent. This is good as most Mexicans have no personal form of transport. However, the fares are rising exponentially. The official inflation rate in Mexico for the past several years is in the range of three to four percent. In the last five years, the bus fare has increased almost 50% in Merida. While the cost of fuel in peso terms has increased, it has not increased by that margin. Obviously, the increase in fares has a very detrimental impact on those who have no other form of transport and can least afford to pay.

Another type of public transport available is what are called *combis*. These are vans with three rows of seats. Combi fares are a little more expensive than buses, but they arrive at their destination much sooner than a bus would. Nevertheless, combis are constantly stopping to drop off or pick up passengers and, therefore create something of a traffic hazard as well.

During combi stops, the coordination between combi driver and passenger is excellent. The driver has a lever at his disposal that operates the double passenger doors on the right side of the vehicle. As the driver pulls up to the curb, he is pulling the lever and you see the door opening. Before the combi has stopped, you can see the profile of a passenger or passengers stooping and moving toward the opening doors. The passenger disembarks and, if there is no one looking to enter the combi, the driver is off in a flash and pulling the doors shut as he drives away. This coordination represents an oasis of efficiency in a desert of chaos.

While combis can have a deleterious effect on traffic flow, they are nothing compared to buses that are sometimes stopped for several minutes at a time while passengers load and pay or disembark. While there is a front door to the bus with signs stating it is only for entering passengers and there is a back door to the bus with a sign indicating it is only for disembarking passengers, nearly everyone disembarks by the front door. This is, of course, totally inefficient and requires significantly more time than following the rules, as embarking and disembarking passengers are clumped together at the front door in a ball of humanity. In the meantime, if you are motionless behind the bus and waiting for the bus to move or looking for a break in the traffic either behind you in the left-hand lane so that you can speed away from the bus roadblock.

Creating additional traffic flow problems are what are known as *topes*. Topes are cement or asphalt humps placed in the road to slow down traffic. They are usually at intersections, but sometimes seem to just appear at random intervals. The purpose of topes is to protect pedestrians. While Merida is teeming with police, it is apparently still necessary to place topes.

Moving from point A to point B within Merida can often be a challenge, not just due to traffic flow issues, but as a result of street planning and layout.

Old Merida was laid out in horizontal and vertical streets that go basically north-south or east-west. The only problem with these streets is that they are very narrow.

However, as Merida grew and expanded outward, the street layout scheme changed. Once you travel outside of the downtown area, streets begin to go in diagonals as well as vertical and horizontal. This, in and of itself, is not a problem. The problem is that the vast majority of streets are one way. Combining the street layout of diagonals, curving streets and the traditional horizontal-vertical design with one way traffic flow, you very seldom can travel in a straight line. Going from point A to point B may create a multitude of direction changes before arriving at point B.

The quickest route from my factory to my home requires nine direction changes registered by my auto compass. This is a five mile trip, with the first four miles in a straight line. I arrive home almost dizzy from the turns I have to make in the last mile.

With respect to one-way streets, you would think that logic would dictate that they would be alternating. This is a false assumption. While it is true in most cases, this lulls one into a sense of security about traffic design that is not warranted. Without warning or any possible understanding of the method behind the design, one may encounter two, three or more streets in a row that are all one-way the same direction. And, there may or may not be a sign indicating directional flow of traffic at the intersection. It is a type of Russian Roulette that you play if you decide to turn.

Once I became aware that the traffic flow might not be predictable and that there might not be signs indicating what the directional flow might be, I began to look for cars parked in the same direction on the street onto which I was considering to turn. While I thought the logic good, I soon learned it was actually flawed. My logic was that if cars were all parked in the same direction that this would indicate that the street was one way in the direction that the parked cars were facing. Not necessarily.

In Merida, drivers traditionally park on whichever side of the street they deem more convenient, regardless of traffic flow. That is, if you are travelling down a two-way street, hopefully on the right-hand side of the street, and you want to stop at a house or business on the left hand side of the street, it is not a problem. You simply cross into the on-coming lane and park if you believe that is more convenient than parking on the right hand side with the traffic flow and crossing the street on foot. Obviously, you cannot predict traffic flow based on parking direction.

With respect to parking, the well-known and universally understood yellow line painted on curbs indicating no-parking zones is used in Merida. However, it appears to be sort of like the white lines painted for lanes in the streets. It is more of a suggestion than a requirement. This is a real problem in the downtown area, as most people don't follow the "suggestion" of not parking in no-parking zones. This drastically reduces the usable space for moving traffic in already narrow streets. Compounding the problem is that double parking, while nominally prohibited, is a common occurrence. All of these "prohibited" means of parking take place in the full sight of police who seemingly have no interest in aiding the traffic flow or enforcing regulations.

In fact, I have noted that along the street in front of the main police station, the curb is painted yellow, indicating no parking. I have never been by the main police station when the yellow line was not obscured by a long line of parked cars.

Meridians know that their fellow residents don't really pay attention to parking regulations. Therefore, you see on many garage entrances a sign saying "Don't Park – We puncture tires free." Despite this relatively aggressive threat, one will still see garage entrances blocked by parked cars.

Stop signs on street corners sometimes present a problem. Most of us are accustomed to looking for stop signs on the right hand side of the street if we are on a two-way street. Don't make that mistake in Merida. While the majority of the two-way streets do have stop signs on the right hand side, not all of them do. Quite a few two-way streets will have the stop sign placed on the left hand side of the street, which, obviously, could create a very unpleasant surprise for a driver not aware of this possibility.

Turn signals and emergency flashers seem to have different meaning for local drivers in Merida. With respect to using blinkers as turn signals to indicate what a driver might do, please don't take these indications too seriously. First, drivers don't appear to take them seriously, so why should you? Turns are usually made without turn signal advance notice. I have a friend who has a theory that Meridians believe that they are saving battery power by not using turn signals. It could be, but I think that it is simply lack of consideration for others.

In the rare instances that turn signals are used, often the signals keep flashing even after the turn is made. It is as if all vehicles sold in Merida lack the auto switch-off of the turn signals. Clearly, this creates problems for those following them. If you are new to the area, you are certain that the car in front of you plans to turn. After numerous blocks of following the car, you become aware that this is not the intention of the driver in front. Usually at about that point, the driver in front will actually turn. But the turn may be made in a direction other than that indicated by the signal. As you become more experienced, you become much more alert in terms of the options that the driver in front may actually be considering.

During highway driving in the Yucatan, you may note that slow-moving vehicles on narrow highways may from time to time turn on their left turn indicators. You will be thrilled that you have a driver in front of you that is following driving norms that you are accustomed to. Accordingly, you will await his turn so as to be driving safely. When you note the driver does not turn and/or that there is no place for him to turn left, you disgustedly pass.

However, over time you begin to realize that left turn signals on the highway are polite driving etiquette used by Yucatecans. They are actually signalling you that it is clear to pass. Just about the time you understand this signal, you place it into action only to discover that this time it is a rare instance of a left turn signal. You narrowly avoid an accident, hopefully, and then ask yourself, "How do I tell the difference between a left-turn signal and a signal that it is clear to pass"? Answer: You can't. So, you just drive as if in a state of constant alert and interpret no turn signals without extreme caution.

Speaking of blinkers, most of us understand emergency blinkers to indicate some type of emergency.

Like left-turn signals, emergency blinkers can mean a number of things in Merida. Meridians seem to be enamoured with the use of emergency blinkers. I would guess as many as 10% of cars on the streets in Merida at any one point in time have their emergency blinkers on. The most common use seems to be an indication that the driver in front intends to be slowing down for whatever reason. Once turned on, emergency blinkers seem to be left on, regardless of the initial reason for use.

Motor scooters are a curious part of the driving chronicle. Entire families of up to four riders are sometimes balanced on these little scooters. The father will be driving with the mother on the back and one tiny child sitting on the gas tank while another is sandwiched in between the mother and father. While it is an entertaining sight, it is obviously very dangerous and disturbing to watch. If there is a law against packing families onto a motor scooter as if they were some sort of circus act, it is never enforced. Thankfully, I have never seen an accident involving one of these families.

Besides balancing people on motor scooters, any number of inanimate objects are also balanced along with the driver. One of the most common sights is seeing a lawn mower tied to the back of the motor scooter with the handle protruding high into the air behind the head of the driver.

While I have not seen accidents involving families, I do see many accidents involving these scooters. Unfortunately many riders do not wear helmets and most of those who do wear a helmet, wear something that looks like a World War II German military helmet. These helmets appear to be made of some sort of plastic; they could not possibly withstand much of an impact.

Accidents involving motor scooters occur frequently because the tradition seems to be that motor scooters do not follow normal driving rules and traffic regulations. These drivers weave in and out of traffic as if they are playing a harmless game of tag. At stop lights or stop signs, they feel no need to wait their turn in line. They simply weave between lanes and cars until they reach the head of the line. This creates a traffic hazard as the little scooters have no power and now they are at the front of the line holding up all the cars behind them once the light changes and traffic moves.

Mexican scooters come in brands that we have never heard of. I have not seen a Honda or Suzuki that I can recall, except for exceedingly old ones. These old scooters always leave a trail of enormous clouds of smoke as if they are on fire. The Chinese have taken over the scooter market in Mexico with a brand that makes a scooter that looks like a miniature version of a Harley Davidson. But it is tiny. The biggest such Chinese motor scooter that I have seen is 250 cc.

Part of the problems of driving in Mexico is that many (probably most) drivers were never properly trained. You do see driving schools with brightly painted signs on their cars announcing driving students are at the wheel. You pass them, noting always, the customary death grip that all driving students in all countries have, clutching the wheel desperately with both hands as though they are trying to strangle a serpent.

I am glad to see these driving schools as many drivers are lacking in understanding of basic driving concepts. Speaking to a friend once about her driving and obtaining her driver's license, she simply stated, "Oh, I bought my license." I came to understand that she simply paid a bribe to get an official drivers license as she feared failure on the test.

The phraseology used by my friend is an interesting example of cultural differences that can lead to misunderstandings. Using the verb "to buy" when the facts would call for the verb "to bribe" is what Mexicans would refer to as being "polite." This politeness conveys a different meaning and those from other cultures could probably see this as an imprecise reference to the facts.

I probably should have "bought" my license, as well. Not due to the tests, but due to the fact that I had to make about four trips to the driving license test and issue facility to obtain my license. The time required to submit or obtain government paperwork in Mexico is astounding. One reason is that different clerks at the same government facility often give different answers to the same question or require different papers for the same bureaucratic issue. So if you return thinking you have all your papers in order but get a different clerk, he/she is likely to patiently explain that you have not brought the correct paperwork. Explaining that another clerk at the same office gave you explicit instructions on what was needed will only cost time. Therefore, it often takes several trips to the same office until you have a stack of papers an inch thick at which point it seems that two or three papers are selected randomly and the clerk is satisfied.

The written test for the drivers license was quite easy. In fact, the administrator of the test essentially gave a lecture on the questions and their answers prior to administering the exam. As a foreigner I was surprised, along with the fifteen or twenty other people taking the exam, that I was the first one finished.

The actual driving test consisted only of parallel parking. You have three chances to get it right. In my case, the officer was absolutely insistent that I park his way—I could not just park my way and get it right—I had to park his way and get it right. His way was different from the way I learned (albeit a long time ago), but his way worked just fine and I now have my Mexican driver's license without having "bought" it. However, the "purchase price" is the same as the official fee, and you don't have to spend so much time going back and forth, bringing in more and more paperwork each time.

Actually, my suggestion for the driving test would be to change from learning to parallel park to learning to park correctly for "straight-in" parking. Straight-in parking is the type of parking that is in most parking lots; you park between two straight and parallel lines. Many drivers in parking lots seem to insist on diagonal parking when the lines are marking straight-in. This is a constant occurrence in supermarket parking lots and creates a situation where fewer cars can park than what the lot was designed for.

I am sure the diagonal parkers are parking diagonally not due to a lack of driving expertise that enables them to fit between the straight lines, but because if they get the opportunity to park by simply turning in diagonally they do so as it is easier. A recurring theme I have discovered in Mexico is that if it is easier and there is no penalty, the easy way will be taken. While this is a very practical philosophy, it creates some hardships, almost always for others. It also creates a sense of chaos and lack of order, at least for me. And, even if the easy way has a penalty associated with it, it may be less costly to look for a way to circumvent or mitigate the penalty by paying a bribe. Take the drivers license "purchase" as an example.

The combination of Meridians only getting in a hurry when they get behind the wheel of a car coupled with the idea that if its easier do it even though against the law—and there is no penalty—creates even more chaotic conditions. There is one particular intersection that I go through on my way home that has a one-way street with traffic going south crossing a two-way street with east-west traffic. The traffic going west backs up from time to time at the stop sign. If the line is more than about three cars deep, newcomers to the line begin to make their own lines to the left and to the right of the west-bound lane. Obviously, this blocks any traffic that might wish to turn east from the southbound street. On the two-lane east-west street I once saw westbound cars squeezing into four lanes going west or wanting to turn south. The southbound cars began to back up in their left-turn lane to go east, as they were blocked from entering. I actually counted two police cars pass by going south without doing anything even though the blockage of traffic was more than apparent.

CHAPTER FOURTEEN
Supermarkets

Like driving, another microcosm of Mexican culture is their supermarkets. This is true in the management of supermarkets as well as in the behavior of customers.

In the States, supermarkets are relatively plentiful and easily accessible. Supermarkets in Mexico are somewhat scattered around town and not so plentiful. Once in one, you are immediately struck by the narrow aisles where merchandise is crammed into every available space.

In my experience outside of Mexico, supermarkets arrange the merchandise in a certain way and that arrangement is maintained over time. For example, bread is always on Aisle Five. This makes for quick shopping by customers, obviously.

However, in Mexico, bread may be on Aisle Five this week and Aisle Nine next week. This always creates consternation for me. At first, I thought this an example of lack of order, reflective of a poorly organized work force within the supermarket. Now that I know Mexican behavior a little better, I believe there is a method to their seeming madness. As is related below, Mexicans see going to the supermarket as an outing. Therefore, changing the location of merchandise may represent an ingenious marketing method. If one has to wander through the entire store to find goods and if the shopper is an impulse buyer, no doubt sales increase by requiring a hunt for the goods. Along the way to buy bread, the impulsive shopper may find some other item they had not thought about buying before.

Adding to the frustration for me is that on the hunt for specific items that I cannot find I ask a clerk where the item might be. The clerk will take you to a location within the store and note that the item you are looking for is not there. He says, "Oh, we're out."

You ask if there might be some stock in the back. Without checking his immediate response will be "No."

You ask, "Do you know when you will get more?"

The answer is always "No," or something like "Maybe in a few weeks." I never recall a supermarket in the States being out of something, much less that it will take weeks to get more inventory.

When I first arrived in Mexico, I assumed that everything would be cheaper, including food. I was mistaken. Very few kinds of merchandise in Mexico are cheaper, including food. About the only food I find cheaper in Merida than in the U.S. is tortillas, beans, and fruit.

Personally, I go to the supermarket as a necessary chore I am required to endure so that I will have food to eat. My experience in the States is that most supermarket shoppers feel the same way. The idea is get in and get out as fast as possible so that you can go on to more productive activities.

However, in Merida, supermarket shoppers never appear to be in a hurry. Instead, they seem to treat their shopping experience as a diversion to be enjoyed. I rarely see solo shoppers. Usually the whole family is along for the fun.

Most shoppers normally come to supermarkets without lists. The result of all this is that shoppers casually stroll down the narrow aisles, viewing with seemingly exaggerated interest each can or package along their blissful way.

If you have ideas of getting through a congested aisle of what appears to be spectators instead of shoppers, forget it. If you ask politely that they move their carts out of your way, you will get a glare that says, "You are a rude, rude person and should be ashamed of yourself for making such a selfish request. Can't you just relax and enjoy shopping in an air-conditioned store like the rest of us?"

It is true that on hot summer days, the entire family will load up in a public bus and go to the mall. They stroll the mall together window shopping for hours. It is not only diversion, but they get a break from the hot weather for the cost of a bus ride.

Another odd situation occurs when you ask a clerk for the location of an item. It is not unusual that in the midst of his explanation another customer will come up and interrupt the clerk. Amazingly, the clerk will stop his explanation and immediately begin responding to the new request as if you were not there. Once finished, he will resume his explanation with you. It is almost as if he has attention deficit disorder and can only handle one request at a time. The last request pushes the first request out of the queue.

This is a characteristic of clerks not just at supermarkets but in all types of shopping. It is maddening.

So, as in driving in Merida, there is an element of chaos that permeates the shopping experience. There appears to be a lack of organization. To me, this represents a sort of take-it-as-it-happens attitude for which I certainly have respect. I wish I could do a better job of adopting that attitude, at least in non-business experiences. However, when it comes to making something happen as you want or have planned for it to happen, forget it.

Of course, the lack of planning through the use of shopping lists further exacerbates the apparent lack of organization built into the management of the supermarket. Since time, or the strategic use of time, seems is not a priority, why would anyone be concerned that a fifteen-minute shopping trip turns into an hour? And if the real purpose is diversion and buying food is only of secondary interest, certainly the longer the experience lasts, the better.

CHAPTER FIFTEEN

Profitable at last

Just as Joe came into OGA's life at the most appropriate moment, we had the good luck to hire someone who was over-qualified, really, to be our production manager. Luis Diaz is a Honduran who had been in Mexico the last five years working for a multi-national U.S. company, which had recently closed its factory doors in the Yucatan.

Luis had been making a market salary. We still did not have the ability to pay a market salary. I convinced Luis to come to work for us for much less money than he had been getting. He was willing to gamble on our future, and it turned out to be a good decision for both parties.

Luis took our production floor to still higher altitudes. As a result, we finally began making worthwhile profits. Along the way, it became clear that our 50,000 square feet were not enough to satisfy our customer's needs. We now had about four hundred employees and could not fit any more into the building.

Another multi-national U.S. company failed at about this time and placed their factory building on the market. This building had about 70,000 square feet and would satisfy our needs. In May of 2005 we moved to our third factory, OGA III. As I write this, we have now grown to over 500 employees and are busting at the seams again.

We were able to hire Luis and acquire the factory building due to the China Effect. That is, many factories in Mexico were closing and simply going out of business or moving their production to China. Obviously, this was a concern to me as my customer could decide to do the same. I knew that my customer already had some contractors in China, and I also knew that there was absolutely no way to compete against the Chinese on the basis of cost. How were we going to stay in business under such circumstances?

Our biggest competitive advantage was obvious: geographical proximity to the United States. This, of course, meant faster turn-around. The Chinese had a turn-around of about six months time unless their product was sent by air, which added too much to the final cost. So geography was in our favor, but the question was would that be enough?

Obviously, quality is important. We had already proven to our customer that our quality was probably among the best that he could get. However, the customer received the same product for almost half the price we charged. Only our customer knew the cost/benefit calculus for cost and quality and where the break occurred in terms of paying more for our quality or relying on a less-expensive Chinese product.

What else could we use to our favor in the search for customer satisfaction? Not much. I finally decided that our only other advantage would be in service. Service is defined in my mind in a broad way, but one of the key components to service is on-time delivery. Among other service components, I began to stress the idea of on-time delivery as key to our success. Included in this concept was customer requests for rush orders. Certainly, China could never do a rush order.

Naturally, once we began to measure our performance in these service components, we became better at delivering not only our product, but also service. In a way, we became victims of our own success. As we improved on-time deliveries, we began receiving more orders and more rush orders. Our production planning department, led by Sergio, began jumping at the customer's request and on the way up asking, "How high do you want us to go?" Our production department began performing miracles in delivering orders on time. But this just made the cycle tighter, as the customer gained more confidence in our ability to deliver on time. Still more orders and more "rushes" were requested. The team kept performing with a minimum of failures, and our quality did not suffer. We were now producing well over fifty thousand garments per month and meeting nearly every ambitious goal that we challenged ourselves with.

The customer's sales began increasing by as much as 20%, year over year. I asked him if he knew why this had occurred. I was gratified by his response: most of his competitors had gone to China. Because China had been inundated in recent years, Chinese deliveries were not being made on time. Even if the boat left China on time, the West Coast ports, where Chinese deliveries entered, were overflowing. He claimed that when his competitors' customers could not get their product on time, they came to my customer, and he was able to deliver. It was a wonderful feeling to receive confirmation that our strategy had been correct and worked to our customer's benefit as well as ours.

Our successes are without a doubt the result of the commitment and dedication of our top people. Our strategies could have been perfect, but without the ability to implement them correctly, we would never have had the success we did.

We were very lucky to acquire the team we have. Their intelligence is astonishing. Yet brains alone would not have been sufficient without the incredible commitment that they demonstrate every day.

When we began the company, I was unable to pay market salaries. I sold the vision for our company to key prospective employees in interviews with the idea that if we were successful, and there was quite a bit of doubt concerning our prospects, that the company would share profits with the key employees. We would all bet on the future together. Profit sharing is not a normal idea in Mexico, so it got their attention.

Once we turned the corner and began to earn profits, I devised a formula based on current salary and longevity with the company. Presumably, salary level encompasses responsibility. Longevity reflects loyalty, and this is a concept very important to me, especially for those who labored for several years at low salaries and no profit-sharing. About 50% of the total company profits are shared by Claudia and me with a key group who are non-stockholders.

The employee in this group who labored the longest with the lowest salary compared to the market was Wendy Nuñez, our CPA and controller. I convinced Wendy to come to work for us before we even had any machinery, leaving a job with an established company to do so. Part of the reason was that she wanted to get back into the maquila industry and partly she was intrigued by my promise of profit-sharing.

Wendy has become our most trusted employee. She is the single mother of two boys and exhibits an incredible dedication to OGA and to her two boys. She has brought to the job not only knowledge and dedication, but a rare ability to be very impartial and objective. She is also a perfectionist, and I respect her judgment immensely.

Mary Solis, another member of the group that shares profits, was hired as an assistant fabric cutter just as production was beginning. It soon became apparent to Claudia that Mary had enormous potential. It was not long before she became our head supervisor and then what we call the Line Chief, who is the direct boss of all the supervisors.

Mary is a self-taught seamstress who had worked in her home sewing for individuals. It is clear that Mary has a very high level of natural intelligence, although very little formal schooling. She could solve sewing problems quickly and understood the implications of alternative sewing methods on the final product.

Once we moved to OGA II, we made Mary our Quality Manager, and to this date she is our only Quality Manager. Mary has come a long way and is making much more money than she had ever thought possible. It was very rewarding to me when she told me one day with obvious pride, "Don Gus, I never imagined that some day I would be the manager of Quality for a factory of this size." Mary has done a fantastic job for us in bringing our quality to its current level.

Sergio Can is mentioned above as one of those employees who Joe Toste brought us. He is now in charge of production planning and participates in profits. He began his career in the sewing industry as a sewer for the company that Joe worked for. Sergio never began high school because of financial exigencies in his family. He went to work traveling from his home town of *Kinchil* to the Canadian company's plant in Merida.

Sergio's abilities were recognized immediately, and he was promoted to distributor, supervisor, engineering assistant, floor engineer and later became Chief Engineer at Joe's former company. Normally engineers have a college degree in Industrial Engineering. Thanks to Sergio's incredibly high natural intelligence, he was easily trained in sophisticated engineering methods.

Once Joe's plant closed, Sergio was without work until Joe enticed him to come to work for us as a supervisor. At the time, Sergio was about twenty-eight-years-old. He worked his way up to his current post by demonstrating commitment and by finding ingenious ways to solve problems.

I am amazed by his intelligence and his maturity. His only weakness is that he sometimes allows his passion for his job to create some negativity that he transmits to his subordinates. Recognizing his incredible potential, I have worked with him to try and redirect this energy in a more positive way. I recognize the problem in him, as I sometimes have the same uncontrolled passion that gets the best of me. I also recognize I have not always been as good a teacher with him as I should, unfortunately. Nevertheless, Sergio has improved on this weakness immensely, despite my shortcomings as a model.

Santiago Peet is another member of the profit-sharing group who is also a Joe Toste protégé. Santiago is older than Sergio. He came to us at about age thirty-eight. Joe and I went to *Uman*, a city just outside Merida, to talk him into leaving his post in what amounts to a cooperative bank to come back to the maquila industry and work for us.

While Santiago does not have the same high level of intelligence as Sergio, he is very organized and committed to company goals. He hates to miss his goals and if he is in risk of not making them, he gets in a nasty mood. San walks around the production floor with his clipboard full of papers that he is constantly checking as he solves production problems and moving operators from one production line to another in his never-ending chess game to relieve production bottlenecks.

The last member to enter the group was Luis Diaz, the Honduran. Luis also has an incredibly high level of natural intelligence that he has leveraged through obtaining his engineering degree. As I already mentioned, he had several years precious experience in the industry working for large factories. His expertise has been invaluable.

Luis' only problem is that, at age thirty-five, he believes he is invincible. He is still young enough to believe that twelve or fourteen years in the business is an eternity, and that anyone with that amount of experience has learned everything one is going to learn. If there is a problem, Luis has the answer and does not want to waste time listening to the supervisors or anyone else who might have something to opine on the subject. I have asked him to slow down and let them get their two cents in, even if what they are recommending is idiotic. I suggested that it is good to tell them why their suggestions won't work and why his ideas will work; in the long run they will feel important for having opined. Besides, occasionally, and I admit rarely, Luis might not have all the facts or the correct answer. He has an astonishingly good track record at being right in solving production problems and he is getting better at listening to his subordinates.

Luis loves to argue. He argues with me on a regular basis. He said he would like to consider me as his father figure. This, of course, is a great honor for me. He must really consider me as a father figure as I often feel like I have a teen-aged son in him; he especially likes to criticize my management philosophy, as I know I loved to criticize my own father's idiotic philosophies (or so I thought at the time). I listen and note that he does have some insight on my weaknesses. Listening to this thirty-five-year-old describe my failings is, of course, maddening. However, Luis and I argue with good faith, looking for ways to improve the company. And he has been instrumental in helping us improve by leaps and bounds.

CHAPTER SIXTEEN
Mike Moser

The contractor who was remodeling the OGA III building, Zacarias, asked me if I knew another Texas named Mike Moser. I answered that I did not. He said, "Well, he's a good guy. I will introduce you to him. I just finished his new factory out on the loop".

Zacarias never got around to the introduction. But one day I was in the gym and heard this guy speaking English and struck up a conversation. It turned out to be Mike Moser.

Mike is a tall angular Texan married to a short and pretty Korean lady. Mike was the owner of a jewelry factory in Merida, and says the smartest thing he ever did was sell the business to his Customer and go to work for his Customer. I think the smartest thing he ever did was marry Young Hee.

According to Mike, he did not graduate from high school out in Lubbock, but got accepted to North Texas State University in Denton on the basis of his college entrance scores. Mike lasted a semester before becoming exhausted from all the partying.

He moved back to West Texas for another semester of partying at a junior college. In the meantime, he was accepted at the University of Hawaii. Off he went on the eight year program of more partying.

Ultimately, he obtained an undergraduate degree in Anthropology and a Masters degree in Archeology of Southeast Asia.

Between studies in Hawaii, Mike played the guitar and was the lead singer in a band that sang mostly country and western. Mike says he was ahead of his time in that he was a long-haired country western singer. He also made money by driving a cab in Hawaii.

Once he graduated, I am sure to the relief of everyone, he returned to West Texas. He was working in his father's business. A close friend's mother was in the jewelry business and counseled Mike to consider jewelry as a career. At this point in Mike's life, "career" was not much of a consideration.

At any rate, he was about to embark on a trip to visit his sister in Maine, and his friend's mom told him to go to New Mexico and buy Indian jewelry to take to a specific place in Boston on his way to Maine. She told him that Indian jewelry was selling like hotcakes in Boston.

Mike spent all of his available cash on jewelry, bought a ticket to Boston and went right from the Boston airport to the jewelry store his friend's mom mentioned. Mike sold everything he had to this jeweler in Boston and more than doubled his money. He immediately traveled to Maine to see his sister. He spent the next months in a drunken and marijuana-induced stupor, enjoying the fruits of his entrepreneurial venture into jewelry.

While in Maine and in a rare state of lucidity, it occurred to him that he could repeat his Indian jewelry sales experience. To his credit, he stayed lucid long enough to buy a return ticket and plan the next sales trip to Boston.

He repeated the cycle about four times. Each time he earned significant money and spent time in Maine visiting his sister. The last trip, while in Maine, he met a very pretty girl, coincidentally from Texas, who was working in Maine during her summer vacations. They immediately hit it off and this girl, Suzanne, was destined to become Mike's first ex-wife.

However, matrimony was not on either's mind at the moment. The primary themes of their relationship were fun and adventure. So, they decided to hitch-hike from Maine to Portales, New Mexico where Suzanne was studying. They did so, but en route the plans somehow changed, and they ended up in San Francisco.

In San Francisco, Mike met up with his former band buddies from Hawaii, and they began singing in clubs. This went on for several months and Suzanne and Mike kept house together. Then one day Mike arrived home and found a note left by Suzanne saying she was tired of the life they had together with Mike playing in bands. She decided to go to Oregon without him.

Mike was devastated. He spoke with a friend, Jason, about the situation. Mike just thought she was too beautiful, and they had too much in common to let her get away; he wanted to go look for her in Oregon. He had an idea where she was, but could not let her get away without trying to find her. Jason said, "No problem, I'll go with you. There is a freight train that passes slowly behind a certain bar, and we can be in Oregon in 30 hours at no cost."

This sounded good to Mike. They would have another adventure and he could search for Suzanne. They packed knapsacks and went to the bar, drinking and waiting for the train to come through.

Once they heard it coming they paid their bill and walked out back. Jason had done this many times before and took the lead. Mike said to me, "While it sounds easy to jump into a slowly moving box car, it really is not. First, the floor of the box car is about chest high. Second, there is a slope from the tracks back to ground level. Third, while the train is only moving about six miles per hour, managing the height, the slope and a backpack all at once is not as easy as you might think. You have to throw your backpack on first, then you have quite a bit of motivation to make sure you get on as well." It does sound difficult, but it also sounds like fun. I felt a tinge of jealousy that Mike had done it and I still have not.

Jason hopped on first and then helped Mike in. Then it occurred to Jason that they would freeze to death this time of year since the train went through the mountains. He told Mike, "Look, we've got to get back to the train car that is transporting the new automobiles. They always leave the keys in them, and we can get in and turn on the heater."

The only problem was that the train car with the autos, three levels of them, was toward the end of the train. They would have to hop from car to car on the moving train to arrive at the train car with the automobiles. They made it and were once again pleased, as well as relieved.

They picked out a nice truck and entered the cab. Jason claimed he knew where they always hid the keys, and it turned out he was right. They spent the night in the warmth of the cab listening to good music on the radio of the truck.

The next morning they woke after a good night's sleep and began to eat fruit they had brought along. Then they noticed three little heads in the truck in front of them. The door opened to the truck in front and a ten-year-old boy made his way back to them. The boy said he and his brothers had run away from home and had not eaten in a day. Mike and Jason shared their fruit with the kids.

Once in Oregon, Jason stayed with Mike a couple of days and then made his way back to California. Mike began the search for Suzanne. He miraculously found her working in a hotel. The two of them got back together, and they both worked in an upscale hotel in Oregon for about a year.

After they became tired of Oregon, they bought a truck and moved back to New Mexico. At this point, Mike decided to return to the Indian jewelry business since he had done so well financially before. Indian jewelry was very fashionable at this time, the 1970s. Mike began to manufacture the jewelry. He had about eighty Indians working for him making in the fabrication process. He soon began earning prodigious amounts of money.

Indian jewelry mostly has stones set in silver. In the manufacturing process, there is a great deal of waste of silver. Mike always had the silver shavings swept off the floor and saved in barrels. In the mid 1970s, silver was fairly inexpensive. Therefore, Mike never re-sold the silver, but only warehoused it in barrels.

In 1973 silver had a market price of about two dollars per ounce. Then in the mid 1970s and early

1980s, the Hunt brothers tried to corner the silver market along with some Arab partners. Their consortium owned about half of the world's deliverable silver by the 1980s. As a result, silver prices began increasing rapidly, leveling out at about fifty dollars per ounce. Mike decided to sell his barrels of silver shavings. He received several hundred thousand dollars out of his silver scrap.

Mike sold at a propitious time. Once the market became cornered, many small investors began chasing silver as well. The trading rules were changed by regulatory agencies in the U.S. Eventually prices bottomed quickly. Silver lost as much as 50% of its value in one day in 1980. The Hunts were ultimately convicted of conspiracy and had to file bankruptcy.

Mike's silver sales windfall, coupled with his very successful factory, enabled Mike to retire in the early 1980s. He and Suzanne married prior to his early retirement. They sold the business and moved to Tahiti to live blissfully in Paradise for the rest of their lives.

In another moment of lucidity, Mike realized in a couple of years that at their current rate of spending, they would not be able to continue as a young retired couple in Tahiti. They returned to the States, this time to San Antonio to be near Mike's uncle, and Mike began working for a jewelry supplier he had used while in business in New Mexico.

Mike and Suzanne had a child, but their marriage was not going well. In the meantime, Mike met a man from Houston who was interested in starting a factory in Korea. He proposed that Mike set up his factory. By this time, Mike and Suzanne were divorcing so Mike accepted the proposal.

The Korean contract was for a one-year period. After he had successfully set the factory up, Mike decided to stay in Korea. He formed a partnership with a Korean to make wax models that are used in jewelry factories. While living in Korea, Mike met, married and divorced his second ex-wife, a Korean.

Following that ill-fated relationship. Mike was getting anxious to return to the United States to be with his daughter. While forming a plan to sell out to his partner, he noticed a beautiful Korean walking past his house to visit a friend. Not a bashful type, Mike decided instantly to meet her. He introduced himself to Young Hee, destined to become his third and final wife.

Within about six months Mike arranged a deal with his partner and was moving back to New Mexico to be near his daughter. Young Hee followed some two months later, and the two became partners in another jewelry factory that Mike started in his garage. This factory soon grew to sixty employees. In the process, he was contracting with a silver factory in Taxco, Mexico for parts he was using in his own factory.

While on a visit to Taxco, Mike met a very wealthy businessman from Arkansas who wanted to form a partnership with Mike for a full-scale factory. The two decided on Merida, and Mike moved there with Young Hee. Their factory grew rapidly to over three hundred employees. The product was going to a large company in the U.S. who Mike convinced to buy the factory. As part of the deal, Mike and Young Hee stayed on to manage the factory.

As one might expect, the security in Mike's factory is extravagant. He has caught employees with gold placed in body cavities as they leave the bathroom in the factory. There is a security room with about twenty monitors that reflect what is being recorded from some fifty different cameras located in various parts of the factory. I am not sure how many security guards are employed with his factory, but it appears to be a small army. The polishing and grinding of all gold is done within a type of glass box that has a vacuum system that sucks all the gold dust generated through the polishing and grinding into a central repository. Every so often the gold dust is collected from this repository and re-processed. This vacuum system, Mike says, cost several hundred thousand dollars, but I suspect it has already paid for itself.

Mike and Young Hee love dogs. They have a Jack Russell Terrier named Rocky who travels back and forth from home to work with them, just like my own dog, Jake. Besides Rocky, they have taken in (at last count) thirteen dogs that live on the factory grounds. All of these dogs are street dogs who were wandering the streets before finding a veritable Dog Heaven with Mike and Young Hee. Mike is spending a small fortune each month just on dog food and vet bills.

I have enjoyed knowing both Mike and Young Hee immensely. They are both very down-to-earth and without pretensions. They are a joy to be around with a wonderful sense of humor and are gracious hosts. I wish I had met them earlier so as to have enjoyed their friendship longer.

CHAPTER SEVENTEEN

Dan and Sofi

I remember being at Pancho's one night at the upper bar. There was a big crowd. A threesome, two guys and a very attractive woman, were together speaking English. Two of the three spoke with an accent. The attractive woman spoke English with an East European accent and one of the men spoke with a Spanish accent, but he was clearly not Yucatecan. The third guy spoke with an American accent.

The third guy was Chuck Nihan. Chuck was mentioned earlier and will be mentioned again. As often happens in these settings, eventually the conversational group begins to expand and we are all introducing ourselves at some point. We all became friends before the night was over.

Dan and Sofi are a delightful couple. Dan is Argentinian. He is tall and lanky with prematurely white hair. Sofi, from Macedonia, is beautiful and vivacious. Both have a great sense of humor.

It is interesting how fate works to bring people together. If it had not been for the breakup of the Soviet Empire and the subsequent ethnic cleansing that was to take place in what used to be Yugoslavia, these two would never have met. A series of events that created such misery for so many people resulted in the happy, and seemingly perfect, marriage of two people from totally different cultures.

Dan was born and grew up in Argentina. He decided to go the United States to attend law school. Dan is very unassuming and not the least bit boastful. Therefore, I found out through Sofi that he did very well in school at the American University in Washington D.C. He took the bar exam in the state of Virginia and scored the highest of all participants in Virginia on that exam. When confronted with this admirable accomplishment, Dan responded in typical understated fashion, "Oh, Argentinians are very good at memorizing."

He soon found employment in the U.S. for a large law firm specializing in international law. The firm decided to open an office in Buenos Aires, and Dan was the logical choice for leading the charge in Argentina.

After several years, Dan returned to the States and became the legal counsel for the Peace Corps. However, the Peace Corps rules require that after five years employees must resign, so Dan then went to work for the American Bar Association.

The ABA had some interesting projects overseas in the developing countries of the former Soviet Union. Dan jumped at the chance to go and began a series of very interesting experiences in Eastern Europe in various countries.

Subsequently, Dan took a position as a consultant with U.S.A.I.D. The projects were always related to developing a western-style legal system in these former socialist or communist countries.

Dan accepted a position to advise on legal systems in Macedonia. He was on the fourth floor of a building that housed several embassies and other entities. A friend said that he wanted to introduce him to an interesting Macedonian lady. He accepted the invitation to lunch.

Sofi grew up in a socialist country with an older sister who excelled at everything. Sofi had the great opportunity to go to the United States as an exchange student. She arrived speaking no English. She says her first semester of high school was horrible due to her lack of English. She made very low grades, including failing grades. Slowly she mastered English and before the end of the school year was making straight As.

She could have stayed in the States and gone to a university, but decided to return to her native Macedonia. There she attended a university and found herself somewhat bored. Her parents, she says, were very disappointed in her because her sister had done so well academically. However, she really did not have much interest, although she had confidence that if she found something she wanted to do, she knew she would be great at it.

After the breakup of Yugoslavia, she found work as a free-lance translator. She was working for five different agencies, all from the U.S., and she was doing well financially. Then she got a call to interview for a job as a translator with the British Embassy. She was chosen over 80 other applicants. The ambassador who hired her said he did so because she was the only applicant who did not claim to be at the top of her graduating class. She says, "I did not tell him that because I was far from the top of my class."

It is clear that Sofi is highly intelligent and the fact that she did not finish at the top of her academic class was a result of lack of interest. She was challenged by her work at the British Embassy which maintained her interest. Over time, her performance was easily noted, and she was rewarded by her competence with ultimately some six different job titles at the same time in the Embassy. When she left, the Embassy had to hire six different people.

Sofi says she was making very good money, at least by Macedonian standards, but was using the money to travel the world over where she could and buy clothes. She met many interesting people. Once Richard Gere visited the Embassy. She was terribly excited to meet him. However, it was anticlimactic. She says he was obviously full of himself. Not so of Tony Blair, she says. The Prime Minister could not have been a more normal and down-to-earth person.

The six jobs she had were very demanding. She would get home late and had to be at work early to give briefings to various embassy officers. When her friend said he wanted to introduce her to Dan who worked in the same building, she really had no interest. She was too busy to take time for lunch and too busy to date. Nevertheless, she went as a favor to her friend.

At the time, a medical condition created some type of spots all over her skin. Doctors told her that it was stress-related. Despite this medical condition, Dan was smitten. Her favorite color, she explained to me, is pink. She was struck by the fact that Dan wore a pink shirt that day.

Dan began courting her seriously. By the second or third time they went out, Sofi passed the point of no return. About a month into their courtship they traveled to Greece for a long weekend. Dan had the ring ready, proposed to Sofi and she accepted. They were married in Macedonia.

Soon Sofi received a promotion and arrived home totally elated. She told Dan. Dan said, "You have to resign. We are moving because I have been transferred to another project in Armenia." The wind was taken completely out of her sails, but she knew she had committed to a life with Dan. She resigned and they soon left for Armenia.

Armenia was not a happy place. Additionally, Sofi suffered an accident at home that almost paralyzed her. The only bright spot was that Dan was making very good money, and Sofi landed a job with the British Embassy again. Her Russian language ability helped in addition to her recommendation from the embassy in Macedonia.

While in Armenia, Sofi received an award: Member of the British Empire, from the Queen of England. The award was given due to her tireless assistance of British sailors while she worked for the embassy in Macedonia during the intervention of U.S. and British forces brought about by the ethnic cleansing taking place in Bosnia and Serbia.

Dan had come to know Merida during his first visit some thirty years before. Like many who visit Merida, he was instantly enamored. He had always had a dream to return to Merida. He discussed this dream with Sofi. The two decided that the time was ripe to bring Dan's dream to fruition.

They moved to Merida for the purpose of building a Bed and Breakfast. They found a location and began. In the meantime, Dan received an offer to go to work in Kosovo. The money was too good; he accepted. The plan was for Sofi to stay in Merida and finish the B & B so that once the project ended the two would re-unite in Merida to run their B&B.

After five months in Kosovo and run-ins with the project leaders, whose main objective appeared to be to spend U.S. tax dollars regardless of Benefit, Dan decided enough was enough. He resigned and returned to Merida.

Like all ex pat stories of starting businesses in Mexico, it was not easy for Dan and Sofi. Most people starting businesses have horror stories to tell about the bureaucratic hassles that are forced on all businesses. Dan and Sofi were remodeling an old home downtown. This creates an extra level of beauracracy, as Merida has rules about remodeling old homes. The idea is a good one: preserve the original architecture and flavor of Old Merida.

However, like many of the good and well-intentioned ideas of government, the consequence is to provide opportunity for government bureaucrats to take advantage of petitioners. Since this is Mexico, it is likely that this consequence was fully understood and intended when the rules were made.

Sofi had to do the initial work on the B&B on her own since Dan had gone back to Kosovo. At that time, Sofi did not speak good Spanish. She did have experience in building, as she had been responsible for the construction of the new British Embassy in Macedonia.

Fortunately, Sofi only had to go to INAH, the government Agency responsible for issuing the permit to remodel old homes, three times. This is a record. Furthermore, she was not asked for a bribe. For my first house remodel job, just to get permission to raise the wall in front of the house, it took three months and the government bureaucrat was clearly asking for a bribe to get the permit, although it was never given. I imagine that the difference between Sofi and me is her beauty and charm. Chauvinistic bureaucrats in Mexico never fail to notice the aesthetics of beautiful women.

Thankfully, Dan returned in only five months, but in the interim, Sofi had to find ways to address problems she encountered on her own. She relied on her beauty, charm and intelligence once again to solve the problem of *Los San Lunistas*. This is the term given to the workers who do not show up for work on Mondays as their tradition is to go on weekend-long drunken binges. The consequence to overindulging alcohol for forty eight hours is that Los San Lunistas are unable to work on Mondays; brick masons are famous for this.

Clearly, the work is slowed if a large group of workers is always absent one day per week. Sofi, who is very classy and normally very subdued in her attire, thought of a solution to the San Lunistas not showing up on Mondays. She went to the store and bought a blouse one size too small and fairly low-cut. Every Monday she would saunter through the job wearing this blouse. After the first Monday, the word got out and absenteeism dropped dramatically in the future.

Dan and Sofi now have a very successful B & B at a great location downtown. It is called *Hotel Marionetas* and has been written up in about twenty magazines, despite an existence of only two and a half years as of this writing.

Sofi laughs explaining that her parents back in Macedonia were appalled once Dan and Sofi informed them of their decision to give up high-paying jobs and move to the Yucatan. As a result, her parents are too embarrassed to tell their Macedonian friends of their daughter and son-in-law's adventure in what the parents think of as the middle of nowhere among Mayan Indians.

Nevertheless, the B & B has been a fantastic success. Sofi's parents would no doubt be proud to know that usually Las Marionetas is booked with reservations for a minimum of 50 percent of the rooms as far out as eight months.

CHAPTER EIGHTEEN

Robbed!

While moving from OGA II to the new building for OGA III, we had to find space to store excess material, such as the copper tubing we had used for our compressed air system throughout OGA II. Some of the material we left out in the factory yard, waiting to make space within the factory.

I was not worried much about the material in the factory yard as the factory had a high chain-link fence around it. Besides we had hired a very good security firm prior to moving to this factory.

The two partners to the security firm were Emilio and Randy. Emilio is a good-looking Mexican who was an ex-policia. Emilio was also mentioned in the chapter on J.W. Barnes and ultimately played a part in helping uncover Tomas' robbery while dismantling OGA II. Emilio's older brother was an important Comandante with the Merida Police in charge of the southern half of the city. Emilio's partner, Randy Ruiz, was a Mexican citizen who had lived in the U.S. most of his life as his mother had been a Gringa.

Randy spoke perfect English. He had served in the U.S. Army. He claimed to have been in Special Forces, the Green Berets. I asked about his military occupational specialties as I know all Special Forces soldiers are cross-trained in two. He was a sniper and a munitions expert. Subsequently, he had become a dog trainer and worked with the canine group of the police in Campeche before coming to Merida.

I used to chat with Randy when I had time. I even invited him to a party where he enthralled some of the guests with a couple of word tricks. He claimed he learned these undergoing psychological training while in Special Forces. Much of this training focused on how to psychologically manage capture. The next time he tried these tricks on a friend, I paid more attention and noticed that he manipulated the responses and I doubted that this was something from Special Forces training. It was a simple trick. The more I questioned him over time about his service, the more I began to question that he was former Special Forces. Nevertheless, both Emilio and Randy were very alert security guards that had helped us improve our perimeter and internal security.

With the security we had in place at OGA III, I was surprised to get a call at home on a Saturday morning from the Director of the Industrial Park asking if I was aware of the robbery that had occurred last night at OGA III. I was not. Strangely, I had not received a call from our security company. I called Tomas Mata our Maintenance Manager and we went together to the factory to get the facts.

We interviewed the park security officer first. On his rounds around the park, he had noticed a car on a dirt road at the back of our plant. Our plant is on one side and jungle is on the other side of this dirt road. The park security officer called the police who were able to catch the driver of the car while the accomplices escaped into the jungle. The car was a small four-door sedan and the back seat was crammed full of copper tubing bent like an accordion to fit inside the back seat. The car was impounded and the driver thrown into jail.

I asked where our security guard was and the park security guard said that after the police arrested the driver, they and the guard went to our guard shack and called out. There was never an answer. Or so they claimed. Clearly, this raised suspicions. Randy was working that night.

When I interviewed Randy he claimed never to have heard the park security screaming at him from about two feet through the guard shack walls. I told him that this was impossible. He said that he agreed and that he believed that the park security guard was lying. Randy looked me right in the eye and said that he would never steal from me after all that I and the company had done for him. Randy was a good liar without a doubt, as this stretched the imagination beyond belief. He never wavered in his story nor the sincerity that covered his face.

Under Mexican law, there are a series of requirements that the robbery victim is obligated to do to ensure that justice is pursued by the authorities. Immediately we had to go to the *Ministerio Publico*, the Public Ministry, to file complaints. Tomas went to do this for the company with relish, as neither he nor Randy liked one another. Unfortunately, the authorities at the Public Ministry refused to accept his complaint for various reasons. This was true for both Saturday and Sunday.

Therefore I went on Monday, but was not able to get to the Public Ministry until the afternoon. I was directed to a particular office within the Ministry. I arrived at this office at 3:10. This was the only office empowered to accept these complaints, and the office closed for the day at 3:00. There was no one else who would accept the complaint.

The next day, Tuesday, I received a letter from the Public Ministry informing me that I had until 5:00 P.M. the last Sunday to file a complaint against the burglar or he would be released! I was astonished. The police themselves had captured the burglar in the act. In fact, on Saturday and Sunday we had attempted to file the complaint and been refused. Now, forty eight hours after the deadline to act, I was receiving an official letter telling me I must be at the Public Ministry or the burglar will be released. I arrived at the Public Ministry as directed only to discover that the burglar was released on Sunday. I was livid, but knew I could not accomplish anything dealing with the Public Ministry bureaucrats.

I was advised by my legal counsel that the perpetrators could still be prosecuted, but that if I really wanted that to happen I would have to hire a private lawyer who specializes in criminal acts to file papers with the Public Ministry. For the *nth* time, I was stupefied at Mexican laws and legal traditions. I wanted to know if I understood correctly that in order to get the government to do its job, I would need to hire a private lawyer at my own expense. The answer was "yes". Otherwise, I was told, the burglar caught red-handed in the act by the police and also set free by them would continue living free without prosecution. Not only that, but the police would not do an investigation to catch the accomplices. The case was closed, as far as the police were concerned. It made no difference that we had attempted to file a complaint prior to that Sunday and had not been allowed.

I called the criminal lawyer recommended by our corporate attorney. He quoted his fees at the approximate amount of $1,500 equivalent and would need half up front as is customary in Mexico. I decided that we would have to do this or that the perpetrators and everyone else would believe that they could steal from our company with impunity. We accepted the lawyer's proposal. Then he told me that this would not include any bribes he would have to pay to get the police to act upon his official legal filings. Again, I was stupefied. I simply told him, "I just want you to do your job. Paying bribes is not legal. Any valid expenses that you encounter above your fees will be paid, but I will not pay a bribe, nor reimburse you for bribes paid in my behalf." That was code for I want no part in bribery, but get the job done and if that includes a bribe, I don't want to know about it.

In the meantime, we had to deal with Randy. Before we could do much, Randy disappeared. Emilio claimed he did not know what was going on, and he had been having trouble with Randy about a number of problems. We began our own investigation based on the identification of the one burglar who was actually caught. He was a former employee and through an internal investigation we discovered that the other burglars were also former employees that lived in the same pueblito nearby. Through other employees we confirmed that the burglars were bragging about the theft and that Randy had been an accomplice.

We turned all of this information over to our private lawyer who gave it to the police. The car had been impounded, and the lawyer did get us permission to go to the pound and extract the copper tubing.

Months went by with no word on any police or prosecutory action. Our lawyer, paid to make things happen, was claiming he was checking on the situation weekly and was complying with all their requests. I decided I needed a meeting with the D.A. to make something happen. I knew I would have no chance getting a meeting with the equivalent of the District Attorney if I simply called him; in fact, I knew he would never take my call. After several months I asked the Director of the Maquila Association, Roman, who is politically connected, to get me an appointment with the D.A. Roman told me, "No problem, I just played golf with him over the weekend."

Roman soon called me back and had the appointment. I showed up at the D.A.'s office at precisely the hour I was told to be there. After an hour of waiting, which is normal for a government appointment, I asked the secretary if I should come back. I was very polite, but was thinking, *Okay, I have paid my dues waiting for an hour proving that the D.A. is more important than me.* For the entire hour from the D.A.'s office was the sound of constant and boisterous laughing. It was a shame I had to disturb a public servant with a plea that the police and prosecutors get about their business, especially when he was obviously having such a good time.

The secretary did go into the D.A.'s office, and the laughter stopped. In about five minutes the friends of the D.A. left and he came out, making a big show that the secretary should always inform him when he had an appointment waiting.

We entered his office, about the size of a small gymnasium. There were three conversational areas with sofas and coffee tables and his desk, which was located appropriately in the corner of his corner office. I explained the situation, apologizing profusely for taking the time of such an important person for something seemingly so trivial as a small robbery. "However," I explained, "I do not want to allow petty thieves to rob from me with impunity, especially since it may erroneously provide an image of a rich American who does not care if he loses small assets, as this will be an invitation to continue robbing."

He responded that he understood completely. Then immediately he asked, "How many employees do you have?" The message was clear: the company needed to be sufficiently big in order to merit his attention. At that time I had about four hundred employees and responded truthfully. He immediately picked up the phone and called the prosecutor in charge of the case.

As usual, the bureaucrat that he was looking for was at lunch. I am sure he intended to return in two or three hours. At any rate, the D.A. assured me that the culprits would be caught and punished appropriately. I left his office with a sense of satisfaction. However, it did not last long. No visible action was taken. My private lawyer seemed to be getting nowhere despite his professional efforts. I began following up with the D.A. by phoning him. He soon became "unavailable" each time I called and despite the secretary's promise to have him call me back, I never received a call.

All of the thieves to this day run free. While I never heard from the D.A. again, I did call Roman to let him know of my dissatisfaction. Roman seemed basically resigned to the idea that this was as far as he could go and gave me the impression that I should live with the result. The lawyer seemed to think that the culprits paid a bribe, not only to get the one who was captured out of jail and have the documents delayed to cover his trail, but also to have the police and prosecutors not act against him. I have no idea what really happened and probably never will know.

CHAPTER NINETEEN
Robbed Again!

Tomas Mata as our *Gerente de Mantenmiento*, Maintenance Manager was responsible for managing all the mechanics who worked on the machines in the factory as well as for maintaining the factory building and installations, such as electrical and air conditioning. His right-hand man was Jaime Sanchez.

Tomas had been raised in Northern Mexico. I believe he told me that he was raised by his uncle on his uncle's ranch. He recounted a number of stories about living the cowboy's life and herding cattle as a pre-adolescent.

Tomas began his career as a mechanic in the northern part of Mexico. He met his wife in the north, who was a pretty Yucatecan, and about 10 years before I hired Tomas, he moved his family to Yucatan. He is smart, so he soon moved up the ranks to become Head Mechanic at the factory that Joe Toste worked for prior to coming to OGA after the other factory closed.

Like most mechanics in factories, Tomas was like a child in a candy store. The vast majority of sewing operators are women. Mechanics are all men. Most mechanics apparently believe that they are God's gift to women. Tomas is a good-looking guy who still looks younger than his 45 years. While the other mechanics *believe* they are God's gift to women, Tomas *knows this* without any doubt. And since discipline where women are concerned is his weakness the combination of these facts created great potential for personal problems for Tomas.

I don't think Tomas slept much on weekends, balancing his family life, such as it was, with his usual stable of girlfriends and their demands for time and money. Tomas also had a habit of getting thrown in jail as a result of too much mixing of drink and women.

One Friday Tomas asked to borrow the company pickup truck for some personal errands. As a trusted employee, I agreed. Tomas was to return the truck on Saturday morning when he showed up for work on a Saturday for overtime. Not only did he not return the truck, but he did not show up either.

Around 9:00 the nest morning, Tomas called and reported he was in jail in Progreso. He also mentioned the company truck had been impounded. I sent Joe out to get him out of jail. Joe reported back asking if he should also bail out of jail the two operators who were with Tomas at the time of his arrest for drunken driving. Needless to say when Tomas came to work the next Monday morning we had a heart-to-heart talk.

Despite this, I always considered Tomas a trusted employee. While my faith in him wavered for awhile, he soon won it back with his dedication to the job. When his mother died and he did not have the money to fly back to northern Mexico for the funeral, the company gave him an interest-free loan to buy his airplane ticket. We did not deduct anything from his pay for the week he was gone.

We made repeated non-interest loans to Tomas over the years. Once he needed to buy a car. Another time he was very short of money. I think he had over-committed around Valentine's Day to the wife and the girlfriends. I was always glad to help him out due to his commitment to the firm.

Then about eighteen months later on a Sunday afternoon, I received a desperate call from Tomas's wife saying that he had been thrown in jail again, and they needed to borrow six thousand pesos to get him out of jail. I went to the jail facility thinking that this was a lot of money for drunken driving. I was also somewhat concerned as Tomas was responsible for taking a technician to the airport that Saturday night who had come to town to help us install a new automatic fabric cutter. I was hoping the technician was home safe and not sharing a cell with Tomas.

I discovered the technician had safely made his flight after he and Tomas had visited some local clubs. After dropping the technician at the airport, Tomas had been detained for erratic driving. What happened next is still in dispute. Tomas's story is that he was beaten by the police. The police version was that Tomas was belligerent and attacked them who then responded with appropriate force. In fact, part of the reason that the bail was so high was that one of the Police had actually sued Tomas for the equivalent of assault.

Tomas did look as if he had been beaten up. Actually, he looked worse than that. He was a wreck. Knowing Tomas, I was sure he said something that provoked the police. Knowing the Police, I was sure that their version was a lie and that they saw this as an opportunity for a little freelance extortion, and no doubt they planned to split the proceeds.

Tomas's lawyer went to the supposedly assaulted policeman and worked out a deal. This, of course, involved another loan to Tomas in order to pay the policeman to drop the charges.

I was once again disappointed by Tomas. Further disappointing was the fact that Tomas did not once tell me "gracias" for getting him out of jail. In our now traditional heart-to-heart talks after jail time, I mentioned my special disappointment in not receiving a thanks. He claimed that he was so embarrassed that he forgot to thank me. I suppose it is possible.

Again, Tomas had a period of dedication to work. No doubt, part of this dedication came from my sincere promise that there would never be more heart-to-heart talks, nor loans of money to get him out of jail. Part of it must have come from the knowledge that to pay off all he owed for this disaster would take quite awhile.

At any rate, in a number of months Tomas had once again worked his way into my good graces. Also the business was growing, and we needed more space than we had at OGA II. The aforementioned factory building that was to become OGA III was acquired. This building was located on the opposite side of town, and we had to manage the move in such a way as to minimize the time that we were unable to produce. Moving a factory of about four hundred people and machines across town in a minimum of time presented a tremendous logistical challenge. Tomas was of tremendous assistance in meeting this challenge.

Our most important goal was to get production up and running again as soon as possible to minimize revenue loss. We shut down on a Friday just after lunch and began moving machines, equipment, fabric, components, work in process and finished goods. Production resumed the next Monday morning. That is, we lost about a half day of productive time. It was really quite a feat. Tomas was invaluable in the implementation of our plan.

However, we still had to dismantle OGA II. OGA III had been bought with feedrail, compressed air and everything in place. We had rented OGA II and installed all electrical, feedrail, air conditioning, and steam boiler system for our presses. All of these installations had to be removed. As mentioned in the last chapter, some of this material was to be temporarily stored within the factory grounds at OGA III.

Tomas was in charge of dismantling all of the installations in OGA II. We had to be out by a certain date, and this was the deadline for dismantling. Tomas left Jaime at OGA II managing the operation. Occasionally, I went by to check on things. The dismantling was taking longer than I had planned.

One maintenance employee was not getting along with Jaime and came to me to complain. In the discussion he claimed that Tomas and Jaime were selling copper tubing from the compressed air system as well as other items. At first, I felt he was simply disenchanted with Tomas. I did not think Tomas was capable of stealing from me after all we had done for him. However, the disgruntled employee continued to accuse him. And soon he was telling me that Tomas and Jaime were threatening him.

I felt there was enough smoke for me to check to see if there was a fire. I went to the old plant and began checking with a nearby buyer of scrap metal that the disgruntled employee had told me was buying the material. He denied it but I saw some copper tubing that looked similar to what we had used in OGA II. I also asked my security guard, Emilio, to check with another neighbour who supposedly had bought some material from our plant. He recorded her conversation where she admitted to buying from Tomas.

I was truly heart-broken. I had trusted Tomas with so much despite his past failings with alcohol and women. I decided to go to the Policia Judicial and have them investigate on their own to obtain objective evidence. Clearly, if it were true, and it appeared more than likely that it was, I would have to fire Tomas. However, I wanted objective evidence to do so.

The Policia Judicial spent about ten days investigating and gave me a written report. The report was conclusive: Tomas and Jaime had sold material from OGA II and pocketed the money from the material that was supposed to have been delivered to OGA III. We filed a complaint with the police and informed Tomas and Jaime. I agreed not to prosecute if Tomas would accept a limited severance and agree not to file a labor lawsuit. I explained my deep disappointment with Tomas, who continued to deny he had stolen and sold the material. The same for Jaime.

Both accepted the conditions we placed on their departure from OGA without argument. When Tomas and I parted that day, both of us were water-eyed. Our public statements to the rest of our team was that both Tomas and Jaime resigned. Clearly, no one believed us, but they did not ask questions. After three months, I dropped the charges against both of them since neither had filed a labor lawsuit.

About two years later I received a notice in the mail that Tomas had not complied with his conditions of the bail that I had put up for the second incident that resulted in Tomas's jailing. I was therefore obligated to pay more money. We located Tomas who agreed to come to my office to clear things up. We then went with my lawyer to the court where Tomas took full responsibility and signed a form letting me off the hook for any further damages.

While at court, Tomas was very friendly, but contrite. He was apologizing for all the trouble he caused me and indicated how much he had always appreciated my help and support. I felt much better about Tomas, but will never be able to employ him again. He remains married, miraculously, and I wish him the best of luck and a more stable life in the future.

In the investigation of the robbery, the police could not have been more helpful. This was not the case with the next incident, unfortunately.

CHAPTER TWENTY

The Police

My experience with the Merida Police described in the last chapter was generally good. This is not always the case. The cops in Merida are quite active, but not necessarily in the way you would expect or hope for. I have encountered police who are very helpful and view their jobs as "protect and serve." However, I do believe that what drives the behavior of most police, at least in Merida, is the opportunity for bribes; there seems to be a definite positive correlation between bribe potential and police activity.

In Merida, police are omnipresent. They are stationed at nearly every intersection, sometimes more than one officer at the intersection. These policemen are on foot and normally do not have radios or any method of communication except personal cell phones. As you drive through or stop at these intersections, the police are usually reading the newspaper or sending text messages on their phones. Most of the time there is really no need for them, so I suppose reading the newspaper doesn't affect their performance. However, traffic will snarl up, and sometimes these men pay no attention or assist in any way.

Besides the police who are afoot, there are cops who ride around in cars. When I first moved to Merida, it was distracting to see the patrol cars because they keep their lights on the roof of the car constantly flashing, even though the siren is not on as they drive through the streets. There are quite a large number of police cars on the road, and these cars move through traffic at a speed of about 15 miles per hour, so their main function seems to be to slow down traffic flow.

Besides these types of police, which are State Police who wear brown uniforms, there are Merida city police, who wear blue uniforms. These police are concentrated in the downtown area. Some ride bikes.

There are Tourist Police, which wear brown and white uniforms. They are found afoot, in cars, and on motorcycles. Supposedly the Tourist Police have special training in politeness and languages. My experience with at least one of them is that their standards for training are lacking.

Another group of police is the SPV. SPV stands for Secretaria de Proteccion y Vialidad), The Department of Protection and Highways a State agency. The SPV Police wear all black and ride black motorcycles. They wear black bullet proof vests over their long sleeve black shirts and have what appear to be M-16s strapped to their backs. They wear black, military style helmets. They look quite ominous as they weave in and out of traffic on their motorcycles. I really don't understand how they last in the heat of mid-day shrouded in black.

Federal Police normally roam the highways but can be found within the city limits as well. They seem to be the best-trained and most respected.

A type of investigative police also exits. They are called the Policia Judicial (Judicial Police). These cops wear plain clothes and investigate allegations of crimes.

The crime rate in Merida is relatively low. As a result, many Mexicans from Mexico City and other areas of Mexico are moving to Merida so they can escape the capitol's high crime rate. With so many police, the crime rate should be low, but I am not sure that the cause and effect is that direct, nor do I think it is a result of excellent police work. In my experience, based on a robbery at my factory which was related earlier, the police not only did not catch their man, but when the thief was delivered to them by private security, they allowed the thief to run free.

I believe the low crime rate is actually more a result of the culture and personality of Meridians. With the large of influx of those from other Mexican cities, this may change. I hope not.

One local Police Comandante who I know told me that crime is maintained at such low levels by making examples of criminals. He claims that about ten years ago a group of criminals were escorted to the Yucatan State boundary with Quintana Roo. At the State line some of the criminals were murdered by the police and the lucky witnesses were let loose to describe what had happened as a discouragement to other criminals who might want to do business in Merida. The truth in Mexico is often an elusive concept, and I believe the comandante's story was told for effect and had little to do with the truth.

I had a very disagreeable experience with a Tourist Police one Saturday morning. I was moving from a house I had just sold. We had to park the moving truck partially on the sidewalk as it was too big for the garage. In Mexico, permits are required for nearly everything. There was a permit supposedly required to park a truck and move household goods using a truck. I discovered later that those permits are not required if the moving is done between 9:00 and 12:00 on weekend mornings. I did not know that at the time, but I doubt it would not have made any difference had I explained the law to this officer.

The truck driver informed me that he had permission to park and load the truck. It turned out that his permission was verbal given by two patrol policemen and the driver had nothing in writing. Soon a Tourist Policeman came riding up on his motorcycle. Before a word was spoken he already had his face contorted into anger either unconsciously or, perhaps because he thought he would be more intimidating if he looked angry.

At any rate, he asked for the permit in a very unfriendly tone. The driver indicated he had verbal permission. The policeman indicated he was going to call the tow truck as well as fine us. I asked him to wait a minute and calm down. I explained that we would only be about fifteen minutes more and that we were not in any way obstructing traffic. I explained that every work day cars were illegally parked along this stretch of the street, which is heavily trafficked on weekday mornings, and I had never seen any police here asking that they move.

This set him off. His next question, delivered in a most disagreeable tone was, "What did you have for breakfast this morning?" I was totally taken aback and befuddled by the question. Before I could answer he asked, "What did you have for breakfast yesterday?" He was shouting his questions, his face even more contorted now. I realized he was really wanting to intimidate and had no interest in what I had for breakfast, but nevertheless I responded, "Nothing." This set him off even more.

He soon had a tow truck there, but I convinced the driver to leave. Then he had two squad cars with four policemen. He ended up writing a ticket. I said, "I note you don't have your name tag on. What is your name?" He seemed not the least concerned that he was essentially out of uniform and proudly wrote his name down for me and sped off rapidly on his motorcycle clearly pleased.

Some Mexican friends were present helping me move and were astonished at his behavior. Later I spoke to my security guard at the plant who had been a policeman, and he told me that the question about "breakfast" was known as a code word for a bribe. He agreed to accompany me to the police station to submit a complaint.

The complaint was accepted with apologies. A date was set to interview us all together. The appointed day arrived, and the Tourist Policeman did show up with his smirk and angry attitude. I was quite surprised to see that he had no fear of penalty for his behavior. We each gave our versions to an SPV official who was acting as an arbitrator. During my discussion I noted once again that this officer did not have his name plate on and that this indicated a lack of discipline, which is dangerous for police who carry firearms.

Soon the arbitrator's demeanor changed and was apparently siding with me. It was only at this point that the policeman began to see he might have a problem. He apparently did get fired, even though I told the arbitrator I did not want him fired but wanted him reprimanded and to understand this was not the image that the police, especially the Tourist Police famous for their politeness, wanted to project.

My very first experience with police in Mexico was twenty-five years before. I was traveling with a Mexican friend through southern Mexico, not too far from Merida, on my way to Belize. I was driving my car, a Nissan station wagon. We were stopped at a barricade on the highway where the police were looking for drugs. One of the policemen became very interested in my car and wanted to buy it. Both back then and today, it is against the law to sell a car that has a foreign title without paying import taxes and going through all kinds of bureaucratic gyrations.

I thought it was some kind of trick, so I, of course, said no I would not sell the car. After leaving the barricade, I mentioned to my friend that it must have been some kind of trap that he was setting for me as it is against the law to do what he was proposing. My friend told me, "Oh no, he was serious. He wanted to buy your car."

I responded, "Well it would be against the law for me to sell and for him to buy."

My friend said simply, "In Mexico, the police *are* the law. You could have sold it to him with no problem." I have come to believe that, at least in their own eyes, the police do believe that they are the law, and no one seems interested in changing their opinion.

My first experience with traffic police in Merida was at an intersection where the officer claimed I had not yielded as I was supposed to. A Mexican friend happened along at that moment. My friend read the riot act to this cop and told him that he should not be harassing tourists. Then she told me to give him five pesos "for a coke." All was resolved.

When I was working on a grant with the government the next year, I rented a car. Thinking I should get advice on how to handle another such traffic dispute with the Police, I asked advice of employees at the government office I was working in. I was told to state very emphatically that I was working for the Government of the State of the Yucatan.

As luck would have it, I was soon stopped by a policeman who claimed I ran a red light downtown. I tried to state nicely that the light changed to yellow as I passed through the intersection. He was not buying it. However, he gave me an opening when he asked me if I was a tourist. I put on a stern face and responded as authoritatively as I could, "No, I am working for the Government of the State of the Yucatan." His face instantly morphed from an aggressive smirk to that of a humble public servant. I drove away with the confidence that I now had the solution to this type of problem.

My last encounter with the police in Merida was leaving our company Christmas Party where we had rented a large cantina that had live music. The cantina took up one complete block with one-way streets on all sides. When leaving, the parking attendant directs drivers to one of two exits, each of which exits on a different street. He directed me to leave on a street that caused me to go the wrong way for about ten feet to exit on to the main boulevard. As mentioned earlier, going the wrong way on a street is not necessarily considered a problem in Merida.

Shortly I was pulled over by a motorcycle cop. He arrived grinning and wanted to know why

I went the wrong way. I explained that the parking lot attendant directed me to do so. Of course, my argument was not persuasive. But he told me that I was in luck because today, he said, "Is the Day of the Police." His grin grew even bigger. Of course there is no such thing as the Day of the Police; I knew what this meant and was tired so with my own grin, so I congratulated him on the Day of the Police and shook his hand with a one hundred peso note inside. And then I went on my merry way. An employee who was with me indicated that he was sure that the attendant and the cop had worked out a deal for the attendant to send cars the wrong way, and the cop would hide in waiting. Then the two would be splitting my hundred pesos and any other bribes they could get using this scam.

Over the years, I had several encounters with the police. In order to avoid paying bribes, two tacks seemed to work in nearly every case, assuming I had the time to take one of these approaches. One is to speak very fluently, never offer a bribe, and simply outlast them discussing the weather, baseball or any other agreeable topic, but never touching on the issue at hand.

In Mexico, the procedure once an infraction has been written up is for the police to remove the license plate from your car. This requires you to go to the police station to pay the fine in cash in order to retrieve your license plate.

While you are trying to avoid the discussion of the infraction, the cops always try to redirect the conversation back to the issue at hand by saying that they will have to take your license plate, and this will cause you much time and effort to go to the police station to pay the fine to get it back. And they continue, stating that their job is not to cause problems for anyone, usually followed with a long pause. When you don't take the bribe bait, they soon realize they are wasting time on someone who is not going to pay a bribe, and this precious time could be used to find someone who will pay the bribe. The result is that you are soon on your way.

The other approach is to simply act stupid and to act as if you don't speak Spanish. My friend Cheryl has perfected this approach; she repeats to them in a louder voice each time, "No Nintendo," like the computer game, instead of saying "No entiendo," which means I don't understand. This seems to frustrate the cops, and they soon go away.

Then there are those accidents where drivers know how to play the corruption game and have the resources to do it. The driver of our company car was plowed into from behind by a very fast-moving, nice car. The driver of this car had resources and immediately pulled the police aside. Our driver was obviously from humble beginnings with not much opportunity to enter into negotiations. Before our company representative arrived at the scene, the situation was already settled in an informal way. Our driver was held at fault and taken to jail. Under the odd legal rules, even though we had complete insurance, the driver was kept in jail for over twenty-four hours. Our insurance company paid all claims.

A friend had her parked car smashed, and totaled, by a drunk driver at nine A.M. When the police arrived at the scene, the officers recognized the drunk driver as a friend. The situation was going to be settled between the drunk and the police when an on-looker realized what was happening and called in more police. Nevertheless, the drunk driver was released and made an official payment to the police for the totaled car of my friend in the amount of about $400 USD. The police accepted this and my friend had to hire a private lawyer to sue the drunk driver for a proper settlement. The case remains in litigation with no court hearing for over a year at this point.

I did have one very favorable encounter with the Police when I ran over someone in my garage. Yes, I ran over a person in my garage.

I had not yet enclosed my garage with an electric garage door. Most people have garages enclosed with an iron gate that is manually opened and closed. This was my case at the time, although I was going to be installing the electric door. It was a Saturday afternoon, and I had come home before going to meet someone at the movies. I had left my iron gate open because within the hour I would be leaving.

Leaving to meet my friend, I started my car and began to back up. I felt the right rear tire roll over something and then the right front tire do the same as I was exiting the garage in reverse. Since the house was still partially under construction, I immediately began cursing the brick masons for having left a concrete block in the garage.

I backed straight out into the street and glimpsed back into the garage. To my horror I saw what appeared to be a dead body that I had obviously run over instead of a concrete brick. I frantically jumped out of the car and rushed over to the body to see tire tracks plainly marking his pants at the thigh level. I was relieved to note that he was alive, but was unfortunately speaking gibberish.

I had recently moved to the house and made friends with my neighbor, a Mexican. I rushed to his house and yelled for him to come out. He quickly did, saw the obvious, and said, "Don't worry. He is inside your house, so you are not at fault," and took on a very relaxed air.

While at some level this gave me comfort, I was exceedingly concerned for the man I had run over. We rushed over and my neighbor, Jose Luis, could not make out what he was saying either.

As luck would have it, a patrol car was passing by, and we flagged the officers down. Soon an ambulance arrived. The EMTs simply checked the man over to make sure there were no broken bones. Miraculously, there were not.

It had become obvious that the man was drunk. He was slowly sobering up as any of us would after having a three thousand pound automobile roll over your legs twice. The fact that he was drunk probably did make his legs more flexible in the moment of impact so as to allow his bones to sort of roll with the punch, if you will.

After about a twenty minute examination, the EMTs left, and the police officers said the victim could go. Before leaving, he politely shook my hand, bid me goodbye, and walked off with a noticeable limp. I am sure that once the alcohol wore off and he woke up the next morning he had excruciating pain.

Jose Luis suggested I give some "help" to the nice policemen as he informed me that the protocol was to take me to the police station and fill out hours of paperwork. They were not going to make me do that, probably because they did not want to be bothered by that nuisance as well. So I thanked the police for their efforts and shook hands with them with a two hundred pesos note that stuck to their hands like they were using fly paper.

Robberies are a fairly common occurrence. Anything not tied down, behind iron bars, or locked doors will disappear within hours, if not minutes. It seems that the risk of capture is fairly low so simple cost/benefit analysis done by thieves results in opting for thievery, since there is a great probability that there is no cost to attempt robbery, and if successful, almost anything can be sold for some amount. This situation results in the theft of odd articles.

In the second factory building that we occupied, we placed large flower pots full of gravel outside our office doors on a porch for those workers in the office who smoked. Our administrative offices had windows looking onto the porch. Nevertheless, one day in broad daylight during office hours, someone made off with these two huge flower pots full of gravel that had been converted to ash trays. Each one weighed between sixty to seventy pounds.

One day my friend Lyman walked out of a house where he had been visiting a friend. His car had been parked on the street for about five minutes. He walked out to the sight of a man leaning in through an open window of his car. The would-be thief was stretching farther and farther into the car with each iterative stretch trying to reach the other seat where papers were on the seat. The thief must have thought the papers were covering something of at least quasi value.

Lyman simply watched for awhile, amazed at the man's audacity in a heavily trafficked area in daylight to try and steal. He clearly had no fear of anyone noting his attempts at thievery, or if they did, not making any effort to thwart the theft.

Finally, Lyman screamed at him, "Hey, what are you doing?"

The thief responded instantly, "I didn't take anything," as though *attempting* to steal was not a crime. He went on, "Look, you can see in my bag." The thief had a bag strapped on his shoulder and showed Lyman the contents. Lyman noted a set of Chevy hub caps inside the bag that must have been the result of a *successful* attempt at stealing.

The thief never ran, even after Lyman yelled to his friend to call the Police. Since this had no effect, Lyman yelled, "Get the pistol." This got the thief's attention. He mounted his motor scooter with his bag of hubcaps again hanging from his shoulder, started the engine, and took off quickly in one very practiced and smooth move.

The police arrived in about fifteen minutes, despite the fact that the main police station was only about seven blocks away. The police did offer to take Lyman around in their patrol car looking for the unsuccessful robber, but there was obviously no point by now. Although Lyman provided the police with the license plate number from the motor scooter, to this date the man has not been apprehended and probably never will be.

Alcoholism is a serious problem in Mexico. Accidents involving drunk drivers occur with alarming frequency. The police in Merida have adopted a zero tolerance approach to drinking and driving. They set up road blocks to find drunk drivers.

If stopped at one of these road blocks, you are asked to blow in the officer's face. As far as I know, there are no meters to register alcohol content. If the officer smells alcohol, you are pulled over immediately. This is when the zero tolerance policy is explained and when the negotiations begin. If you are not too drunk to negotiate, it is likely that you can escape jail and will soon be on your drunken way. I have one friend who does not speak Spanish very well. He was unable to negotiate a bribe, and the zero tolerance policy in this instance meant jail.

Another friend was pulled over after one beer and made to pay a bribe. He said he was clearly not drunk. My friend asked me if it would be worthwhile to complain to the equivalent of the district attorney. I told him it would be a waste of time. It was. The district attorney took the side of the police and claimed that zero tolerance meant no alcohol permitted, not that you were necessarily drunk.

I frankly believe this is a police policy applied in the absence of any existing law. Given how the policy is applied, it is obvious that it is meant to be a method for extracting bribes, and there is no real interest in removing drunk drivers from the streets.

The drunk driving road blocks are set up at night. During the day road blocks are also established by the police. They are set up so often that you would almost think you were in a Police State. There is one location in particular that they seem to like. It is a four lane road, and usually there are about four patrol cars and eight to ten policemen standing on the side of the road with rifles. I have been stopped at this location several times without incident.

An article appearing in the November 18, 2006 issue of *The Economist* noted that there are some four hundred thousand police in Mexico in several hundred different agencies. The average policeman has only advanced through six years of formal education and received two weeks of police training. The average pay is the equivalent of $370 per month. The authors of this article set the rate of drug use among police at 35% and the turnover at 40%.

The article spoke not only to the police but to the attorney general's office as well, mentioning that the reputation for crime busting is so bad that 75% of crimes are not even reported. Of those that are reported, only 10% are prosecuted, but those that are prosecuted have a conviction rate of 97%.

Police conspiracies and cooperation with drug lords, especially in the border states of Mexico, is a well-known phenomenon. As of this writing, Calderon, the new president has sent the Mexican Army to the border states to re-take police control of the drug situation. It is a courageous move and the right thing to do. Hopefully, this will be the first step in cleaning out the corruption. Clearly, the police need to be professionalized. This will require more training and more money. But the government has the resources to do so, especially with oil prices continuing to rise. It will be a question of will and leadership that creates a change of priorities within the government that focuses on security for its citizens.

My opinion is that Merida is one of the safest places in Mexico. This opinion is also held by many Mexicans, as Mexicans from all over the country are migrating to Merida in droves. While the police have endemic problems, and the system is littered with corruption, Merida is still a safe place, relatively speaking, and the police in the Yucatan, with all their warts, are due some of the credit.

CHAPTER TWENTY-ONE

DIVERSIONS IN MERIDA

There are many interesting and fun aspects to living in Merida. Eating and drinking are sort of national sports and are nearly always a topic of conversation.

Depending on your location and on the direction of the wind, you may be treated to the unique and odiferous smell that large groups of pigs generate when they are congregated in farms. This smell comes wafting through the air when you least expect it. There is good that comes from living around a large population of hogs; the Yucatan is known for some of the best pork in the world.

COCHINITA is a regional specialty. Cochinita is pig normally cooked underground wrapped in banana leaves. Once done it is pulled apart into sort of shredded pork. It is incredibly greasy, delicious and, no doubt, terribly unhealthy. A local favorite that is often eaten for breakfast in TORTAS DE COCHINITA, which is a COCHINITA served between two pieces of French bread. Real connoisseurs, like myself, ask the preparer to dip the bread into the pig grease in the pan with all the shredded pork. It is good to add SALSA DE HABANERO, which is made from the habanero pepper and is about a thousand times more hot than a jalapeno pepper.

Poc Chuc is another regional specialty. Poc Chuc is grilled pork that is sliced very thin. A special tomato sauce and grilled onions usually accompany the pork. Poc Chuc is a Mayan name.

On Mondays, a tradition is *FRIJOL CON PUERCO*. This is chunks of boiled pork that go in a bean soup. Usually it is accompanied with rice, radishes, raw onions, and a salsa that you put into the soup as well.

Another traditional meal that is not made from pork is *Panuchos*, which are usually turkey or chicken shredded with lettuce and tomato on a tostado that has refried beans on it. *Salbutes* are a version of this but have refried beans inside a tortilla and is not fried like a tostado.

Vaporcitos are a type of tamale that can have either pork, turkey, or chicken inside. It gets this name because it is steamed in banana leaves.

Another traditional dish that is eaten normally only on Day of the Dead is *Muc bi Pollo*, sometimes called simply, *Pib*. This is a tamale stuffed with either pork or chicken and sometimes also has black beans inside. It is cooked underground wrapped in banana leaves and has a smoky flavor. This is a Mayan name and Mayan scholars may question my spelling. No one I have asked can tell me why it is traditionally eaten only on Day of the Dead.

My mouth is watering as I describe these dishes. None of them are healthy, but all are delicious. They make the occasional pig smells worth it.

Speaking of smell, at night as you travel through Merida, you receive the tantalizing smell of grilling hot dogs and onions. On many street corners there are carts with tiny mobile kitchens selling hot dogs. It is doubtful that they have permits to sell food or that the food is made and kept in sanitary conditions, but the smell always gives me an instant apetite.

The weekends are always enjoyable in Merida. They are exceptionally pleasant, from about October through March, since the weather is perfect. But even in the summer months, there is nearly always a very pleasant breeze that reduces the temperature to the low 70s and sometimes it feels much cooler due to the breeze and humidity in the air.

Every Sunday, downtown is closed to motor traffic, and there are thousands of people wandering through downtown. There are many street vendors selling all kinds of wares. Big tricycles can be rented that will take three to four people at a time. Families and fun abound. Any of the various downtown plazas is great place to go to have a drink and do some people-watching.

The city provides free music delivered from musical groups, and spectators are encouraged to dance and have fun. Restaurants set up tables and chairs in the street. While you would think there is much potential for problems, not once have I seen a problem requiring police intervention during these so-called *Merida en Domingo* celebrations.

Many Saturday nights the city will also close downtown. Every Saturday night, there is something called *Noche Mexicana* that is a sort of mini concert at the beginning of *Paseo de Montejo*, the main boulevard in town, with street vendors and live music.

Every week at designated days and times, there are free exhibitions at various plazas in town. For example, at Plaza Santa Lucia, each Thursday at 9 PM there is a folkloric dance that is offered for whomever wishes to view it. On each Sunday morning at this same plaza, antique dealers set up tables from 9 AM until about noon.

Merida also has a *Carnaval* celebration that is growing each year. This goes on for about ten days with parades every day culminating with a big blowout street party and parade on Fat Tuesday. Hundreds of thousands attend that parade.

Obviously, Merida is a fun place to live in a social sense. Something is almost always going on. And it is not just always raw fun. Merida has a very good symphony orchestra, and plays and operas are fairly common at the opera theatre downtown. These performances are either free or offered at amazingly low prices.

An interesting pastime in Merida is going to the cantinas. A cantina is not necessarily what you might think. There are cantinas that promote themselves as family cantinas. There is no stigma associated with alcoholic drinking in Mexico. Alcoholism is definitely a serious problem, and there is a stigma associated with excessive drinking. Mostly, excessive drinking occurs in the pueblos and among the lower socio-economic classes.

In the family cantinas, you will find just that: families. The parents and the children eating and drinking alcoholic and non-alcoholic drinks. In Merida, most cantinas serve *botanas,* which are appetizers. As long as you are drinking, the waiter continues to bring botanas. The botanas are varied and usually quite good. I have friends who go to these cantinas instead of going out and paying for a meal, as they make a meal from botanas.

There are cantinas where you would not be interested in taking the family. These cantinas usually have very scantily clad waitresses, and the clientele is nearly 100% male. Botanas are still provided, but most customers are not there for the botanas.

Finally, there is a type of cantina that is more like a club. At these places, the waitresses also dance. There are no free botanas or anything else that is free at these establishments.

Speaking of dancing girls, one of the more outstanding characteristics, so to speak, of Meridian women is big breasts. Of course, this is a typical conversational theme of bored males the world over. I remember that Bill, of Bill Simpson fame in the first section, had his Theory of Big Breasts. He believes that because Mexican women have a tendency to have many children and many of them breast feed, that over time this has naturally resulted in some type of gene for big breasts. I suppose it is possible.

Some of the most interesting diversions in the Yucatan have to do with the many small pueblitos around Merida. Each pueblo has an annual fiesta that has some religious significance, or at least some vague religious excuse for the fiesta. All of these fiestas of the pueblo have bull fights in a hastily erected bull ring usually made from tree limbs that look as though they could not retain a twelve-year-old child, much less a raging bull.

My friend Lyman lives in a little pueblo called *Caucel* (pronounced Cowkel), which is about two miles outside of the loop around Merida. I have attended the town fiesta a couple of times. All of these fiestas last about a week, with the final big bash culminating on Saturday, which means the fiesta begins on Saturday and usually continues until the next Sunday afternoon.

At any rate, once I attended the bull fight in Caucel on Saturday. This was worth more than the price of admission, which was about twenty pesos. It was great entertainment, not for the matador's expertise but for the entire spectacle.

First, fully half of the spectators were drunk. Occasionally, a drunk would either fall from the spectator stands into the bull ring. Sometimes one of the local spectators, emboldened by drink, would simply walk out into the ring to take on whatever was in the bull ring at the time. Thankfully, I saw no one hurt.

Nor are the bulls hurt. The bulls are brought in by about twenty cowboys on horseback, each with a rope around the bull's horns. The bull is then directed to the middle of the ring where a tall tree trunk shaved of all its limbs has been sunk into the ground. The cowboys go in circles around the tree trunk until the bull is essentially lashed to the tree trunk by his horns and not able to move. Two men take each rope off of the bull after tying it to the trunk with two of their own ropes.

As each cowboy's rope is disengaged form the bull he prances on his horse freely around the ring, posturing for the crowd. Finally the cowboys leave and the bull is untied from the tree trunk. By this time the local matador in all his gala has entered and plays with the bull for awhile with his cape. The bull is not killed.

When the matador is done, the twenty cowboys come back into the ring, each roping the bull again. Once all or most of them have the bull roped, they lead the bull out of the ring and back to his pasture.

The best show is saved for last. The final bull fight is with the best local matador. One group of cowboys bring in the last bull and prance around for awhile in the ring. Then another group of cowboys tries to enter. The entering group is met by the group on the inside at the entrance to the bull ring where the two groups clash with their horses. It is a mad clash of hooves and horse humanity, the horses banging against one another. No cowboys fought with other cowboys; they simply had their horses bang one another around for about twenty minutes. I never understood what the purpose was but I am told it is done each year.

Caucel, like many other pueblitos, has the tradition of burning *viejos* at the stroke of midnight on each New Year's Eve. Viejos are dolls made of straw or hay that is stuffed inside clothes. They are placed outside of the homes, usually on the side of the street and firecrackers are stuffed inside these viejos. At the stroke of midnight, the firecrackers are lit and all Hell breaks loose. It sounds like a war; the sky is full of exploding rockets that shoot out from the viejos. The viejos obviously catch on fire. I don't understand how major disasters are averted, but they are. The idea behind burning the viejos is a symbolic burning of the past year. The Old Year is gone, and the New Year is starting.

All holidays are big events in Mexico. After New Years and Carnaval the next major holiday is Easter. School is usually out for two weeks. Many families take these two weeks off and go to the beach where they either have their own beach houses or rent them.

Good Friday is not a legal holiday, but for tradition most companies take Good Friday and Holy Thursday, the day before. Some companies shut down the entire week of Holy Week.

The following national holiday is Labor Day, which is always May 1. For a country with labor laws like Mexico, I suppose having Labor Day on May Day is appropriate. Shortly after Labor Day is Cinco de Mayo, which most of us know celebrates the Battle of Puebla. In 1862, the French invaded Mexico. A Mexican militia directed by General Zarragoza defeated a larger French Army. While Cinco de Mayo is a big celebration in the States, it is not a legal holiday in Mexico and goes almost unnoticed by Mexicans in the Yucatan.

May is a big month for holidays. May tenth is always Mother's Day, which is not a legal holiday, due to the almost sacred view of the matriarch in Mexico, but is often taken as one.

Father's Day is celebrated the same day as in the States. However, in Mexico it seems to come and go without the emotional fanfare of Mother's Day.

There is a long stretch of no holidays through the hot summer until September. September 15 is the celebration of the Declaration of Mexican Independence and September 16 is Independence Day. For centuries Mexico had been under Spanish rule. The conquerors treated the native and mestizo population in very bad ways. Finally, in September,

1810 led by the shout of Father Hidalgo, "*Mexicanos, viva Mexico*" (Mexicans, long live Mexico), the revolution from Spanish rule began. These two days represent very big celebrations, perhaps as a result of much pent-up celebration fever after a summer of no holidays combined with the natural patriotism that Mexicans have.

Halloween is not celebrated, but Day of the Dead is on November 2. Day of the Dead was brought to the New World by the Spanish Conquistadores. However, the Aztecs had a complicated belief system about death, which to some extent fused into the Day of the Dead brought by the Spanish. It is traditional to make temporary altars in homes, dedicating them to the dead family members and/or friends. The altars have flowers, food, and pictures of the deceased. They light candles and place them next to the altar.

The Anniversary of the Revolution is celebrated November 20. In 1910, a revolution began against Porfirio Diaz who had been president for thirty years. This was an interesting period in which the likes of Pancho Villa and Emilio Zapata made names for themselves.

December 12 is the Celebration of the Virgin of Guadalupe. The Virgin of Guadalupe appears to be more revered than the Virgin Mary. The history goes something like this. One of the first Aztec converts to Catholicism after the Conquest took the name of Juan Diego. On December 9, 1531 he says a blinding light stopped him on his walk and an image told him she was the Virgin Mary and that it was her desire to have a church built on this spot, which happened to be the site of a former Aztec temple. Juan Diego was to give this message to the Head Catholic Priest at the time.

The Priest was very busy, and Juan Diego very fearful of the priest's reaction to his story. But on December 12, the image appeared again telling Juan Diego to pick flowers from the site of the temple and deliver them to the priest as a sign of his sincerity. Juan Diego did so and obtained permission to see the priest. As the flowers spilled out in front of the priest, a perfect image of the Virgin appeared on the cloak of the priest.

The image on the cloak is preserved. Scientists cannot place the origin except to confirm that the fabric is from the 16th century. The pigments from which the image appears have not been identified.

On December 12 all over Mexico, caravans of runners honor the Virgin, running from a pre-designated spot to another locale carrying a torch, much like the Olympic Torch. Police and other cars form a barricade of protection from other traffic on the streets.

Finally, Christmas is an enormous celebration. During the entire month of December there are constant parties. Many businesses shut down for at least a week as they do with Easter. From about 15 December until the first week of January do not expect to get anything much accomplished.

During all of these celebrations, it is as if a war were going on. The sound of fireworks goes well into the early morning hours of the next day.

One of the great things about Merida is its proximity to the beach. Merida is only twenty miles from the coast. The beach is white sand, but not the sugary sand of Cancun. Progreso, the closest beach town, is still considered part of the Gulf of Mexico. The Caribbean Sea does not officially begin until about Isla Holbox east of Merida about halfway around the coast to Cancun. The water is a pretty, blue-green, but not as clear as the water in Cancun.

The coast is now starting to develop rapidly. Not only are Americans and Canadians coming to purchase single-family homes, there are new and large developments springing up all along the coast from Sisal to Santa Clara and no doubt will soon make it to DZILAM DE BRAVO, where supposedly the famous pirate Jean Lafitte is buried.

Lafitte helped defend New Orleans during the War of 1812, even though at that time he was embarking on a career of piracy. About five years later, his reputation for piracy created the need for the authorities in New Orleans to assist him in leaving. He went to Galveston and continued his ways until the U.S. government asked him to leave, which he did peacefully. From there he went to the Yucatan and his powerful reputation diminished, and he apparently died and was buried.

Over the two weeks in Easter and the months of the *temporada*, the school holidays, which are June, July, and part of August, the beaches are packed with people. The rest of the year the beaches are almost abandoned. Homes get boarded up and the prices at restaurants are reduced during the rest of the year.

The only problem after the temporada for those of us who like the beach on a year-round basis is that cruise ships come to Progreso about twice a week. The good thing is that the passengers pretty well limit themselves to the *malecon* and the beach at Progreso. Other than that, you can have the beaches to yourself.

Cancun and Playa del Carmen are close enough that they can be driven easily for a weekend trip. Playa del Carmen used to be a neat little place to visit, but has become a mini Cancun. Nevertheless, from time to time I enjoy getting away to one of those places.

Mayan ruins are another interesting diversion. *Chicen Itza* is on the way to Cancun. It is an incredibly interesting place. It is huge; supposedly at one time there were five hundred thousand inhabitants. There is no way to appreciate it in one day, but it should not be missed even if you have only one day. *Uxmal* is another large ruin close to Merida. It is much smaller that Chichen, but many think it is more interesting.

The entire peninsula is littered with ruins. There are many more than the two biggest already mentioned. Each has its own particular "feel."

Many of the Mayan customs are still respected. There is one belief that is maintained today about rain. It is supposed to rain each May 15, according to Mayan beliefs. Supposedly, this is the rain that marks the planting season. Over the years I have noticed that while it may not rain on exactly May 15, it does seem to rain for the first time since the dry season begins very close to May 15, if not on that specific date.

Another interesting custom is the belief in *aluxus*. Aluxus are supposed to be little man-like creatures, like gnomes, that only come out at night. They are not believed to be evil. I had a night watchman who was Mayan and would tell me when he had seen the aluxus; he was certain he had seen them. I have never seen one.

Then there are the stories of the *chupa cabras*. This translates literally as goat sucker. Supposedly these are types of man-beasts that attack at night to suck the blood of humans or of livestock, like Dracula. There are many stories reported in the newspapers concerning sightings of chupa cabras or of people claiming to have been chased by chupa cabras. There have been photos of livestock that are laying dead in the pasture, legs frozen stiff by rigor mortis and pointing up toward the heavens, supposedly drained of blood. Fortunately, I have never had an experience with a chupa cabra.

The chupa cabra stories reported in the newspapers are normally reported in the local equivalents of *The Enquirer*. There are an incredibly large number of newspapers in Merida. There are two that report serious news for the most part, EL DIARIO DE YUCATAN AND POR ESTO!. Each, of course, has its own political slant. Despite the fact that Merida has a population of about a million, the reporting style is perhaps something that you would have seen in a small town weekly in the 1950s.

⁂

As a general rule, everything that can be exaggerated in the news is exaggerated. This is beyond sensationalism that we are all used to in the news media. For example, recently there was a story on a mafia-style hit on an illegal Cuban who was reportedly involved in drug dealing. The facts themselves were apparently not sensational enough, so it was reported that this particular Cuban was on the FBI's Ten Most Wanted List. A quick check to the FBI web site made no mention of the Cuban drug dealer, but it does make a good story.

There are numerous newspapers that specialize in sensational reporting such as chupa cabra stories. These papers also like to report on automobile wrecks, especially if there are photos with bodies and blood. These papers always have provocative pictures of buxom women who are movie stars, singers, or some kind of celebrity placed right on the front page. The pictures are usually accompanied by a very short story about the personality. The sales of these papers is apparently much higher than the two serious papers. They are especially popular among the lower socio-economic strata.

One of the interesting aspects of the want ads in the newspapers is the blatant age discrimination reflected in them. It is especially true of sewing factories, but I have noticed in all ads a tendency to specify ages eighteen to twenty–five. There is one sewing factory that routinely fires sewing operators over a certain age, I think thirty. There are also ads that specify the applicant can only be male or female. These kinds of ads would be a lawyer's heaven in the U.S., but are perfectly legal in Mexico.

Another great-selling publication among locals is adult comics. These comic books are more like pamphlets, a little larger than a man's billfold. These publications are raunchy. All construction sites are littered with these comic books and newspaper photos of buxom women in provocative poses.

CHAPTER TWENTY-TWO
LABOR LAWS

One of the greatest challenges to managing a business in Mexico is the labor laws. Nothing proves Mexico's non capitalist bent more than these laws, which came into existence about eighty years ago, as I understand it. The laws must have been an understandable reaction to the system in place in those days in Mexico, which was built around the exploitation of the worker. Ironically, often this very law enables further exploitation under the auspices of the government system that administers the law.

There are a number of odd features to this law. Minimum salaries are established under the law, and they are adjusted each year based on inflation. These salaries are expressed in amounts per day and sometimes vary depending on the region of the country. The rates vary depending on the trade in question: a worker classified as a professional sewer has a minimum daily wage set at 59 pesos. A brick mason has another, higher minimum daily wage.

Further, this minimum daily wage translates to a minimum weekly salary based on seven days, irrespective of the number of days actually worked. For example, in my company the standard work week is the maximum allowed, 48 hours, without paying overtime. These 48 hours are worked over a five-day period. One might think that if the pay is stated at, say 60 pesos per day, that those workers would receive 300 pesos for a week's work. Under the Mexican labor law, if the worker came to work each day, his pay is calculated over seven days or in this case a total of four hundred and twenty pesos for the five days actually worked. Therefore, the minimum of sixty pesos per day is actually over 80 pesos per day for each day worked. That is a significant increase in wages that some foreign investors do not calculate into their analysis before coming to Mexico.

Furthermore, if an employee works on Saturday, he will earn an additional amount based on double pay; if he comes to work on Sunday, he will earn triple pay. Our employees earn significant more than these amounts because they also earn incentives.

Social security taxes are paid only by the employer, and the rate is approximately 35%. Many Mexican owners do not pay social security, paying their workers on what amounts to a black market, an underground economy. If workers are not enrolled in the social security system, their pay is not deductible by the employer. Most of these owners who do not pay social security are not paying income taxes either. That is, they do not give a "factura" for the sale of their product or service. Those buying the product or service may not deduct the cost because there is no factura. Therefore, not only are income taxes evaded, but the IVA (*IMPUESTO VALOR AGREAGADO*) tax is avoided, since IVA must be collected with all facturas. IVA is a value-added tax. As already mentioned, a great part of the Mexican economy is underground, and there seems to be no will by the government to attempt to catch those involved, which could be the majority of citizens.

Additional onerous features to the labor law include the requirement that if you fire an employee, you must pay what amounts to severance pay of three months salary. If the employer company files for bankruptcy and has to close the doors to the business due to lack of resources, there is no exemption to the severance pay requirement. When bankruptcy occurs, sometimes the owners, especially foreign owners, flee the country. This is because the government embargoes all equipment and assets of the company that has filed bankruptcy and sells the assets. If there is not enough revenue to cover the severance taxes, the government can imprison the owners until the debt is paid. Basically, the government has made it a crime to go bankrupt.

As one might expect, a requirement to pay severance taxes if an employee is fired creates some unintended consequences. Clever and malicious employees often try to get fired so that they can receive three months severance. For many employees in Mexico, three months pay received all at once is an enormous windfall. So their strategy is to be very inefficient, forcing the company to fire them.

I remember asking our labor lawyers once, "If I have an employee who has a very low efficiency and is not becoming better over time through training, surely I can fire that employee with cause." The lawyer's response has stuck in my mind all these years, "The law does not contemplate firing for low efficiency." I was dumbstruck.

When a company has an employee that has a strategy of getting fired in order that he can collect his severance, a chess game develops between the employee and the employer. The idea is to get the employee to resign. If he resigns, there is a legal requirement for certain payments, but they are reasonable, such as accrued vacation pay, but no requirement for the three-month severance pay. Therefore, when it becomes clear that the employee has a goal of getting fired, the company begins to create problems for the worker. For example, if the worker has previously indicated he does not like certain jobs, management makes sure he gets those jobs. The law does contemplate legal suspensions of a worker if he does something negligent. In the case of an incompetent employee, every legal excuse is found to suspend the worker without pay. Over a period of time, the disenchanted worker usually gives up and resigns, thereby saving the company three months pay.

However, this process takes a long time and results in paying for very inefficient workers. Nevertheless, this inefficiency is built into the system through the culture and a very paternal legal system that eventually gets distorted and creates unintended consequences that damages the worker in the long run, as will be clear later.

There are other unfavorable economic effects of this system. Disreputable lawyers sometimes hang around the larger factories at quitting time and approach workers claiming to be able to get them thousands of pesos if the worker will agree to hire them for a labor lawsuit. If the workers get conned into doing so, the result is that they usually lose their job after claiming to have been unjustly fired, and the lawyers get most of the settlement so that what the workers are left with in the end is less than they would have received if they simply resigned and walked away; only the lawyers benefit.

These labor lawsuits are very strange from my perspective. Actually, they are not lawsuits as we know them. The government has established reconciliation agencies that use government bureaucrats to hear the case. It is a well-established fact that the laws and these reconciliations, a type of arbitration, are all stacked against the employer.

The normal procedure for these events is that the company receives a notice of an arbitration. In the notice, the facts are related by the complaining former employee. These "facts" are usually egregious lies. I remember one in particular where the employee claimed that I had personally come from my office to scream at him, "Get out of here. I never want to see you again. Get off the premises and never come back!" It further stated that I had done so with no reason.

After receiving the notice, you are given a certain day and time to show up for the arbitration. If you, as the defendant, do not arrive on time, the case is automatically awarded to the plaintiff, the complaining former employee. However, if the lawyer and the plaintiff do not arrive on time, there is no consequence; you simply wait a reasonable period of time and if they don't show, the arbitrator re-schedules.

Once the arbitration begins, a sort of deposition entails in which the arbitrator reads a series of questions from a list prepared by the plaintiff's attorney, which purport to give the facts. Some of these questions have truthful answers that are correct: Did Juan Perez work for your company from 1 January to 1 June. Most of the questions are based on outrageous propositions such as: Is it true that Juan Perez worked 80 hours per week during this time and you never paid one cent of overtime. My lawyers instruct me to reply to every question asked of me, "No lo reconozco," I don't recognize that fact, regardless of the veracity of the question. I was told if you ever say, "I do recognize that fact," we have most likely lost the case regardless of the actual truth, due to a nuance in the law. All legal issues in Mexico seem to be decided by form and not substance.

The arbitrator is careful to tell you before the questioning begins if you do not tell the truth you are subject to jail time. I found that almost humorous, as it is well established the entire legal system in Mexico is built around the ability to be untruthful. At any rate, I played the game. After two or three of these deposition-like episodes, subsequent to the arbitrator's warning, I finally began asking the arbitrator, "OK, and if there is a question that is not representative of the truth, will the lawyer who wrote the question go to jail?" This threw everyone for a loop. It was clear that this had never come up before. Eventually, the arbitrator responded, "Yes." At the end of the deposition, I told the lawyer, "I guess one of us is going to jail, because I did not recognize any of the questions as the truth, which means one of us is lying." He laughed.

I have been told that sometimes the arbitrator will make a deal with the plaintiff's attorney to take part of the settlement in order to find in the plaintiff's favor. This was probably a more prevalent practice in the past. I have to say that my experience with arbitrator's has been favorable in the sense that they do apply the law objectively, which is definitely in favor of the plaintiff. For the most part, I have found them to be reasonable.

Fortunately, by Mexican standards, we do not have a large number of such lawsuits, perhaps three to four per year. But sometimes those cases can be maddening. I remember one such suit where our former employee had signed his resignation letter. This normally is considered *PRIMA FACIE* evidence that he resigned and has accepted his full settlement and would, therefore, negate any further legal action. However, one of these aforementioned unscrupulous lawyers brought a lawsuit against us claiming that we had forged the former employee's signature.

Once forgery is claimed, the arbitration system requires a handwriting expert to certify the signature as being that of the plaintiff. The defendant has to pay this cost, which is a standard cost of about $1,000. The plaintiff's lawyer was asking for about $1,500 in the lawsuit. Obviously, this tactic was designed to force us to settle without paying for the handwriting expert. I felt this would set a precedent that would come back to haunt us, so I said we would pay for the handwriting expert.

Shortly after we did not fold on this case, the plaintiff's lawyer offered through our lawyers to "make the case go away" for a direct settlement to the lawyer of about 600 USD equivalent. The lawyer claimed he would tell his client that the case was lost. I said I would pay the money direct to the lawyer, and the distribution of it would be between him and his client. However, I wanted a written statement from the lawyer that he had accepted the money in full satisfaction of the lawsuit. He did not accept, and the case continues without resolution to this point.

The most astonishing example of the labor law's slant toward employees occurred the first week after we moved to OGA III. A particular employee who had worked at OGA II never showed up for work after we moved to OGA III. Obviously, we assumed she had resigned. We were wrong.

She showed up on payday, a Friday, wanting her paycheck despite the fact she had not come to work all week. Clearly we thought we were within our rights to explain to her that we would not pay her as she had not come to work. She became infuriated. During her tirade, she explained, "I did not resign. You renounced your address at OGA II and moved to OGA III. OGA II was right around the corner from my home. It was not my idea nor my fault that the company moved. I was not in agreement with the move. It is my desire to continue working, but you decided to move. It is too inconvenient for me to come to this location."

Therefore, by her reasoning, we owed her for her salary and would forever owe her salary because we decided to move and she was not in agreement. Of course, we did not pay her the salary she so adamantly thought she deserved even though she did not come to work. She hired a lawyer who has sued us and despite the ludicrous basis for the suit, the government has allowed it to go forward.

Besides ridiculous laws, unscrupulous politicians encourage idiotic behavior. After a hurricane came through Merida, although it did not create much damage, the public busses were not running for a day. A politician went on the radio to announce that all businesses owed their employees their salaries for the missed day; that it was an obligation of employers to pay. Even though the laws are very slanted toward workers, there is no such obligation in the Mexican labor law.

Nevertheless, immediately the workers began to say that we were being unfair not to pay them for the day they could not come to work. There was no damage done by this hurricane. All of our employees forgot that after Hurricane Isodoro the city was devastated, as were many of their homes. We did not work for two weeks but all workers were paid in full during those two weeks. We felt a moral obligation to help our employees during this very difficult period, despite the fact that the company had no revenues for two weeks. Under the circumstances we felt it was the most prudent and compassionate strategy. No one in the government ever recognized what we had done. In this case, no one was disadvantaged. The government and politicians simply seem to teach workers to fight against the economic future of their employers without regard to the consequences.

Once I was complaining about the labor laws to a Mexican owner. His response is an example of how Mexican owners work around these laws, which are so stacked against the employer. He told me, "Look, it's simple. On the same day you hire the worker, you have him sign a resignation letter and you leave the date blank. Once you decide to fire him, you simply do so and you have his resignation letter; you don't pay any severance." I am sure that system would work, but we do not use it as it clearly goes against the spirit of the law. To my knowledge we have never broken a law no matter how onerous its requirements. While it would be unethical to do so, there is a practical side to my reluctance to knowingly break laws. It makes no sense to even consider doing so because as a foreigner I would run substantial risks that Mexicans don't, such as deportation and loss of my business.

An additional onerous burden imposed by the law is mandated profit sharing. This is known as PTU (*Participacion de Trabajadores en Utilidades*), workers' participation in profits. PTU is required to be calculated at 10% of net profits. This is not a voluntary contribution that the company makes for workers; this is required by law.

Again, Mexican owners handle this in a very flexible manner, shall we say. For example, if profits will be, say, a million pesos, the owner will declare himself a bonus of, say, nine hundred thousand pesos, leaving a hundred thousand to distribute to workers. Technically, this is correct, but again, skirts the intention of the law.

I have never "played" with this number. We have had the good fortune of having profits increase each year after our start-up losses. As a result PTU at OGA has increased each year.

Due to our situation, we elected "safe harbor" rules. In nearly all countries, the national government establishes such rules to ensure maximum taxes in the home country of the corporation that receives the revenues. Certain companies, and OGA is one, for various reasons might elect and have the power to control the price of the product. For example, if the product is sold for $10, with a cost of $5, the seller might instruct the buyer to pay $4 to another company in the US and pay $6 to the Mexican company in this case. Profits in Mexico would be calculated as $1 instead of $5.

The Safe Harbor Rules basically state that instead of having to prove in some fairly rigorous ways that something like the aforementioned example is not occurring, a taxpayer can elect "Safe Harbor." Under Mexican law, the Safe Harbor Rules require that income be set at the higher of actual net income calculated under Mexican GAAP, a set percentage of expenses, or a set percentage of assets owned by the company making the product. This situation will result in the company electing safe harbor to always pay taxes. In our first years of operation, even with substantial losses, we were paying taxes. Since we have grown rather significantly and both expenses and assets have increased substantially over time, our PTU has increased each year, a fact not lost on our workers and appreciated by them.

This has relieved us of some problems traditionally experienced by Mexican companies. Mexican workers, knowing tradition in Mexico of exploitation, *ALWAYS* suspect distortion in anything that relates to their pay. By law, the PTU must be distributed by the end of May the following year. Naturally, most companies wait until May to distribute these profits. Workers suspecting some kind of number manipulation when their PTU is less than they expected have work stoppages and strikes. I don't remember a single year when at least one company has not had this problem in the Yucatan in May or June.

Besides PTU, the law also requires that each worker receive a minimum of two weeks' pay as a Christmas bonus. Some companies actually pay more for trusted employees.

The law also requires that each worker receive a minimum of six days vacation. The law requires additional vacation days for each year of employment.

IMSS (*INSTITUTO MEXICANO DE SOCIAL SEGURIDAD*), The Mexican Institue of Social Security, is the government agency that administers the social security system. If an employee for which you are paying social security is sick, the employee has the right to medical attention at a Social Security Hospital without cost. A Social Security doctor determines if the employee is deemed *INCAPACITADO* (incapacitated). If incapacitado, the worker does not have to go to work until he is cured as determined by the doctor.

If incapacitado, the worker receives pay for a certain time from the employer and after a certain period receives some percentage of his regular salary paid by the government. In this case, the employer has no further responsibility for salary payments until the employee returns to work.

There appears to be no defined criteria for when a worker is classified as incapacitado and when not. Once classified as incapacitado, there appears to be no uniformity with respect to how many days of incapacitation that he/she will receive. Sometimes, the time period seems ridiculously long and sometimes ridiculously short. As an example our Import-Export clerk had a slight, hairline fracture that she received from an accident while gardening in her home one weekend. There was no splint required or any overt medical treatment given. Nevertheless, the doctor gave her twenty-one days of incapacitation. Her injury may have slightly affected her ability to type for a few days, but it was against the law for her to come to work during that time.

Stomach problems are a serious issue due to lack of clean water, lack of sanitary kitchen and bath facilities in homes, and proper food preparation.

As a result, on any one day a factory of five hundred workers will have a number of workers who are incapacitated. Nevertheless, I have seen some sewers who have returned from social security and appear deathly ill, yet have not received a doctor's permission to miss work. If no such permission is obtained and the worker does not come to work, his pay is docked and he is liable for a suspension that creates further financial hardship.

I learned that if suspensions are not applied in these cases, workers look for ways to take advantage of a good heart. The most common way to do this is to claim you were sick but to give an excuse for not having received a doctor's permission. In my naïveté I initially negated my management's advice to give suspensions in these cases; I soon learned that the Mexican managers knew what they were talking about. Taking the attitude that you can believe the workers simply creates additional absences and, in production, the more unexpected absences, the more difficult it is to maintain a smooth production flow.

After a Mexican company reaches a certain size with respect to employees, the law requires that the company employ a company doctor to attend to employees in the company, despite the availability of free health care sponsored by the government. The company absorbs the cost of the doctor, but in mild cases of illness, the employee does not have to leave work and spend a day at the social security hospital. In or case, the company doctor was a double-edged sword. He is young, single and very good looking. We noted the incidence of mild illnesses increased among the female population almost immediately. Actually, even those fairly ill wanted to keep working so that they had a chance to see the doctor each morning.

All of these issues create hidden costs that most investors would not think about. At least, that was my case. There are other hidden costs that are not mandated by law, but are essentially mandated by culture. For example, only a small percentage of my employees have automobiles due to their poor economic plight. As a result, we have to pay private carriers to bring our employees to work. This is a huge hidden cost that most Americans without experience in Mexico would never consider in their analysis. We are currently paying about $20,000 per month to transport our people. These costs are unavoidable if you want to ensure that the workers who wish to arrive at work actually have the ability to do so.

Another hidden cost is the tradition, at least in the Yucatan, to pay a bonus for workers who arrive on time and who come every day. All companies of any size in Merida pay this bonus. That's right: You are paid more than your salary if you actually come to work every day and come on time. This was difficult to understand, but all companies pay it and without doing so, you will not be competitive in the market.

The labor law is almost communistic. Its application creates many unintended consequences and often makes worse off the very workers it is intended to protect. It creates hidden costs that companies must absorb and assists in creating a work ethic that it not always admirable. That is, workers often feel they will be better off if they are fired in order to get a windfall payment, rather than being efficient and maintaining employment. Personally, I believe this is one component of Mexican law and culture that is having a wave of deleterious effects on Mexico's competitiveness and society in general. The labor laws need to be changed, but they have become so ingrained and politicians would certainly demagogue the issue to the point that any attempts at change would be shot down quickly. To me, this is a tragedy of enormous dimensions, as Mexican workers in general can be very productive when given the motivation. They are being limited by their own government's laws.

CHAPTER TWENTY-THREE

The Adventure of Managing OGA

At some point OGA became my life and my identity. I became so wrapped up in the business that the most important thing to me became the satisfaction of making OGA successful, but not just financially. In this sense, OGA was my child and I needed to learn every nuance necessary to make the child grow in a responsible manner. I had managed people before, but always as an employee of some organization and always in my home culture.

Mexican cultural traits obviously have an impact on how one manages. A pure American management mentality does not work for many reasons. Basically these reasons can be classified as cultural and/or economic. The cultural differences manifest themselves in the work place and American-style management can cause initial confusion for all concerned.

Trust in any aspect of life in Mexico is in short supply. The effects of the Conquest are not lost in the work place. Recall the discussion in the Introduction concerning how the conquistadors came to crush the indigenous population and the cultural effects that this has brought to the country. Those with the power use it, and those who don't have it, cede to it.

The power discrepancy creates natural suspicion and distrust. Often, those with the power tend to abuse it; those without it tend to look for ways to avoid the brute application of this power.

Economic differences in culture primarily devolve from the federal government's attitude about not caring for its citizens and/or the unintended consequences of labor laws. Labor laws were already discussed.

In my opinion, the primary cultural difference that creates the biggest challenge is what Hofstede classified as power distance. This was discussed briefly in the Introduction. Power distance, in brief, means that the Mexican culture is accustomed to great differences between the power that is vested in certain individuals, whether it be economic or authority. That is, Mexican employees are stand-offish from the boss. The boss is stand-offish from employees as well. The two do not mix in social situations nor is the boss accustomed to being questioned about decisions. To some extent, I believe it is a residual effect of the Conquest.

Mexican employees seem to like this arrangement. One of the reasons is that employees in Mexico often try to avoid responsibility. While this is a natural human characteristic, it seems exaggerated in Mexico. If something goes wrong, employees simply say they did as told by the boss and can't be held responsible for mistakes if they are simply following orders. Bosses don't like it when something goes wrong either. In Mexico, they simply blame the employee or someone else. Among other problems created by this attitude, suspicions run rampant. Once we grew to a certain size, it was necessary to attack this sentiment and we had varying degrees of success.

I also soon realized that in some cases my approach, based on American culture, simply would not work. Due to the great distances in power and the natural tendency for those with the power to abuse it, suspicions are rampant between boss and subordinates. This lack of trust seems to nurture the idea present in other parts of the culture that everyone is out to take advantage of someone else if the opportunity arises.

At some point, I began to make rounds of the production floor each morning. Every day I still walk through each production line in the plant greeting operators and supervisors along the way. I have two purposes. One is I want them to know that to the CEO of the company they are important, and I want all of our management team to see that the operators and supervisors are important to me. These employees are where "the rubber meets the road" as the old saying goes. We won't produce anything without them, and I know we will produce more if they are happy, content, comfortable, and made to feel important. I probably greet 150 employees each day and call them by name. I joke with them and over time I have gained their trust. They will grab me in my rounds and tell me, for example, that the light above their machine is out. In that moment I call the Maintainence Department on my walkie-talkie and ask them to change the bulb so the operator can see better. They tell me about their personal problems, and I think it is important to take the time to listen and provide any help or guidance that I think is prudent.

The second reason I make these rounds is that while making them I am able to notice problems or potential problems present on the production floor or in the building. Without getting physically out on the floor and moving around, I might never become aware. Eventually someone would notice and correct the situation, but I want to know about it and let the managers know of my involvement and interest.

There is nothing new about this walk-through technique, but it is true that many of my managers were somewhat suspicious of my motives for making these rounds. I believe even the operators were suspicious as well; they were not accustomed to bosses doing this, much less owners. At first there was very little interchange between me and the operators, only stilted and polite responses to my questions. Over time they opened up.

The managers were certainly suspicious and worried about the quarterly meetings held with representatives from each production line and department within the company. No bosses are present, only Claudia and me. After each of these meetings, I noted how nervous my managers were and that they always asked about how things went at the meeting, with that tentative look that children always give their parents when they know they are about to be punished. It was at this point that I became aware of the extent to which many Mexicans are concerned, almost terrified, of being "caught" or held responsible for something that did not go right; the aforementioned cultural tendency that responsibility is to be avoided at all costs.

This avoidance of responsibility is even reflected in the language. For example to say "I dropped the bottle," in Spanish, one would say "*SE CAYÓ LA BOTELLA*," which literally translates as "the bottle made itself fall." In Mexico, one does not drop a bottle, the bottle is responsible for its own falling.

Mexican bosses are almost always more autocratic than those in the U.S. Do it my way. Why, you ask? Because I am the boss. Subject closed.

As mentioned earlier, the autocratic boss concept is often fine with employees because if something goes wrong, the boss can be blamed, thereby avoiding responsibility. Unfortunately, since the boss is autocratic, all-powerful and wants to avoid responsibility as well, often the blame is easily shifted back to the employee, regardless of actual facts. Imagine the difficulty in trying to find out what actually happened when something does go awry. Obviously, the idea is not so much to find blame, but to determine what happened so that the root cause can be fixed and we all learn from the situation so that it does not repeat itself.

I learned that if something did go wrong, one cannot simply ask what happened. The first story was always about 50% truthful. That was especially true if the first phrase out of their mouth was "*LO QUE PASO. . .*" (What happened was. . .), which is the preamble they all seem to use when they had at least a part in the problem but are looking to shift blame. When there was a problem, I had to interview every person involved until I developed a basic picture of what really happened. While I explained carefully that the purpose was never to assess blame and point fingers, but to find the cause so that the problem could be eliminated in the future, for a long time no one believed that that was my intention.

In these meetings to discover the truth, all of the managers were extremely uncomfortable at first.

They saw this as a type of confrontation in which at least one person, if not more, was going to lose face or receive some horrible punishment. Therefore, the truth became a very elusive concept. They all dreaded when something went wrong because they knew there would be a meeting to discover why, rather than just blaming some faceless employee and moving on. Eventually, they learned the idea that discovering the source of a problem was the way to learn from mistakes and represented the road to improvement was accepted and overcame their cultural fears of unpleasant repercussions.

I tried to explain, while no one seeks blame, the idea of shifting blame or managing autocratically goes against the grain of modern management practices. The farther down the chain of command a decision can be made, normally the better, assuming parameters about decision options are defined. Therefore, the idea of empowerment had taken hold in most developed economies.

I broached the concept of empowerment with my managers. I did not know the word in Spanish and made up a word that should have worked, "*EMPODERAMIENTO.*" No one knew what the hell I was talking about. I described the concept: it was anathema to them. I could not find the word in a dictionary for a long time but finally found it: "*APODERAMIENTO.*" I gave the Spanish definition to them from the dictionary. Puzzled looks abounded.

I saw I had a challenge but, after all, I had been a university professor and enjoyed the opportunity to discuss these concepts with my managers who obviously had an interest. Over time they have come to understand not only the concept but that it can be beneficial in managing their subordinates. The concept of empowerment was completely foreign to them, but because they are a smart group and truly wanted to learn, they did learn and applied the concept with great success.

At about the same time that empowerment school was in session, I noticed another feature of the autocratic management style. Once we became a bigger factory and needed a more professional work force, the production management team made the point with me that to become more productive we needed more discipline with the operators and supervisors. I agreed. But I realized that their method of managing to increase discipline was based entirely on negatives. If an operator or a supervisor did not perform as expected, punishment by an autocratic manager was needed, at least in their view. I began to understand better why no one wanted to sit in meetings to find the root cause of problems because their experience and their own management style was to punish, thinking that punishment was the tough medicine needed to create a solution.

A simple example will illustrate the situation. On my morning rounds one day, an operator told me that she would like to work at her machine in a sitting position rather than standing. Since the machines are designed so that they are adjustable, I told her no problem. I called over the supervisor asking him to ask a mechanic to make the adjustment. He said he had already asked his boss, the Line Chief, about this, and the Line Chief said it could not be done due to an electronic box that contained the computer that operated the machine.

I looked at the box and saw that it could be a limiting factor to lower the machine beyond a certain point, but appeared to have sufficient clearance to lower the machine enough that the operator could sit. I told him to go ahead and try.

In a few minutes I was approached by the Line Chief. He told me, "Don Gus, we can't lower the machine due to the electronic box."

I responded, "There are still several inches of clearance, so let's lower it as far as possible to see if she likes it." He told me that it could not be done. I said, "Maybe I don't remember well, let's go look at it." We got there, looked, and noticed sufficient room.

It was then that the real reason he had not lowered it surfaced. He pulled me aside and said, "Don Gus, the problem is that Doña Juana does not cooperate with us when we need overtime and so we don't really want to accommodate her. We need more discipline in the production line, more commitment to the company, and when we need to work Saturdays, she never comes to help us."

I raised the possibility that maybe she is not committed because we are not accommodating her, and if we were more accommodating it is possible she would feel more of a commitment. He was really focused in on the punishment aspect. His response was, "Well, she does not really need for it to be lowered. She is working just fine with the machine at its current height. Doña Ana does the same operation, and she does not want to have her machine lowered."

To make his point, he drug me over to Doña Ana, who when asked if she preferred to work in a standing position responded, "Yes," as if this was all the proof necessary.

"Look," I said, "Maybe Doña Ana would like it or maybe not, she has never requested that her machine be lowered. The point is that Doña Juana wants to have it lowered and now all the operators around her have heard her asking for our help. Let's lower it and give it a try. To not do so will give the impression to her and her co-workers listening to her complaints that we are not really interested in the operators, and that is the last impression we want to leave."

He reluctantly agreed that it would be lowered when she went to lunch. The next day on my rounds, I asked Doña Juana how the sitting position was working out.

She responded with a big grin, "Just fine."

Then as I passed Doña Ana, I noticed she was now in a seated position instead of standing. I said, "I thought you liked the standing position."

She responded, "I was confused, I like seated better."

I never said anything to the Line Chief about this incident. But this is one of a thousand examples where managers got their feathers ruffled by an employee and wanted to punish them for not doing as the manager wanted, as if the manager's desires alone and without explanation or understanding of the situation of the employee, are sufficient cause for punishment. The overall objectives of the company were lost in the equation by the Line Chief.

I became convinced that managers found it easier to punish, or to threaten punishment, than to convince employees of the wisdom of their decisions through leadership. They were taking the easy way out in the short run without concern to long-term implications.

I remembered a friend paraphrasing what some famous person once said: "assault is not leadership."

I spoke with our group and using the example that you could get someone to do what you wanted by telling them you were going to hit them with a hammer if they did not. Obviously, it is more than likely that under these circumstances, the employee will 1.) do exactly as you have asked and 2.) immediately begin looking for another job. Turnover and the associated training is costly, so it is best to find a way to sell ideas without threatening employees with some kind of punishment.

This sort of management by brute force is cultural. Why would an employee need to know the reasoning behind any decision or even be considered prior to making a decision? Employees in Mexico have almost been thought of as expendable soldiers for many years.

I had an important opportunity to manage by example with respect to the benefits of informing employees about the reasons behind certain decisions. Through a misunderstanding of the labor laws, we were working three hours less per week than actually allowed without paying overtime. China was just coming on strong, and we knew that we had to become more productive. One way to do so is to work another three hours, but pay the same amount we were currently paying. Workers are paid by the week based on the number of days worked. As long as workers did not work more than forty-eight hours per week, no additional pay was required for overtime under Mexican law. Hours above forty-eight per week are paid at double time. At this time we were only working forty-five hours per week.

One can imagine what an employee's reaction would be to the proposition that he or she put in another three hours per week for the same pay. Clearly, the reaction would be unfavorable. We began to float the idea, and it was not well received. We found threats in the suggestion box of a work stoppage and going to the press to indicate that the workers were being exploited. While we would be acting within the law, we certainly did not want the press involved nor a work stoppage. Also, there were threats of massive resignations, which would cause associated severance pay, creating potential cash flow problems and putting in jeopardy production goals if we lacked employees.

This was a worrisome situation, to say the least. However, I had been explaining the concept of selling your ideas to employees and now had the perfect opportunity. I made up a speech and went with Claudia and the other top managers to each production line, one at a time. My speech essentially sold the idea that we were all in the same boat together and that this boat was going to make it to the destination or was going to sink, but, regardless, we were all in the same boat. We were not competitive with China and increasing the work week to the maximum that the law allowed would make us more competitive. Furthermore, the China Threat was real. Over twelve thousand jobs had been lost in the Yucatan in the last few years to China. Finally, if they resigned and went to work for another company, that company would already be working the legal limit of forty-eight hours. We were not doing anything but increasing the work week to the limit that all the other factories in the Yucatan were already working.

It took two complete days to give the speech to each line and to answer questions. The following week the new, longer work week would be implemented.

We waited with bated breath for the next Monday. As far as we could tell, only three workers, out of about two hundred and fifty at that time, resigned due to the longer work week. There was no work stoppage, and no one called the press. This experience convinced me without a doubt of the power of the POR QUE?— the why. That is, the vast majority of employees are reasonable and if the reasons behind actions taken by management are explained and justified, employees will get behind the decision. While culture can make some difference in the degree to acceptation of management actions, it seems that the power of the POR QUE? can overcome a great deal of resistance.

Instilling a quality culture was also a sales job. As part of our incentive plan, workers' pay is based on individual production efficiencies or the amount of an individual's production. Without any inspection of quality, a sewer will only focus on production. Obviously, production without quality is production that cannot be sold. We have no need for un-saleable products. Therefore, the Quality Assurance function inspects production and sends repairs back to the source of the problem for correction when necessary.

I remember one situation in particular when our quality people explained to a seamster that it is company policy that each worker repair his own bad workmanship. This seamster was livid, claiming he had never been required to do this before and literally got up from his machine and walked out the door, never to return.

This is the attitude of many workers in the Yucatan who in the past made inexpensive and simple products like T-shirts. We had to sell the idea that quality is part of their jobs. Our Quality Team, led by

Mary, did a great job in instilling this culture of quality over time. We started with the supervisors and convinced them first. Walking through the factory now I see sewers inspecting their own work before passing it on. The first couple of years this did not happen. But we installed a bonus scheme that paid incentives once operators were above a certain individual efficiency percentage only if their quality was at a preset acceptable level. Then we explained the obvious: each time you have to stop to repair a garment for bad quality you are losing time that could be used to produce another garment and get closer to earning incentives. Therefore, it is more efficient to ensure the job is done correctly the first time. This is simple logic, but it had to be explained and once sewers saw what is in their best interests, they began inspecting their own work. At some point, we were able to remove Quality inspectors from process inspections in each line because they were not needed since operators were doing their own inspections.

Speaking of incentives, we noted that all operators only wish to do one operation. It is clear why this would be; if they practice only one operation they can become very proficient and increase efficiencies and, therefore, their pay through incentives. In the Mexican culture, in general, there is a lack of a teamwork ethic. We solved these issues by installing a packing bonus—the more garments finished and packed for shipment, the more each worker earned in this bonus. Now it was in everyone's best interest to move around where the trouble spots were in order to increase the packing bonus.

These were clear examples in practice of the management principle to align company goals with individual goals. Goal congruence between employees and the company gets everyone on the same page and pulling together for the same outcome.

With respect to changing the corporate culture, there was much resistance from the managers. From the perspective of a Latin boss, the masses should not be given much authority or leeway, as they are going to take advantage of your good heart. It sort of goes back to the theory of the Conquest; punish and squash if you can and if you see an opening, take advantage of it in every way.

Our Mexican managers were right in cautioning me about allowing workers to take advantage of the company and my management style. I learned the lesson several times before it sunk in. Mexican employees are incredibly adept and agile at playing the system and getting something for nothing. While they may have very little formal education, they are not stupid, by any means. They can calculate to the exact centavo what their pay should be, and they calculate it each week using our fairly complex bonus scheme to make the calculation.

I remember once that an employee's mother had died and she did not have sufficient money for the burial. In my morning rounds, she explained her situation asked if there was any way the company could help her. She used the word "help". I responded that the company could help her. I directed her to follow our procedures for this type of thing and that she should go through the procedures with her boss. Eventually, the Line chief came to my office saying he thinks there has been a misunderstanding. He says that this particular employee had interpreted my agreement for "help" to mean the company would simply give her the money. We had to explain that if we began giving money to each employee, even in these dire circumstances, the company would soon be broke. By "help", I had meant an interest-free loan.

I was constantly cautioned by some on our management team about not appearing to lenient or good-hearted with employees because they would take advantage of it. Of course, I thought they were exaggerating. I was wrong. The old adage that no good deed goes unpunished is a truism in Mexico.

As related earlier, one of my most trusted employees, someone I considered a loyal friend, robbed from the company. The company could not have been more generous with him, including sharing profits and paying for airfare for him to return to Northern Mexico to bury his mother when she died. Obviously, he was truly devastated, and he was without funds to pay for the flight. So, I have learned lessons that the Mexican managers tried to explain to me the hard way. And I have had to find that balance between proper treatment, concern and compassion for employees and maintaining the discipline necessary for success. It is certainly a different balance than one would use in the States.

The massive mistrust that employees have for the company as an institution still exists, despite my attempts to make transparent our honesty and motivations. I hope our top management team has come to really believe in "enlightened" methods to motivate employees. I know they have taught me to be less naïve in dealing with workers so that our styles have morphed into a management approach adapted for the reality of the culture.

I also had a heated discussion with Luis when he informed me in his thirty-four-year old, all-knowing way, that my philosophy of management was going to reach a point of failure before long. I listened as he lectured me, albeit in an endearing, but infuriating way, that people like Doña Amey would have to be eventually run off.

Doña Amey is our oldest worker. She is now sixty and works at a much slower rhythm than the young operators. However, Doña Amey had been with us almost since the day we opened the doors. Each Christmas she would make me a present. She often worked through her lunch period in order to produce more and get her efficiency up. She also never missed a day of work.

However, she had some infinitesimally small impact on lowering plant efficiency. Since Luis's performance was partially judged on plant efficiency, he wanted no slow operators in the plant. I attempted to explain that there are certain operators who formed a part of the soul of OGA when we were a tiny, fledgling company who I wanted to be with us until the moment they decided otherwise. And, furthermore, all our workers should be made to feel special.

I am reminded of Jorge, our warehouse foreman. As the business grew, Jorge began to lose some control over our components in the warehouse. The situation deteriorated rapidly and was creating problems in the production area. At the time, Jorge reported to our Production Manager, Joe, who had his hands full with the customer's demands for increasing production. I thought I could help Joe by alleviating one of his problems and enable him to solely concentrate on production if I had Jorge report to me.

During this time, I had a lot more time to dedicate to Jorge than did Joe.

Over a period of time, Jorge gained control and did a much better job administering the warehouse. I did not interpose myself very much in his operations except to be physically present and begin to ask questions and make suggestions. Afterwards, I asked Jorge, "What caused the change in your operations from the point that your controls were failing until you regained control?"

He responded something like, "Once I had someone asking questions and poking their head in the warehouse, I just became more motivated to stay on top of things." I believe what he was really saying is that he felt special having his boss show interest in his job.

We tried to use the cultural prominence of the family to our advantage. This was a lot easier when we were a tiny company. We wanted to create a family atmosphere to attract and retain workers. As we grew, it was difficult to do so, but we did try to maintain a balance between disciplined production and a relaxed, almost familial atmosphere.

As part of creating the family atmosphere, the company would make interest free loans to employees. Since there was always some kind of severance payment if the employee quit, we usually did not loan an amount greater than the expected severance. The reasons for the loans would sometimes break my heart. Usually it was for medicine or buying school books for the children or money to bury a deceased loved one. The last employee loan I signed off on gave as a reason on our internal loan application: needs a front door.

CHAPTER TWENTY-FOUR

Another Car Accident and My Take on Mexican Driving Philosophy

My second auto accident, again judged to be my fault, occurred also under strange circumstances. It was a Saturday afternoon and I was returning home from the plant. There is an intersection of two large thoroughfares where one side of the intersection has a rare left-turn-only signal. This left-turn-only feature was recently installed. This is one of those intersections that goes from three lanes entering the intersection to two lanes after passing through the intersection. Theoretically, this is not a problem as the third lane is left turn only so traffic should not continue straight from that lane, only the other two.

Since left-turn-only is an oddity and this feature was recent to this intersection, I had already noted that many drivers were confused when the left-turn-only light would change to red for those in the third lane. The drivers in lanes one and two would also stop even though they had green lights for their lanes. So, I was prepared for this eventuality, I thought.

Approaching the intersection, I noted that, indeed, a car stopped in lane two despite the green light as the left turn light in lane three went to red.

Lane One to my right was occupied by another car moving parallel to me. I began slowing and honking and knew that at some point the idiot driver would proceed through the intersection. Of course, he did not. I hit him from behind. Fortunately, I had slowed to a speed that did not create great damage.

Immediately, the police, who are stationed at each intersection, sprang into action. This had bribe possibilities. I jumped out of the car screaming at the poor driver, "Why the hell are you stopped with a green light?" He claimed that there had been a bus in lane One that he thought was coming into his lane. So, of course, it made perfect sense that he would come to a complete stop.

Eventually, the situation was ironed out with insurance adjusters, and I felt very badly for having screamed at the clueless driver. I apologized and all was well. Except for the problem of my hitting him from behind, despite the fact he simply stopped at a green light. The police explained as they always do that they were going to have to take my license plate and write up a ticket, which would cost 250 pesos for the infraction. However, they did not want to give me a hard time and would not do so this time. After this explanation there is the long pregnant pause and the pleading eyes of the police. By this time I had lived long enough in Mexico to know the protocol. I thanked him and asked, "Is there something I can do for you as a result of your generous treatment?" There was.

As I have mentioned previously, I am amazed that there are not more accidents, given the local attitude about driving. In Merida it is as if drivers are determined to take advantage of whatever situation that will enable them to become better-positioned, regardless of effects on fellow drivers. The attitude could not be described as driving friendly. It is as if many Meridians are constantly looking for opportunities to take unfair advantage and all Meridians are forever thinking of defenses against those who may be looking to take unfair advantage.

For example, take an intersection with three lanes, one of which is a left-turn lane. Further assume that the left turn lane is open and the stop light is red for the other two lanes and the line in the other two lanes is long. Some drivers may not wish to wait in the long line so they simply take the left turn lane until they arrive at the stop light and position themselves in front of the car at the head of the line waiting for the light to change. Of course, their car ends up blocking part of the intersection and sometimes even part of the left turn lane. No matter, they have improved their position in line, regardless of fairness to, and consideration of, other drivers.

The first time I saw this happen, I thought there had to be some emergency for the driver committing the infraction. However, I came to note that this is a daily and frequent occurrence. The same attitude seems to be true in business and in other situations discussed in other parts of the book.

Recently I read a front page story in the local paper. The story reported that two days earlier the Pope had issued an announcement from the Vatican that it was a sin to drive discourteously. The reporter went to the Merida Police to see if tickets were being given for discourteous driving. To my surprise (see the chapter on The Police), supposedly some twenty tickets per day were being handed out for discourteous driving. I don't believe the statistic. The fine for discourteous driving, like all traffic fines, is quoted in terms of number of days' minimum salary, in this case five days minimum salary, or about $25.

Cars on the road in Merida are a sight to see. In terms of personal wealth, Merida is quite a wealthy city. That is, there is a high percentage of wealthy families in Merida. This means a relatively high percentage of very expensive cars—BMWs, Jaguars, Range Rovers, and Porsches. Nevertheless, there are also an enormous number of vehicles roaming the streets that in the States would be condemned.

You see cars with rusted out bodies that are hanging to the chassis literally in pieces. One could only imagine what the chassis would look like from underneath. Some cars move down the road yawing and pitching so that they look like deformed crabs, their chassis bent and springs missing on one or more wheels. Many cars have various body parts of different colors, all of which are faded like an old calico blanket. You may see one red fender on a blue car, or a purple hood on a green auto.

Since there is no car inspection in Mexico, anything that can propel itself down the road is allowed on any street or highway in the land. The safety issue is obvious, but the government has no apparent interest in solving it. I would assume that the vehicles used in public transportation must have some sort of governmental inspection, but if required it must be very light. You often see broken-down buses being repaired right in the middle of busy streets. Sometimes buses lean dramatically to one side or the other and have squeaking brakes that seem to be saying, "I am doing my best to stop. Please just bear with me." Of course, if inspection was required, bribery would surely play a part in obtaining inspection permits.

There appears to be no concern for exhaust and pollution. I would venture that in Merida alone, there is more air pollution than in the entire Untied States. Nevertheless, I have never seen a Green Peace activist in Merida nor anyone mention any concern about the clouds of smoke billowing from exhausts of vehicles, private and public.

There is no requirement for liability insurance. If you have the bad luck to be hit by a driver in a rusted-out car with no brakes, you are simply out of luck unless *you* have insurance. There will be no way the driver can pay, nor, that I know of, any consequence to the driver without insurance who smashed into you.

Mexicans have a fascination with American-made cars that are imports from individuals. That is, there are American-made cars sold in dealerships in Mexico, but in the past these cars did not have the normal American options, such as cruise control. Cars originally sold in the United States to individuals and imported to Mexico are subject to heavy import duties. Many Mexicans get around these import duties by paying bribes and getting Mexican titles and license plates issued for the illegally imported car. For some reason these cars are called "chocolates."

Road signs are interesting. There are signs on the highway that say "Don't leave stones on the pavement." I am not sure why anyone would want to leave rocks on the pavement, but they are warned against it by these signs every few miles.

My favourite sign is "Respect the highway signs." This is my favourite because the vast majority of these signs asking for respectful behaviour are rusting and riddled with bullet holes. This despite the fact that guns are outlawed.

Then there are the signs indicating distances. On the road to Cancun, for example, you may pass a sign indicating the distance to Cancun is two hundred and ninety kilometers. You drive ten kilometers closer to Cancun and you see another sign stating the distance to Cancun is now two hundred and ninety-FIVE!

When I first visited Merida as a tourist, I soon became aware of the driving protocols and my first impression was the obvious: driving was a chaotic situation. This led me to believe that there would be an inordinate number of accidents. Fortunately, my expectations were not confirmed. How could this be? I observed that Meridians seemed to drive guided by the theory of every man for himself, but, at the same time, with a heightened state of team work. This, of course, seems highly contradictory, but Mexico is a land of constant and prevalent contradictions.

As a tourist, with no real time schedule, I found driving in Merida interesting. Living in Merida, I have found it incredibly frustrating. I would arrive at work in a foul mood after having spent twenty minutes en route dodging maniacs behind the wheel, who seem to be driving based on random decisions. Over the years I have slowly settled into the driving rhythm of Merida and can get to work most days without getting too upset. I have even found that I have adopted some of the local driving techniques.

Driving is surely a microcosm of Mexican culture in almost all senses. First, there are many traffic laws and regulations, but almost none of them are obeyed with any frequency. And what is the penalty for disobedience? Nothing of much consequence. If you are stopped by police for a driving infraction, you simply pay a small bribe to a policeman, the problem goes away, and all is forgotten. Until the next time. Corruption plays a part in every aspect of life in Mexico.

Actually, the idea that you should get a second chance is a good one. But, as is discussed in succeeding pages, second chances in Mexico have become a way of life. Rarely are there consequences to unwanted behaviour. My perception is that the U.S. is tending toward this same characteristic, so it is not unique to Mexico.

Mexicans are a very warm and caring people on a one-on-one basis. However, in general or in impersonal situations, they are often very selfish. This is exhibited in driving where if you can gain an unfair advantage, you take it. If someone else is inconvenienced, that is their problem.

This is an extension of the theory mentioned in the introduction that the Conquistadores left a heritage of squashing others when you can. That is, if you have the power to take advantage of someone and obtain personal gain, you do it, and if you don't do it, you must be stupid.

There is little concern for safety or well being of Mexican citizens by the government. There is no governmental requirement for inspections of cars nor insurance.

For years, I saw little or no road rage despite the often aggressive and selfish driving patterns coupled with very poor design of road systems. In recent years,

I have begun to note more and more rage and disgust exhibited by Meridians while driving. The good thing is that guns are almost nonexistent in private hands within cities. But there is much waving of arms, hurling of verbal insults, demonstration of obscene gestures and so forth.

The horn in Mexico has been converted from a driving tool into a weapon of personal insult, and is used mainly for that purpose. The horn is not used for short beeps to advise another driver of a potential problem. It is used in long bursts when the honker does not like what the honkee is doing. It is as if the automobile itself is belching imprecations to the other driver. When one wishes to issue the ultimate insult to another driver, he simply beeps the horn in a cadence that is widely recognized to mean "*C*H *TU MADRE*." However, I have never seen any kind of confrontation become physical, which I believe is another trait of Mexicans: physically, they are rather passive.

The concept of planning, in general, is not well developed in Mexico. This is clearly manifested in driving *MORES*. As mentioned above, turn signals may or may not be used, and if used, may or may not be indicating turns, or even turns in the direction indicated. But beyond this, turns represent other types of threats. Since planning seems to be of little importance, drivers often arrive at intersections without planning and are not in the correct lane. When drivers arrive at an intersection and wish to turn left or right, the idea that they are not in the correct lane to do so is not an obstacle. Turns are often made from the incorrect lane. While this can happen, although rarely, in any culture, it is an everyday and common occurrence in Merida and often happens in the clear view of police. Apparently, turning from whichever lane whenever the need strikes is accepted tradition.

Driving, as a microcosm of Mexican culture, reflects many structural obstacles that the government does not appear to have much interest in removing. At least in Merida, if traffic studies are done, they are not done well. Rules are on the books but selectively enforced. As a result, drivers simply decide what their best interests are regardless of the rules, and there are very few adverse consequence to doing as one pleases. It's an every man for himself attitude. Police corruption is enhanced by having so-called "zero tolerance" policies for alcohol, which are clearly designed to enable corruption since no technical data is collected. Cops simply smell the motorist's breath and make a determination of the degree of inebriation on that highly subjective basis. Furthermore, since the inspection of vehicles does not exist, pedestrians and other drivers in placed in constant danger. There are no laws requiring insurance.

The government could improve all of these structural deficiencies if it had the will to do so. While the system works, it has a high cost in dollars, time and safety. It does not have to be this way. But these deficiencies can only be cured by the government taking the responsibility to properly govern.

CHAPTER TWENTY-FIVE
Tucker Johnson[9]

---

[9] Fictitious name for a real person

  Tucker was pronounced dead of mortal stab wounds by the attending emergency room physician in England. Since Tucker was a U.S. citizen, the United States Embassy was advised of the death, which was ruled a murder. The Embassy followed normal procedure and notified Tucker's family in Chicago. The family then notified various other friends, family and newspapers in the U.S. including in Tempe, Arizona where Tucker had attended college.

  The orderlies were called to move him on a stretcher to the morgue. The body was covered with the familiar green hospital sheet. As the stretcher's wheels squeaked down the hall en route to the morgue, the orderly pushing the stretcher noted that the body's feet and toes were exposed since the sheet was pulled up over the body's lifeless head. The orderly thought that if this were a live patient he would be stopping to cover the feet so the patient would not be cold.

  At that moment, the orderly noted a twitch in the big toe. He thought he must have hit a bump or maybe something was stuck to one of the wheels causing an uneven roll. He stopped the stretcher and was going to check out the wheels when he noticed another twitch in the toe. He realized that was not caused by an uneven roll and that the patient was actually still alive. He spun the stretcher around and raced back to the emergency room. Tucker owes his life to this alert orderly.

It was sometime around 2002. I was seated at the bar at Pancho's and Tucker was telling me the story. "Oh, man," he said, "It was wild. Once I recovered from my wounds, I went back to the States and went out to visit some old friends in Tempe. We were entering a restaurant, and I saw an old girlfriend just as she saw me. I was going to go over to give her a big hug and she fainted. A few months earlier they had published my obituary in the Tempe paper and she had read it. Now she thought she was seeing a ghost."

"How did you get in a situation where you got stabbed?" I asked.

"Oh, man, you won't believe it. I was spending the night with a friend in England. My girlfriend was with me. We had been partying most of the night. We had all gone to bed, and I had to get up to pee. The owner of the house, my friend, was still up, and I think he had mixed some drugs with the alcohol. Man, he freaked out and started screaming and pulled a knife on me. He thought I was someone else. He stabbed me several times."

Tucker had been a fixture, coming and going, in Merida over the last fifteen or twenty years. "Tucker," I asked, "How did you come to be in England in the first place?"

"Oh, I went over to Europe about 1970 because a friend had a charter boat over there that he wanted me to crew with him in the Med. He had been doing it for awhile and was doing pretty good financially, so I flew over to join him. I was supposed to meet him in

Mallorca, Spain where he planned to be docked. I got there and discovered he had just disappeared. Apparently, he and one of his other crew had some kind of problem with illegal drugs and my friend and his boat sailed out under the cover of darkness just before I got there. I was to meet up with him again years later in Puerto Rico, I think it was."

Tucker is a very outgoing guy and makes friends easily. Being alone in Mallorca was not a problem for him. He began talking to other charter boat owners and soon made friends with several of them. He went to work as crew on a boat and learned the ropes. They travelled the entire Med, and he had a ball doing it.

He learned the ropes and eventually became a partner with one of the owners of another boat. Tucker had a great time for about seven years and made money while doing it. He was visiting his knife-bearing friend in England when all of this came to an abrupt end.

"OK, Tucker, how did you get to Mexico then?"

He responded, "Well, after I came back to the States, I went to Arizona to recover from my stab wounds. While I was there I received a postcard from a friend who was visiting Progreso, the port just outside of Merida. He claimed Progreso was like what Puerto Vallarta was fifteen or twenty years before. This was about 1978. So, I was intrigued by his description and decided to come down and visit."

Tucker liked Progreso and Merida. Shortly he had to return to England to testify in the trial. After the trial, he returned to his hometown, Chicago. He found himself thinking often of Progreso and Merida. And, it was not long before he decided to drive from Chicago to Merida. He became even more enamoured with Merida during this trip. Once he arrived in Merida, he just sort of hung out and had a good time. He met Peter Munro, a Welshman, who was engaged in the shipping business. He also met Denis Lafoy, a Canadian, who also has the distinction of being Wayne Trotter's brother-in-law. The three of them, Tucker, Peter, and Denis, began going out on a fairly constant basis and enjoying what Merida had to offer at night. The fact that Denis and Peter had jobs (and wives) was no obstacle to the late nights and fun.

However, even Tucker, without the obstacle of a real job, began to get a bit tired of the constant partying. Fortunately, Tucker heard from a friend from Europe who had obtained a job as the Owner's Representative on a freighter. He invited Tucker to go along on the maiden voyage. Tucker accepted.

Tucker's friend was affectionately called either "The One", or "The One and Only". This handle was given to "The One", sometimes just shortened to "One", as a result of an unfortunate motorcycle accident several years before. The force of the accident had thrown "One" over the handlebars of the motorcycle, impaling his groin area on the handlebars and causing one of his testicles to be left behind on the way over the handlebars.

While on the maiden voyage, "One" began having one of his bouts with infections in his groin area and had to return to the States for medical treatment. "One" asked if Tucker could take over for him as the Owner's Rep, and the Owner agreed. Tucker remained as the Owner's Rep for a year or so travelling all though the Caribbean on a freighter.

However, Mexico continued to beckon and Tucker returned. He travelled throughout southern and central Mexico for several months. At some point, he met some guys who worked for Con Agra and were trying to set up an office in Mexico City. These guys did not speak Spanish and requested that Tucker work for them setting up the office. Later, Tucker began a trading company that bought coffee, shrimp and other commodities in Mexico and sold them in the States.

Then, the disastrous earthquake of 1985 occurred in Mexico City. While Tucker was not injured, he decided it was time to move out. He moved to Merida and began buying fish, packing it and selling to the States. Things went well, and he even began chartering some fishing boats and buying all their catch.

Business was good for several years but, for family reasons, Tucker returned to the States. However, he would continue to come to Merida for months at a time to hang out and visit old friends.

During the mid 1990s, Tucker went into business again, buying land in Tulum on the Caribbean coast not far from Cancun to develop as a resort property. He constructed various casitas on the property. However, his health began to fail, and he looked for a buyer just as tourism on the Tulum coast began to surge.

I have found Tucker to be a very entertaining and fun-loving man. He is also a very kind and gentle person. He has maintained a close relationship with Denis, Peter and Wayne for all of these years. He returns to Merida periodically where he keeps a hotel room at the Hotel Colon for months at a time, across the street from Denis' travel agency office. I always enjoy seeing him.

I don't think Tucker has a job in the States. We all worry about him because he is constantly fighting a drinking problem. In recent years, he has done a better job at staying on the wagon and we have tried to encourage him to do so. He falls off from time to time and it is hurtful to see him in an inebriated state. Regardless of his situation, he always maintains a very gentle personality.

He has not been to Merida in about a year and a half. However, I did speak to him by phone not long ago. His health is beginning to deteriorate. He called to tell me that he was hoping to come down as soon as his health permitted. I hope it will be soon.

CHAPTER TWENTY-SIX

Public Utilities

Like nearly everything else in Mexico, telephones are relatively expensive by US standards. Not that many homes have land lines since the cost is the equivalent of about $20 per month. Twenty US dollars is the equivalent of about four days' minimum wage. For that $20 you only receive one hundred free local calls per month. Each local call above a hundred costs the equivalent of about twelve cents each. Long distance calls within Mexico are expensive and calls to the U.S. are more than a dime a minute. If you want to have a land line installed in your home, be prepared to wait between thirty to ninety days. Since there are not that many people demanding land lines, I am still baffled by the wait. Making land lines even more difficult to obtain for the average Mexican is the installation cost of about $200.

The phone company, known as Telmex, is not really a public utility anymore. It was government-controlled until 1990. President Salinas privatized the company and his close friend, Carlos Slim (the richest man in Mexico and recently named the wealthiest in the world according to *Forbes Magazine*), became owner of the controlling interest. Mr. Slim and his family control over 70% of the voting shares of Telmex.

Telmex was granted a monopoly by the government for six years. Once competition arrived, the government ministry responsible for licensing competition became very slow, even by Mexican standards. The minister, it turns out, had been an executive with Telmex. Reportedly, the minister showed Telmex the business plans of all competitors. Telmex has been adept at using regulatory power and the courts to block competitors' effectiveness.

As a result, Telmex continues with 94% of all land lines, 78% of mobil services and 70% of the broadband market. Essentially Telmex maintains monopoly power, and Mexican citizens pay the cost.

Another problem with land lines is that the bill has to be paid every month in order to maintain service, obviously. Since many Mexicans literally live day-to-day, they do not always have cash available to pay the land line. Therefore, if service is cut there are also fines involved, which makes the re-establishment of service even more expansive.

Due to the high cost of land lines, cell phones became popular, especially for the economically underprivileged. When these consumers have extra money, they buy a phone card, which gives them minutes available for use depending on the card. Again, the cost is relatively high, the equivalent of about forty U.S. cents per minute of talk time. But by buying cards they are not obligated to a fixed charge per month. As mentioned above, Telmex has the vast majority of the market operated through their subsidiary, Telcel.

Another interesting feature of land lines is that it is customary to sell a house with the land line account intact. No doubt this came custom about as a result of the time and effort involved to get a land line installed. However, this creates additional problems. There is a cost to change the name registered in the directory in money, time, and effort. Therefore, many of the entries in telephone directories have the names and addresses of former residents. While there is an operator information service that you can call for telephone numbers, those operators have the same data as the telephone directory unless it is a new phone with the name registered for the first time.

The fact that the phone is in the name of some other person can create other problems when the house is bought. If there is an outstanding balance owed by the former home owner and it is not paid, your service is cut. There is no need to argue that you just moved into the house. The only thing Telmex wants is their money, and they are not interested in who made the phone calls. You will have to pay the outstanding balance if you want telephone service.

When I sold my residence to gringos, I asked them if they wanted the phone line since I was going to another house that already had a phone line. They said they did not want it, not knowing what kinds of problems they were going to have in the future. There was no way I could explain to them in a way that would make any sense. They were first-time buyers in Mexico. I decided to do the right thing and go to the Telmex office and cancel my phone line and pay the remaining balance.

Trying to do the right thing in Mexico never goes unpunished. The first problem was that when the Telmex office told us their hours of operation, they gave the wrong times. I arrived after they were closed at 4:00 P.M. Trip Number One. Trip Number Two, I arrived at 10:00 A.M. and the wait was in the range of one hour just to get to the head of the line; I was advised to come back when they opened at 9:00 A.M. Trip Number Three, I arrived at 9:00 A.M and they would not attend me because the name of the line was in the name of a person from two owners ago, and they would not allow me to cancel since I have a different name! Since it was impossible to find the homeowner from so many years back, I was advised to write a letter and obtain all kinds of seals from government agencies verifying that I was the owner of the line. Trip Number Four: the order to cancel this time was accepted.

Shortly thereafter a bill arrived that showed rent beyond the date of cancellation and long distance phone calls made on the line, despite the fact that the new owners had not yet moved into the house. Trip Number Five: I asked that the corrections be made and was told I would have to speak with the manager. The manager said I would have to prove that I did not make the long distance calls but would cancel the rent. Since there was no way to prove I did not make the calls, I paid him. I again thought the matter closed.

Next month the new owners showed me another phone bill and nothing had been corrected. Trip Number Six: I went right to the manager, and he said he did not know what happened but would correct it as I waited. He went into the computer system and made some entries. He said he would have to wait for a certain type of approval to finally terminate but that the problem was solved.

About three months later the new owners provided me with another bill showing amounts due for rent. Trip Number Seven: I was beginning to get perturbed and went back to the manager again. He assured me he would solve the problem this time without a doubt. I was not convinced.

At some point subsequent, the new owners received a letter addressed to me at the old house from an attorney's office saying that Telmex had referred my delinquent bill to them and under some statute they had the right break down my door (which now belongs to someone else who paid for the house) and enter the house with the police and remove whatever assets that in their opinion had sufficient value to cover the bill. Trip Number Eight: The manager was very apologetic indicating there was some kind of miscommunication and that he would immediately solve the problem. Thankfully, it now appears solved, but not without extreme effort on my part, the customer.

Telmex is the primary internet service provider in Mexico. At my factory we have fairly demanding needs for broadband due to heavy dependence on our connections to our customer's database and our dependence on Voice Over Internet Protocol. We obtained video conferencing equipment, which further increased the need for band width.

A year previously we had contracted one gig and Telmex gave us another gig in a promotion they were running. Therefore, we thought we had two gigs. This was sufficient for our needs. However, the video conferencing equipment was barely functional. We began measuring our bandwidth and discovered it was actually at .7 gig, despite paying for two gigs. In true Telmex customer service form they insisted we make numerous tests and changes of wires before they would even investigate.

After notifying Telmex of our tests that showed the problem was indeed with Telmex, they began their own investigation. Subsequently, the problem was that their equipment was at capacity and would have to increase capacity. In two months all would be solved, they promised. We did not think it would be productive to ask why we were sold two gigs when they could not provide it, as we knew that we would not get a response that bore any resemblance to the truth.

After three months we still had the same problem and called Telmex. Once again we had to make a number of tests. After notifying Telmex of the test results we were told, "Ah, yes, there is a problem. We are going to have to change some ports and you will be without internet for about thirty minutes." Twenty four hours later still no internet – we were stopped dead in the water due to our dependence on internet.

Our MIS people had dealt with someone named Victor. No one else at Telmex could help us. It had to be Victor since he had started the operation. Victor was gone to lunch and would call as soon as he got back at 5:30 that afternoon. He did not, of course.

So 8:00 A.M. the next day we called for Victor. We were told he would not come in until 10"00 A.M. At 11:00 A.M. Victor called to tell us the problem was solved. In the sense that we now had internet, the problem was solved, but the bandwidth was exactly what it had been before.

Once again we had to deal with Victor. No one but Victor could help us as Victor was the person with whom we made initial contact. By the end of the day, Victor did give us the two gigs for which we had been paying for over a year.

I had the same problem with JAPAY, which is the public utility supplying water to Merida. First, the previous owner had not paid the water bill in about a year. I was stuck with the bill or my water would be shut off. I found this out once I remodeled the house and the meter remained on the inside of the garage, but legible from outside. JAPAY demanded that the meter be placed in a certain way on the outside of the house, and this would be at my expense.

I did so and then received notice that the meter was pointed in the wrong direction and had to be changed again, although completely legible in its current position. I did so and went to the JAPAY Office to complain about my bill. He said I had been charged the maximum for months as supposedly they could not read my meter. The clerk would not allow me to see the history of the account and demanded I pay right then or that my water would be shut off.

I left and immediately went to PROFECA, the government-run legal office for small claims. There I was attended by a government lawyer at no cost, and after two days of bringing in forms and going to the main JAPAY Office, the last month's bill was forgiven. But the other ten months or so I had to pay.

As mentioned in the introduction, the Comision Federal de Electricidad, CFE is the government-owned supplier of electricity to the entire country. The CFE's slogan, remember, is "Committed to Honesty."

While the CFE claims its commitment to honesty, theft of electricity is a common practice. In lower economic echelons of the society, neighbors sometimes sneak up to the pole and somehow re-connect wires to their own homes that go to meters of others.

This is sometimes done with the complicity of CFE workers who might do this in order to earn an extra 100 pesos on the side.

The cost of electricity is incredibly high. Part of the reason is that if you work for the CFE, the CFE supplies you with electricity at no cost. Part of the problem, no doubt, is that it is government-owned. Presumably the "profits" of this company are converted into taxes for revenues to operate the government, as in the case of PEMEX, since tax revenues are abysmally low.

The gringos who bought my house received a shock upon receiving their first electric bill. I had installed air conditioners in each room in the house. Due to stucco construction it is difficult to install central air. I had installed high-efficient mini splits, which are common air conditioners with a separate compressor and thermostat. As we always do in the States, the newly immigrated gringos left the air conditioner on all day even if they were not in the house so that when they returned everything was cool and comfortable. After only ten days they received a bill of over $1,400 equivalent!

The electricity in Merida goes out with the advent of a high wind. Nevertheless, the situation has become better over the years. When I first moved to Merida, I recall losing electricity on average about once a week. The loss of electricity seemed to always occur around one o'clock on the hottest night of the week.

Whether you called or not to report the outage did not seem to make much difference. The average time in the past to repair a problem seemed to take anywhere from two to five hours. That time has now been reduced to about thirty minutes to two hours, so progress is being made on the repair front as well.

The capacity to generate has improved. Nevertheless, brownouts are fairly common. In my house, the fan will sometimes slow to the point that it barely moves air, like in one of those old Humphrey Bogart movies. The lights become dim as candles. Once, the electricity worked fine on only one side of my house, while I had a brownout on the other side. It fixed itself in about thirty minutes.

Despite all of these problems with infrastructure, the situation is getting better. However, with the population growth Merida is experiencing, I hope infrastructure improvement is able to keep up.

CHAPTER TWENTY-SEVEN

CUSTOMER "SERVICE"

It is doubtful that there is a single recorded instance of a customer ever being considered right in Mexico. At least, this has been my experience. I suppose everything is relative, so if all service is bad and the market does not demand better service, service remains generally bad.

In the case of receipt of bad service or product, it also seems to come down to who has the power at the moment. If the customer has already paid for the product or service, the seller recognizes that he is in the cat bird's seat. The seller already has what he wants—the money. The buyer, the customer, has something he does not want, but has already paid for it. Like many decisions that are made in Mexico, it seems that future implications take a back seat to considerations in the present. That is, there seems to be little interest in building customer loyalty.

On the rare chance that the seller might return money for a product or service already sold, the seller makes it as onerous as possible for the buyer. Part of this is due to constant fear of being defrauded, which is a justifiable fear in Mexico as the national sport seems to be fraud. Certainly, there must be proof of purchase, but even if the product remains in the original, unopened box, the seller will be convinced that the buyer has caused some damage to the product and has repackaged it somehow to return the damaged product and get his money back. This scene takes a long time to play out with buyer and seller jousting back and forth. In my experience, in the vast majority of cases, the seller prevails, as he has the power.

The legitimate fear of fraud plays out every day in the purchase of products. Inordinate controls are placed on the purchasing system to mitigate potential theft and risk of fraud. For example, at a drug store you may be waited on by a salesman/pharmacist. This person obtains your medicine, writes or prints out a receipt, and gives the receipt to you. Don't try and pay him or take possession of the medicine at this point. You will be directed to the cashier and given several copies of the receipt. The cashier is ensconced in a separate booth, giving the impression of security.

The cashier takes your cash and seems to make change at the slowest possible speed. He takes all copies of the receipts, normally three, and stamps each one. He gives you back two and tells you to return to the salesman who will give you the purchased merchandise if you give him one of the stamped receipts.

This entire process obviously takes a good deal of time. Therefore, the customer is delayed, unfavorably impacting customer service. I suppose Mexicans have become accustomed to this level of service.

In this day and time with the technology available it would seem to make much more sense to place modern controls to discourage employee fraud. The company would save money on labor, and the customer would have a better experience. It is changing to some extent, but at a snail's pace.

Banks are perhaps the worst offenders when it comes to customer service. Services that those of us from the States have come to believe are necessary, such as internet banking, are provided free in the States. Not so in Mexico. Internet access to your account in Mexico is relatively costly.

Hopefully, you will not have to go physically to a bank on Fridays. Bank lobbies are packed with people, and customers literally take a ticket. A two-hour wait to be attended on Fridays is not uncommon.

Banks, as well as many retail outlets, have TVs hung on the wall blaring a soap opera or some Mexican game show. Customers are transfixed. TV has become an addiction in Mexico. I suppose this is customer service from their perspective, but the volume is turned up so high you can barely have a conversation in the lobby.

Once you arrive at the teller's window, there is much stamping of forms, receipts, and other paperwork. Money will be counted various times. A teller from another station may come up with questions for your teller. Your teller will immediately stop what he is doing to attend the other teller.

If a check is being cashed, you will need several forms of identification. This still may not be enough. Once I attempted to cash a personal check at one of the branches of our bank. Branches in Mexico are almost like stand-alone banks. The business and my personal account were opened at a different branch than the branch of the same bank where I needed to cash my check. The branch manager knew me and our company. However, because my signature card was only on file at the branch where I opened the accounts, he was not authorized to cash my check drawn on the very same bank. This was true even though the teller could pull up a digitized copy of my signature on his computer screen.

I have had several checks that the bank has refused to pay, even though written by me. Due to fraud, if the teller notes the slightest difference in the signature and the digitized version, the bank will not honor it. In these cases, the bank never called me to verify if I had written it. The bank simply sent the bearer of the check packing and wasted his time as well as mine once I had to write another check.

The most flagrant example of lack of customer service occurred with the first bank we used. Our customer was transferring money from Boston to our account in Merida. I had chosen this particular bank because it had promised to give credit on bank transfers within twenty-four hours, beating the other banks who were only guaranteeing forty-eight hours at the time. I had a hard time understanding why it could not be almost instantaneous, but twenty-four hours was the best option I had.

The first few transfers went well. However, this happy situation did not last very long. We confirmed a transfer had been made from our customer's bank to our account, but the money did not show up. After several days of concern and complaints, the bank's response was that I was going to have to prove that the transfer had been made. I did show a faxed copy of the customer's confirmation, but this was not enough. I was still without the money in my account. A week later the money showed up in my account with no explanation. I complained that not only did I want an explanation, but I wanted interest in the money, or I would leave the bank. I had to move my account, since I the bank had no interest in accommodating me even on the explanation for why a wire transfer would take over a week to be credited to my account.

I moved to the largest bank in Mexico, Banamex. The service was better for awhile. In those days we paid in cash as the vast majority of workers had no bank accounts. Obviously, it is risky to have large amounts of cash on hand each payday. Two of us would leave the bank each Friday with about 250,000 pesos in cash in a big duffel bag. I felt like a drug dealer, which did not worry me nearly as much as the possibility of assault, either on the way back to the office or at the office.

Four employees would spend all morning putting the cash in pay envelopes. After one pay day, the next Monday an employee returned a 100 peso note that a store did not accept saying it was counterfeit. Close examination led us to believe it was counterfeit.

We called the bank, asking them to replace it with a good bill, as we had obviously obtained the counterfeit bill from them in the cash payroll. The bank's response was, "Can you prove you got it from us?"

We responded, "Of course not, but it is only logical to assume so."

The bank manager said it is possible that the worker had obtained from another source and simply wanted to convert to a real bill. We admitted this as a possibility, but never before had we had this situation occur. The bank still refused to pay the 100 pesos, or about ten USD unless we could prove without a doubt that the money had come directly from the bank. Of course, there was no way to do so.

We had a meeting in my office. We were reprimanded by the bank manager for not checking the bills we received from his bank before stuffing them into envelopes. I was incredulous. I told him it was only logical for us to assume that he was providing non-counterfeit money and that it was physically impossible for us to take the time to do what he was suggesting. I threatened to leave the bank over the principle if they did not make good on the 100 pesos. While our account was not huge, I could not believe that they would want to lose a customer over ten dollars. I could possibly understand it if this was not the first time this had occurred.

The bank manager said it was against bank policy but that he would pay it out of his own pocket. I accepted his offer. But after a month during which we never got the ten dollars, we moved to another bank where we have been now for about five years.

Several years ago it was announced that Citibank was buying Banamex. There was quite a bit of excitement in the business and foreign community because it was assumed that this would bring service up to American standards. I predicted at the time that the Banamex culture would devour the Citibank culture in Mexico. Unfortunately, for Banamex customers, I was correct.

A relatively recent development is payment of invoices over the internet. This is a success story of massive proportions in terms of efficiency. Since there is no reliable mail service in Mexico, one cannot simply mail a check. To pay bills in the past, you had to contract a courier service, send an employee, or go yourself directly to the business office to pay the bill. Obviously, this was very time consuming.

Once banks introduced this service, even though it has a high cost, it was a great savings in cost and time. However, the bank's internet page and the controls placed on payment are typically very user unfriendly. For example, to access my account on the internet, I was given a special card with numerous codes on it. To access my account I go through five successive internet pages before I can see my account balance. At the same time I am required to input two different secret codes that I obtain from my special card with codes over and above the use of a password. If I wish to pay a bill, I still have two different additional codes to input before the transaction is done.

For the payment of utility bills, besides going through the bank's security measures, I have to input numerous numbers and verifying digits that appear on the statement. Believe it or not, the CFE has a series of 30 digits that must be inputed. Twenty of the digits are on one line and the last ten on another. But despite all of this, it is much easier than going to pay in person, so progress in this area of customer service is being made.

Since there is no reliable mail service, your electricity on telephone service can be terminated with no warning. This is because your bill may or may not get delivered, and if it is delivered, it may or may not be before the deadline to pay. There is no requirement that the electric company, or any other utility, warn you that service termination is imminent.

When service is cut off without warning, you cannot call and have it re-connected. One must physically go to the office and pay in cash the bill as well as a fine for the inconvenience of the utility company. A friend went through this procedure and at the office made the mistake of complaining that this was unfair since the bill never arrived. This complaint infuriated the clerk, who, as part of her rant at my friend, said that customers had the obligation to note what day of the month the bill should come. If it did not come on that date there is a further customer obligation to go to the office and obtain a statement, pay the bill, and avoid further penalties and disruption of service.

Gas stations are another area where there is a complete lack of understanding about customer service. The government-owned oil company, Pemex, does not allow competitors in the market. So all gas stations are Pemex. Nevertheless, Pemex has begun to grant franchises to individual owners, although service is inferior in all of them.

Since there is no such thing as self-service, it is somewhat curious that full service is lacking. All gas station attendants expect a tip, regardless of what they actually do. They will normally put gas in the car and sit by the gas pump chatting with another attendant or just day dreaming. If you ask them to wash the windshield, they seem perturbed, but if they do not get their tip, usually about one percent of the bill, they are even more perturbed.

Most gas stations are relatively large with various islands with pumps. Some of the islands are not manned; if you go to one of these islands, you will not be attended. You must go to an island where there is an attendant. Once you have asked for gas, many honest attendants will show you that the pump is at zero before pumping.

The meters on the pumps are supposedly inspected for accuracy and usually have stickers on them. However, Pemex is notorious for manipulating the meters so that you pay for more gas than you actually receive. I once spoke with a lawyer who had a Pemex client who was caught with inaccurate meters. The station was closed immediately by the government bureaucrats in charge of the operation. Once the lawyer negotiated a bribe to be paid to the bureaucrats, the station was re-opened and the inaccurate meters continued to defraud all of their customers. The lawyer thought this amusing.

Another relatively new development is the ability to use credit or debit cards to pay for gas. This came about as a result of the *HACIENDA* (Mexican IRS) deciding to crack down on false facturas at gas stations. Recall that facturas are special invoices that allow the amount of the invoice to be deducted for tax purposes. For a price, false facturas can be purchased. The hacienda was justifiably bothered by this practice at gas stations and wanted to stop it.

There are two ways to get a factura. The traditional way that creates a long wait while all the data for the factura is slowly written out by hand. Or one can obtain one through the use of a business debit or credit card. The credit card option was a great development hailed by all as an improvement. Raising expectations even higher was the use of wireless point of sale terminals at gas stations. The only glitch is that each gas station has been allocated only one wireless unit. Because the wireless unit is portable, no one ever seems to know where it is. Due to the large expanse of area over which most stations are built and the clear lack of sense of urgency by the attendant in locating the device, you can wait up to five minutes for the results of the search. But, again, it is only time that is being wasted so why would a customer feel short-changed on service?

Mexico's lack of infrastructure is somewhat surprising. Tourists may think it charming that electricity is not always available on demand, like in the States. However, the charm wears off after awhile. And it is not the least bit charming when the electricity goes out and you have over five hundred employees sitting around in the dark not doing anything but certainly expecting their pay for this non-productive time.

The charm also wears off when you call the CFE to report an outage. Whether you are reporting loss of electricity in your home or in a business, the receptionist, assuming you can get through to her, will not take your report of an electrical outage unless you can give her the "contract number" of your account. That is located on your electric bill. No matter how serious the situation, that number must be provided before the CFE will go further. This is exasperating, but you learn to keep your electric bill handy.

I would think American fast-food companies would be checking in some manner how their franchisees in Mexico are interpreting "fast food." One particular hamburger chain is sprouting restaurants all over Merida. I don't understand their success. I usually go through their drive-thru and would guess that 15-20% of the time I receive a different product than what I paid for. I have also waited up to fifteen minutes in the drive-thru with only two cars in front of me.

The same thing happens at airports. All the major airlines use the same ticketing and software. At the counter of a major U.S. airline in Mexico, it takes four to five times as long to get my boarding pass as it does in the U.S. It is a mystery to me.

Everything eventually gets done. The only casualty is time and patience, but Mexicans have much more of both than the average gringo.

CHAPTER TWENTY-EIGHT

The Incredible People at Work

Already mentioned is the enormous respect that I have for the vast majority of workers. Most of us in developed countries are exceedingly lucky to have been born into a culture and a system that enables, rewards, and promotes productivity. Unfortunately, the ability to move up the social and economic ladder in Mexico is virtually impossible.

The inability to advance, in my opinion, is not due to exploitation of workers, although such exploitation does exist. Workers at the lowest level receive a livable wage in the context of the Mexican economy. However, there is essentially no ability to obtain loans or other beneficial perquisites that most citizens have in developed countries. This, in conjunction with the government's cultural and socialistic approach, prevents real advancement.

That is, the structural obstacles for workers in Mexico are so great that I am often astounded by their ability to maintain such good attitudes. It is true that many have the attitude that as a foreigner and business owner, you must be rich and, therefore, owe some social and/or financial debt to all workers. At first, I thought this group represented the majority. I now believe that those such people are a minority.

Most of our workers, I believe, get it. A case in point is Doña Chary. When we moved to OGA III, we were concerned that we would lose many workers, thereby disrupting our ability to maintain production until the workers who resigned were replaced with new hires. We suspected we would lose quite a few workers for the transportation problem; many of our workers in OGA II lived fairly close to the plant and did not have to spend such a long time traveling to and from work in our privately contracted or public busses.

As a result of our concern about loss of workers due to the move, we planned a trip to the new plant, OGA III, with entertainment, a professional video and a speech promoting the idea that our workers should stay with us after the move.

The entertainment was a band and two different local comics that truly entertained our group of workers with the theme of why they should stay with OGA after the move. Nearly every one of our workers appeared in the professional video, filmed while they were working, and the theme of the video was to create pride in all that had been accomplished and that the move was necessary in order to ensure our future and the future employment of all. A speech given by Claudia and me re-enforced these concepts.

Then Doña Chary asked to speak. Unbeknown to us, she had prepared a speech to give to her colleagues. Her speech was very touching. She spoke of the financial capital that had been invested and placed at risk, trusting in the abilities of each of our workers. She showed a true appreciation for the risks undertaken and for her employment and asked that her colleagues take into consideration these factors.

The speech she made left me near tears. I truly believe that Doña Chary has a better understanding of risks and sacrifices of investors than most of the government employees charged with economic development.

⁂

In my morning rounds through the production floor, as I am greeting workers I noticed that several have a strong scent of wood smoke on them. I asked one of the production bosses why this is. I was told that many workers still use wood to fire their stoves or COMALS. Comals are used to make tortillas.

I was also told that many do not have hot water heaters and so they often heat water in the mornings for their baths using wood. I am not sure why this particular fact affected me so. It just further enhanced my appreciation for their efforts and the obstacles that they must overcome.

⁂

Most of our workers are of Mayan descent. Mayans are very short in stature and normally somewhat stocky. Their faces are usually round and could almost be thought of as having an oriental look. The Mayan language has an oriental sound.

At any rate, I began noticing that the girls from a particular village were all quite attractive. Their faces did not have the familiar Mayan features to which I had become accustomed. After awhile, I also noticed that the guys were attractive as well. Furthermore, many of them are taller than the normal Mayan.

We have about a hundred and thirty workers who are bussed in from *Maxcanu* (pronounced Mashcanoe), the village that produces all the attractive workers. I have always had a great deal of respect for the workers from Maxcanu since they have to travel so far and long to get to and from work. Besides, there is another maquila located in Maxcanu, so I am particularly grateful that they spend so much time in transit to work with us rather than walking to work in Maxcanu. Perhaps one of the reasons they preferred to work with us is that the other maquila is Chinese-owned and has a reputation of being tough with their workers.

The workers from Maxcanu have a great work ethic. It is rare that one of them misses work. It is very rare that one of them misses work without a justification of some kind. This is a village that does not seem to have such a problem with alcoholism. For all of these reasons, I became fascinated with the little village.

Over time, I had become very friendly with one of the girls, Veronica. I would stop and joke with her on my morning rounds. Veronica is very attractive with a face that has some Mayan elements, but they are not dominant. Eventually, two of Veronica's sisters came to work for us and one of her brothers. They are all very dedicated workers.

I had been telling Veronica that because of my fascination with the people from Maxcanu that I wanted to come visit. We made plans for a particular Saturday. She and one of her sisters were going to be in Merida to see a doctor on that Saturday morning, so I picked them up at the doctor's office, and we traveled together to Maxcanu.

My plans were to take her and her siblings to lunch in Maxcanu. We arrived at their very humble home and some other siblings had already prepared lunch for us all. They spread a white table cloth in the one-room house, and we all ate together. They made sure I had the biggest helpings and the best seat in front of a fan.

Both parents had died, the mom most recently. After lunch, they took me across the street to meet their grandfather, who was sleeping in his hammock in a *choza*. A choza is a typical Mayan home that is oval shaped with a thatched roof made of palm leaves. Chozas only have one room and a dirt floor. A choza's walls are made of wooden sticks that have a type of stucco made from crushed limestone and mud that is plastered over the stick walls.

The sisters lived in a block house with a flat concrete roof. It was still not totally finished, although it did have a concrete floor. I do not believe it had a bathroom.

After meeting the grandfather, they suggested we go to the CERRO. A cerro translates as a hill or small mountain. We were led to the cerro by Veronica and accompanied by two of her sisters and a couple of friends. The cerro is an interesting place. It was fairly flat on top with areas of very low scrub brush as well as areas of dense jungle. The trail leading to the top of the cerro from town ends at the entrance to a small construction with walls on three sides. Inside this three sided shelter is an altar constructed by local townspeople.

Veronica led us to several caves. The Yucatan is littered with caves as a result of its limestone geology. We only explored the entrances and did not go deep. Several years prior I had contracted histoplasmia from a spelunking adventure. Histoplasmia is contracted from bat dung and creates some sever lung problems; sometimes it is fatal. I had no intention of ever going deeply into another cave as a result of my experience with histoplasmia.

We also walked to another part of the cerro that had what appeared to be a dry cenote. A cenote is a sinkhole formed out of the limestone that normally has water. Many cenotes are believed to be connected by vast underground rivers. However, this sinkhole is dry. Many types of vegetation was growing out of the sides and the bottom of the hole, which may have been about sixty feet deep and about thirty feet wide.

We rested for a period of time around the cenote. It was quite a tranquilizing place. There were a number of bromeliads growing on the trees that I took back for my garden.

After a while, we returned to town and drove around. In the process I was greeted by several workers. They seemed surprised to see me in Maxcanu.

Returning to the sisters' house, while in the front yard I asked to use the bathroom. Veronica became very nervous and asked one of her neighbors if I could use the bathroom at the neighbor's house. The neighbor acquiesced and took me inside her house. She led me to a spot that had a cloth curtain that was opened and left me there.

I pulled the curtain and found myself in an area about three feet by five enclosed completely by a curtain. There was no plumbing whatsoever. I saw a bar of soap on the floor and a hole in the floor.

Presumably, Veronica was embarrassed to either tell me she had no bathroom or to send me to a similar area within her own house. I will never know.

At any rate, I left shortly to drive back to Merida. I was even more impressed by the people from Maxcanu after my visit. We continue to hire more workers from Maxcanu. They have proven themselves as good employees and persons in many ways.

About a year after my visit to Maxcanu, Veronica informed me that she was going to get married. She invited me to her wedding which, unfortunately, was planned while I was going to be out of the country. Therefore, I could not attend.

Her two beautiful sisters and her brother continue to work with us. They never miss a day.

※

Mexico has a developed what could be described as a culture of thievery. One of the reasons for this is the abject poverty in which many live. Another reason, as is clear in the chapter on the police and subsequent chapters in this section on the robberies, there is little consequence to thievery. However unfortunate this is, it is a fact of life in Mexico.

While the vast majority of our workers are honest and committed to their, there is a portion that reflect the bad part of society. This is true of any company. One of the things that caught my attention is that we cannot put toilet paper rolls in the bathrooms in the production area. The reason is that if we do this, the toilet paper will be stolen. We buy something like two thousand rolls of toilet paper each month, and one roll every week is distributed to each worker. If we did not do this, toilet paper would be stolen each day several times.

Our fears concerning toilet paper are not just speculation. We award a concession to a company that cooks for our workers in our commercial kitchen at the plant and feeds them in our company dining room. Just last week I was informed by the owner of the concession that he bought new eating utensils, and that within three days over one hundred sets had been stolen.

Each of our sewing machines has a low voltage light that is very powerful so that the sewers can easily see the results of their operations. We began to buy a very good bulb instead of the normal refrigerator-type bulb that goes into these light fixtures attached to the machines. These bulbs were very powerful, but very efficient in energy use. Soon operators were coming to work and noticing that they had no bulbs. We, of course, had to replace them. The operator always claimed they did not know what had happened to the bulb. It became very clear in a short period of time that the bulbs were being stolen and taken home. There was no way of knowing if it was the operator reporting the lost bulb or someone else who was stealing it. We finally had to go back to the cheaper bulbs and soon there were no longer missing bulbs reported.

CHAPTER TWENTY-NINE
Don Jose

Don Jose is a very special person that is part of the incredible people working at OGA. He is sixty-three-years- young and the only Yucatecan I know who looks younger than his actual age. His youthfulness is no doubt a tribute to his positive attitude and his sweet disposition. I have never met anyone so positive and completely devoid of maliciousness.

In actuality, he is not a Yucatecan; he is from Campeche, the neighboring state. Therefore, he is most accurately described as a *Campechano. Campechanos* are the most ridiculed group of native Mexicans in existence. *Campechano* jokes abound. For those of us who graduated from the University of Texas, a *Campechano* is like an Aggie from Texas A&M; so now you know there is no limit to the amount of justified ridicule one could heap on a *Campechano*.

Don Jose works as a security guard at the factory; he maintains security at the main pedestrian entrance to the factory. If there was a contest for the most loved employee, Don Jose would win a unanimous decision. Therefore, Don Jose is the only living *Campechano* who does not merit ridicule.

His full name is Jose Jesus Canul Sosa. He is approximately 5 foot 2 inches tall, only slightly short in stature for the average Yucatecan of Mayan descent. He is powerfully built; his forearms still ripple with definition. He shaves what little hair remains on his head and is almost never seen without a baseball cap covering his shaved head.

He runs everywhere he goes in the factory yard, which is enclosed by a security fence. When vehicles arrive that are going to enter the factory premises within the security fence, he opens the gate to the vehicle entrance, which is located about seventy yards from the pedestrian entrance. It is a common sight to see his short legs churning like a dervish and propelling him along to the vehicle entrance at an astonishing speed, especially considering his sixty-three years.

Don Jose had explained to me that his parents were still living and in their nineties. He and his wife live in the same house as his parents and his brother-in-law and sister. One day Don Jose asked to see me in the office. Immediately I knew there was a problem as his eyes were red and watery. He told me that he had just received a call informing him that his mother had died. He said he had no money for the burial. I asked how much he needed; it was the equivalent of about $400. It was close to Christmas, so I loaned him $200 and gave him another $200 as his Christmas gift. Instantly he broke down, cried, and hugged me. He must have told me "Thank you" a thousand times over the next week.

Then about two months later, someone mentioned to me that Don Jose was in debt to an *agiotista,* a loan shark. *Agiotistas* abound because there is little chance of the average Mexican obtaining a bank loan. Don Jose had to borrow more money for the burial of his mother and did not want to ask me for an additional loan. He was having to pay something like 500 pesos every two weeks and all of this money was going just to pay interest on the loan. There was no way he would ever come out from this debt. I asked Don Jose if he was indebted to the *agiotista*. He admitted that he was, and I immediately loaned him more money so that he could pay the loan shark off. Don Jose always paid back all his loans to me on time.

When I first met Don Jose he was working for the security firm we had contracted for round-the-clock security. However, we had encountered several problems involving this security firm. We decided to fire the security firm, but hire Don Jose as an employee to do security during the day and contract security from another firm for nights and weekends. Don Jose had been hired specially for our plant, and the fired security firm had no other work for him. I called Don Jose into the office to tell him that we were cancelling the contract with his firm, but that we wanted to employ him directly as a security guard. Immediately his eyes watered and he said, "Don Gus, thank you, thank you" and began crying. He told me he needed the work, and he knew that at his age it would be impossible to obtain employment. Don Jose is a tough guy and these moments of sensitivity and vulnerability only make him more lovable.

Part of what makes Don Jose so lovable for me is his interest in my dog, Jake, a big yellow Labrador Retriever. Jake goes to work with me. Sometimes he stays in the office with me for awhile, but most of the time he stays outside on the grounds of the factory running free within the fence. Don Jose, who loves all dogs, has a special love for Jake. He talks to Jake constantly in a normal conversational tone and appears convinced that Jake understands everything he says. He takes Jake on his rounds with him, and I have heard Don Jose chatting away as the two of them diligently scout for intruders.

Sometimes Don Jose becomes the practical joker with Jake. He has told me that when suppliers, or other visitors, come to the factory that Jake greets them as well as Don Jose at the entrance. When he opens the gate and the visitors enter, Jake often begins sniffing their legs and shoes as dogs are prone to do. Jake's size scares some of the visitors, and they look at Don Jose with that worried, questioning look that is asking implicitly, "Does he bite?" Don Jose tells me he tells many of them, "Don't worry, he doesn't bite. He is sniffing for drugs." He claims to tell them with a straight face, but as he is telling me he is doubled over with laughter at his practical joke.

His love for Jake is so deep that he will ask me, "Don Gus, if you have a date or plans for the weekend, call me and I will baby-sit Jake either at your house or at the factory. Poor thing, he should not be alone as he gets lonely." Don Jose wanted to be clear he was only asking to do this for Jake's benefit, but I know Don Jose, and I know he wants to be with his friend, Jake. Since he began asking, I nearly always leave Jake with him as I run errands or have plans on the weekends so Jake does not stay alone at the house.

Don Jose does not want to be paid for keeping Jake. However, like nearly all our employees, he does not have a car and relies on public transportation, which is slow and costly. Once, I asked Don Jose where he lived so I could take him home rather than him taking a bus after I would come back to the factory for Jake. He was effusively appreciative, but said, "Don Gus, I don't know where I live. I can only get home by taking a bus, and the bus wends around through neighborhoods until it arrives at the point I know I have to get off. I don't know how to describe to you to get there." Nor does he know the name of the Colonia where he lives.

This is another characteristic of Don Jose that is so endearing. He is so innocent. He must be the only living, mature Mexican who has retained his innocence, and it is truly refreshing. However, as one might suspect, this innocence has created problems for him in Mexico.

He told me about an experience he once had while still living in Campeche. In order to make more money, he started a small neighborhood store. These small stores are located throughout Mexico and are usually family-run. The store was operated between Don Jose and his wife. During the day, he worked at a plywood factory, and his wife ran the store.

Apparently, he arranged with the supplier of goods for the store. The supplier would finance the purchase and send an auditor once a month to check inventory and obtain payment for the amount of goods that had been sold.

This arrangement worked perfectly for a year or so. He had a good working relationship with the supplier's auditor who was assigned to his store. However, this auditor got transferred, and a new auditor was assigned to Don Jose's store. There had never been shortages while the original auditor was involved. The first month the new auditor arrived, he found a shortage of 500 pesos, which Don Jose had to pay. Don Jose told me, "Don Gus, these were the days when 500 pesos was a lot of money. I could just barely come up with the money to pay." These were the days when the OLD PESO was in use. The dollar equivalent of this amount was about $200.

The next month the auditor came back. This time found a difference of 10,000 pesos, the equivalent of about $4,000! There was no way Don Jose, who earned in those days the equivalent of about three dollars a day, could possibly pay this back. It was evident to me that the new auditor thought he had found a way to make additional money on the side, taking advantage of humble Mexicans who were only trying to get a little bit ahead. Don Jose would not have purchased so much merchandise in only one month.

He and his wife were devastated. He told me, "I was really scared, but not so much for me as for my wife. She had signed the papers to start the store with the supplier because she understands numbers better than I do. Now they were telling us that we had to pay or my wife was going to prison."

Eventually the local COMISARIO intervened. Don Jose's wife was spared and the debt forgiven. I am sure he never understood that it was a scam that was taken too far.

I asked Don Jose about his past and told him that I heard he was really from Campeche. His response was, "Well, I guess you could say I am from that region, but I am really a LERMANO. LERMA is a city on the coast in the State of Campeche. But the capital of the state of Campeche is CAMPECHE. I don't think Don Jose was trying to clarify for me the difference between being from Lerma and the City of Campeche. I think he does not understand that CAMPECHE is the state and if you are from anywhere within the state, you are considered a *Campechano*.

He said he had worked 30 years in Lerma in a plywood factory. One day the owner of that factory told him that there was going to be a cut-back in personnel, and if he could learn more jobs within the factory his job would be more secure. Accordingly, Don Jose told me that he learned every operation with the factory and stayed employed until the factory closed for lack of ability to obtain raw materials at a price that made the end product saleable.

Since I knew Don Jose to be 62 and to have arrived in Merida only about two years before, there were about 30 years unaccounted for in his life story. So I asked, "Don Jose, what did you do before the plywood factory?"

He responded, "I was a CAMPESINO. Primarily I raised watermelons."

"Well, why did you give up that for the plywood factory?", I wanted to know.

He said, "Well, in those days we would plant in planting season and harvest when they ripened. All planting and harvesting was done based on the rains. But then someone invented sprinkler systems. The government came to the assistance of the big farmers who got the sprinkler systems and now they have watermelons year round. The price of watermelons became very cheap. I had to find something else to do."

I have had the good fortune of getting to know numerous inspirational people. In the case of Don Jose, I would hope to emulate his exceedingly pure heart. His faithfulness and loyalty to my business and me, personally, will never be forgotten.

CHAPTER THIRTY
Doña Tere

I can't write about Don Jose without thinking of Dona Tere, who is my housekeeper. Her complete name is Terecita del niño Jesus Gorocica Moguel. She comes two days per week, which is a minimum requirement, given the amount of dust and sand that is constantly in the air. Without a cleaning and washing every few days, a film of dust and sand forms on everything.

She knows the day that she began working for me; it is a date in June. Every June she will tell me that we are having our anniversary. I had been through numerous housekeepers before her. Most of them were dishonest, and I would find any number of items missing.

However, Doña Tere is different. I can leave money, or anything else, in plain view, and she will never touch it. So she now has over six years with me. I got her a job with the gringos who bought my other house. They are pleased with her, too.

My only complaint about Doña Tere is that she does not see well and, therefore, does not clean well. However, she is incredibly loyal and protective. She knows every trick in the book that dishonest Mexicans will pull and is constantly advising me of how to ensure that no one will be able to take advantage of me. If someone comes to the house and says they were sent by me, she will not let them enter until she calls me at the office and confirms that I have sent them.

Doña Tere's life is probably a bit more difficult than that of the average Meridian. First of all, she is a widow. Her husband died about ten years ago and left her with no assets and two daughters. One of the daughters has a serious physical condition. The daughter has some type of a disease affecting her spinal column, which prevents her from leaving the house except to visit physicians. This creates quite a hardship for Doña Tere. Despite these problems, Doña Tere has never missed a single day of work.

These difficult life experiences have taken their toll physically on her. She is about five feet tall and must not weigh over ninety pounds. She is younger than me, but looks a good bit older, in my opinion. She has one eye that looks off in another direction and clearly does not see well. Her complexion is dark. While she seems frail, she is amazingly vigorous and her leg muscles are very well developed. This latter attribute is no doubt a result of all the walking she must do.

There is no job that she will not undertake. I am never sure how long she stays at my house cleaning as she leaves long before I arrive home from work. I know that she will work in the garden if she sees a problem. She arrives at my home between 6:15 and 6:30 in the morning. This means she must leave her home by around 5:30.

To arrive at work, Doña Tere takes two buses. The round trip cost for her to go to work and return home is approximately twenty pesos. She will make special trips to my house without advising me just to check on matters if she suspects there might be a problem. She will not accept money for the transportation in these cases.

I am so happy to have found Doña Tere. She is a joy to be around and never complains, despite what I know has to be a difficult life. I have enormous respect for her.

CHAPTER THIRTY-ONE
Alberto Castillo[10]

---

[10] A more complete story of Alberto's life can be found in Oaxaca to Yucatan: People and Their Recipes by Lyman Morton, Coyote Cherokee Books.

Continuing with the theme of lovable and caring Mexican friends, I am compelled to write about Alberto Castillo. I first met him on one of my initial trips to Merida. I don't remember how we met, but it was most likely at Pancho's.

I know of no one who does not like Alberto. In fact, I find it inconceivable that someone would dislike him. He is now eighty-five or eighty-six years old. Or so he claims. He is the favorite son of Merida, an artist with an artist's flair in the way he dresses and in the extravagant jewelry he wears.

The fact that I know of no one who dislikes Alberto is probably because Alberto seems to like everyone. Well, almost everyone. The very few times over the years I have heard him say something about someone that could be construed as negative were cases that were much deserved. He laughs often and keeps a perpetual smile on his face; a positive aura seems to be with him always.

Alberto is now frail, but only a few years ago one could still see the vestiges of the well-maintained body that he must have had in his youth. He is bald and sometimes grows a moustache. He has the flat nose of a prize fighter. He told me that his grandmother gave him the nickname of "Chato," which translates to a person with a flat nose. I sometimes call him Chato, and I think he likes it.

Although Alberto is now frail, he is a vigorous octogenarian. Until a couple of years ago, he would stay out dancing until two in the morning or even later. He loves to dance, especially with younger women. In truth, it is difficult to find anyone that is not younger than Alberto in Merida. There is one particular Canadian lady who is half his age who comes to Merida once a year. Alberto used to take her dancing and would only leave the dance floor because she could not keep going.

His paintings hang in most ex pats' houses and many have been taken back to the States over the years. His commissions for doing paintings are too low, but he refuses offers of more money, saying "No, you are a friend. I can't charge you any more." He punctuates this sentence with his unmistakable Alberto laugh, becomes adamant and will not allow you to argue with him.

He has at least one painting in Pancho's. Alberto has remarkable status in Pancho's, as he has his own engraved, pewter beer mug that is kept behind the bar. When he comes in, there is no discussion, the bartender simply takes out his mug and fills it with beer and hands it to him.

Alberto lives alone in the family home that he inherited. The home is over two hundred-years-old and located just south of downtown. The property is very deep and until recently Alberto worked constantly on the garden by himself, keeping it in immaculate shape. I have noticed the garden becoming a bit overgrown now that his health is not as good as it was.

The artist in him comes out in various ways. One such reflection of his artistic bent is the interesting furniture he makes from scrap lumber and other items he finds discarded by neighbors and others. He decorates the furniture with fibreglass adornments that appear to be wood for which he makes molds and places on the furniture. These adornments he usually paints gold. The result is a very unique piece that only Alberto could design and build.

Alberto's house is a mix of rustic architecture with Alberto's special artistic touch, a museum that holds a complete collection of the old television series, Sanford and Son. Nowadays guests enter the house through the side door because he says his front door has been broken into so many times that instead of using conventional locks he places wooden timbers across the door as in olden times to keep would-be robbers out. He claims conventional door locks don't work. In fact, there is a collection of broken door knobs and twisted locks on the table by the front door.

Because the front door has a timber placed across it, Alberto cannot enter his house by the front door. If it is at night and someone is accompanying Alberto home, he has to enter through the side door while his companion waits for him to negotiate his way to the light switch located in another part of the house. Once lit up, the passageways can be seen to the main part of the house. The passageways are cleared through a litter of old wooden and metallic debris that he has collected, no doubt waiting to be turned into some artistic object.

Once into the house, the first thing anyone notices is Alberto's unique interior design touches. There are mannequins dressed in outrageous ways, unique Alberto-made furniture, beautiful door casings salvaged from other homes leaned up against walls, a chandelier in the dining room that has an artificial Christmas tree intertwined in it with lights perpetually shining. Other odd collections of adornments hang in various places throughout the house. While the description sounds odd, the house has Alberto's artistic touch and is very tastefully done.

His art studio is the "terrace" across the back of the house. Terrace is not the right word, but is used for lack of a more appropriate term. Most of it is covered by a tin roof. There are places where the tin does not completely cover the interior. Here Alberto has placed plastic tarps on the roof to keep the water out. One of the tarps has partially filled with rain water and droops into the room between tin sheets forming a sort of bubble hanging from the ceiling. I don't know how long ago this happened, but I can't remember a time when that bubble was not there.

The studio is also sometimes used as a part time warehouse. Last time I went into the studio there was an old refrigerator there. Alberto asked, "Do you need a refrigerator?"

"No, I really don't, Alberto. Where did you get it?" It was about thirty years old and rusted.

"Oh, someone gave it to me, and I don't need it," he responded nonchalantly. Neither of us broached the subject of why it was in the studio.

The studio, like most of the rooms, has extension cables draped from the walls at random intervals as if they are part of the decoration. Some are extensions of extension cables. These are not decorations, but functional. There are those who believe there is only one electrical outlet in the entire house from which all these extension cables emanate like the arms of an octopus.

Not only the roof of the terrace, but much of the roof of the house is of rusted sheet metal. As a result, there are quite a few leaks. My friend Lyman, who wrote the more extensive history of Alberto mentioned in the footnote to this chapter, tells the story of noting a newly installed drain on the floor. When he asked about it, Alberto responded, "That is so the water from the leaks on the roof can be drained out of the house."

Lyman asked the obvious, "Why not just patch the roof?"

Alberto responded, "Because it's easier to work on the floor than the roof." This logic is indisputable.

Alberto left Merida as a young man to study art in Mexico City. While there he had the good fortune of studying under the renowned Diego Rivera and his wife Frida Kahlo. Alberto has a number of interesting stories about Diego and Frida. During his stay in Acapulco, Alberto married.

The young couple moved to Acapulco from Mexico City. This was during the hey-day of Acapulco. In a rented apartment, Alberto set up his studio, which also served as his home. At night, he converted the studio into a restaurant.

During the years in Acapulco, Alberto's young wife died. They had a son together, but Alberto was unable to care for him. The son went to Mexico City to live with his grandparents, Alberto's in-laws.

Alberto, the young widower, was apparently quite the ladies' man, and Acapulco was certainly the place to be in those days, All the rich and famous flocked there from all over the world. Alberto met a number of movie stars while living there. He also relates stories of attending parties nearly every night and sometimes more than one per night.

Over the years in Acapulco, Alberto met a couple from Ohio who owned a restaurant-bar. Each year they asked him to move to Ohio and tend bar at their restaurant. One year Alberto decided it was time to leave Acapulco and accepted their invitation. He stayed in Ohio about eight years and ultimately moved back to Merida to live in the ancestral home, which his mother still occupied at that time.

Once back in Merida, Alberto continued painting. He also set up a restaurant in his home, just as he had in Acapulco. Alberto lent his festive personality to the ambience. Apparently, the restaurant did well. Unfortunately, the restaurant was closed once his mother's health became too bad to help out in the business.

Not long ago, Alberto's son and wife came to visit. They brought their son, Alberto's grandson. Alberto's son lives in France and married a French woman. It had been a number of years since he had seen them. The visit evoked a good bit of emotion and pride for Alberto.

Several years ago, Alberto was in his back yard, pruning a Papaya tree. Somehow one of the pricks on the tree punctured the index finger of his right hand. He thought nothing of it and self-doctored the slight wound. However, the wound did not heal and became infected. It got worse and worse until it became gangrenous.

He went to his family doctor for treatment, but it did not improve. Some friends, led by Diane, a nurse from Boston, finally insisted he go to a specialist. She made the appointment and took Alberto. The specialist cleaned it and gave a series of cures to be done as well as set follow up appointments. Alberto did not like this specialist and quit going. He ultimately went to another doctor who did the best he could with a wound that by that time had developed into a still more serious infection.

Over a period of maybe two years, the finger was cured, but is still deformed and gives him some pain. I think as a result of this war with infection, Alberto's immune system weakened. And, as a result of a weakened system, his health has began to deteriorate. While one would never hear of complaints from Alberto in the past, he is now in a constant state of pain, mainly in his back and legs.

It worries all of us, but Alberto remains positive and upbeat despite his ailments and continues to paint. He continued to dance until recently, but did not stay out until two in the morning.

His health continues to deteriorate and now must use a cane to walk. He no longer dances at all. However, I note his head bobbing to the beat of the background music in Pancho's. Alberto is an inspiration to all of us in so many ways.

CHAPTER THIRTY-TWO

Real Estate, Building, and Remodeling

Dealings in real estate in Merida are quite interesting, frustrating, entertaining and somewhat risky all at the same time. There is no organized real estate market as we are accustomed to. That is, there is no multiple listings service, nor are there real estate appraisers as we know them that check comparable sales. Comparable sales are uncheckable because there is no way to discover the actual sales value of any particular sale under current rules, laws, and traditions.

Furthermore, there is no such thing as a legal real estate license in Mexico. If you want to sell real estate, you just do it. There is no such thing as a sanction for acting unethically. There is no normal commission. In fact, what many real estate "agents" do is obtain permission to sell a property from the rightful owner to sell at the owner's price, say one million pesos (about $100,000), and then market the property for, say, a million and a half. If the agent is lucky, he finds someone willing to pay this sum. So instead of making a paltry 6% t as agents do in the states, he makes a whopping 50%. But this is a tricky deal since the property is in the owner's name, there is no such thing as a listing agreement, so ethics often become an issue. A common practice that agents must guard against is the owner attempting to cut the agent out and dealing direct with the buyer.

There is no county courthouse as we know them with deeds recorded. However, there is a central place operated by the government, called el CATASTRO, where owner's names of properties are listed. While this sounds as if it is a satisfactory alternative, it is not. Owners do not necessarily record their purchases. They often wait until ready to sell the property to do so. Therefore, any information obtained at the Catastro is most likely not updated.

The deed equivalent is called the ESCRITURAS. You cannot legally purchase property without having the original escrituras from the owner. Most experienced buyers will ask for a copy of the escrituras so that their lawyer may check ownership. This is not easy as, again, there is no county courthouse that will have trustworthy data on ownership. And since escrituras can be typed up by anyone and made to look official, fraud is rampant. A recent and welcome development in Merida is title insurance that can be obtained from an American company doing business in Mexico. It is a worthwhile expense, although I have noted that many practicing lawyers in Merida are not aware of its existence.

At the closing, the happy buyer and seller meet with the lawyer. This lawyer cannot be any lawyer, but a lawyer known in Mexico as a NOTARIO PUBLICO, a notary public. What we know as a notary public in the States is a totally different concept. This special type of lawyer in Mexico has powers that other lawyers do not have. As I understand it, this lawyer actually maintains in his offices the legal documents that would be needed in the case of legal disputes. That is, the notary public's office is the repository for some legal documents that we might normally find in a county courthouse in the States. However, the notary public does not maintain the escrituras; these are given to the new owner.

Since there are numerous notary public in any given city, I don't quite understand how titles are researched. That is, there is no central clearing house for legal documents like a courthouse. To search all the legal records you would have to go to each notary public's office, at least as I understand it.

At the closing, it is mandatory for the lawyer to read out loud the entire escrituras. These lawyers read like the fast-talking guy in the old commercial; it is impossible to understand anything, even for Mexicans. After this reading, the parties sign and the deal is done.

The escrituras list the presumed purchase price. The contract between buyer and seller is private and will have the agreed-upon purchase price. However, because there is a tax of 2% percentof the value listed in the escrituras, it has become traditional to place a lower amount in the escrituras. So, the buyer wishes to list a lower amount than the actual sales price. The seller often wishes to do the same due to the fact that Mexican laws use the listed price in the escrituras to determine the capital gains. The actual amount from the sale deposited in the bank account of the seller is irrelevant for Mexican income tax purposes.

Be careful, because besides being illegal this type of manipulation of official facts can trap you in the future. I have one friend who purchased property, and the buyers did not want to pay income taxes on the full price. Therefore, they talked him into placing a lower price in the escrituras, selling him on the idea that he would pay less in acquisition tax.

Supposedly, although illegal, this was a win/win. Until my friend wanted to sell his property to a business that wanted the entire purchase price listed in the new escrituras. Since what was listed in the original buyer's (now the seller's) escrituras was an amount that was about half what he really paid, he now had to pay taxes on a relatively large, but fictitious gain.

If you are a foreigner and wish to buy property in the "forbidden zone," within fifty kilometers of the border or the coast, you cannot do so. But like everything in Mexico that is "forbidden" by law, there is a solution. One can buy property as a foreigner by obtaining a *fidecomiso*. This is a trust with a Mexican bank as the administrator of the trust and the owner of the property in a legal sense. However, the bank stipulates that the property is being held for the beneficial interests of the foreigner and will be sold at the foreigner's direction. This is a solution, but it does have a cost.

Another tradition, at least in Merida, is that on signing the contract to buy and sell the property the sellers will want a down payment of as much as 50 percent of the purchase price. Since lawyers do not maintain escrow accounts, this money must be paid direct to the seller. Obviously, this is risky business.

Some of the real estate agents who are Americans deal mainly with American buyers. To make these people feel more comfortable, the real estate agent will have his own escrow account in the U.S.

Instead of paying the money direct to the seller, the money goes into this U.S. escrow account. This works fine when the seller is also American, but if the seller is a Mexican, he or she may not be willing to accept this arrangement.

I have bought and sold numerous times. Merida is full of old and very interesting homes. The really old homes are built with MAMPOSTERIA, the term used for walls made of stone and cement. These homes have walls of a foot to eighteen inches thick and keep the houses quite cool. The old homes usually have ceilings as high as four to five meters (thirteen to sixteen feet.)

I moved into my first purchased home that I remodeled to discover in a couple of months that the previous owners had left the water and electricity unpaid for quite some time. Since Mexican utilities tend to go with the home regardless of whose name is on the bill, the current resident must pay or lose the service. I was stuck with a hefty bill.

Also, the real estate agent told me that some chandeliers went with the house. In Mexico, anything not completely removable is normally not sold. So air conditioners, light fixtures, ceiling fans, are removed by the seller upon vacating the premises. Based on the agent's information, I was surprised to see two very valuable chandeliers removed. The agent told me that since my lawyer wrote the contract and did not stipulate that the chandeliers remain, I was out of luck despite her verbal comments that the chandeliers remain. I was also out of luck with getting any kind of reimbursement for the utilities bills they left.

When I sold this particular house, a different real estate agent made the sale. Remember, there are no exclusives, so all real estate agents try and sell the same house at the same time. Most of these agents are Americans who have web sites. This agent was an American, working for an American who owned the Mexican real estate agency. I will call this fellow Chris.

Chris told me the deal on the house was to close in November. I reminded him of one slight detail: I had sold the back part of the lot to a Mexican neighbor, and knowing the traditions here, I doubted that the land sale had been recorded by my neighbor. I later discovered that in fact he had not recorded the sale but would start the process so that the data at Catastro would match the data in the new escrituras. Chris said, no problem we have sixty days. I respectfully reminded Chris that it had been my experience that these sorts of things, which seemed so simple, took forever in Mexico due to the bureaucracy.

Again, Chris said it should be done easily within the sixty days. I began to wonder how much experience he had. Soon my concerns were verified.

Of course, the paperwork could not be done within the sixty days, and Chris began to become upset with me, as he had not informed his buyers of this possibility, and they were coming to town expecting to move in. While I reminded him he was advised from the beginning, he still believed that this was somehow my fault. I finally had to deal direct with his boss who turned out to be very competent. He told me that Chris had only recently begun to sell real estate in Mexico and had never sold it in the U.S. This was obvious. The deal did finally go through, although late.

I grudgingly admit that I respect Chris, because he has now begun a construction company. This despite the fact that he speaks only a few words of Spanish and knows even less about construction than he does about real estate. I am told he is charging unsuspecting Americans moving to town U.S. prices for very poorly done work. I have respect for him because he somehow has stayed in business despite these very serious handicaps.

While constructing or remodeling, it is interesting to watch the work going on and talk to the workers. The word for brick mason is ALBAÑIL. Albañiles can do miracles. My experience with them is that they will do whatever is asked and do it well. However, some Mexican contractors and architects tell their albañiles not to do anything without their permission. This creates a problem as Mexican bosses have a tradition of not being very involved. While this is not true of all bosses, with some contractors and architects this cultural characteristic means that they are not on the job very much. So you ask an albañil to do "X" and he has to wait until his boss comes on the job before he can do it. If he does it without permission, he may be fired or have his paycheck reduced.

I gained the trust of many of the albañiles on various jobs. Some of them would tell me that their paycheck varies from week to week, although the number of hours worked was the same. I asked them why. Their response was that they did not know and were afraid to ask why for fear of being fired. They also explained that none of them were on the books for Social Security so that if they were hurt on the job, there was no medical care for them.

As an entrepreneur in Mexico, I have some liberal acquaintances who accused me of coming to Mexico to exploit workers. Of course, one reason I came is due to lower wages. But I have never broken the law that I know of, nor made attempts to exploit laborers, as seems to be the tradition among some Mexican employers. So I find my liberal friends' comments, not only ironic but ill-informed.

The work habits of the albañiles are questionable for sure. Merida has an incredibly hot climate. As a result, you would think that construction workers would arrive early to avoid the heat of the day. Not so. Starting time is supposed to be 8:00 A.M. Most arrive between 8:10 to 8:25 A.M. Their supervisors arrive around 9:00 A.M. and the contractor or architect is probably just finishing breakfast around that time.

The first thing the albañiles do on the job is eat breakfast. The breakfast is small, maybe just crackers and/or tortillas and a coke. Then they begin to read the newspaper. Slowly, one by one, they start to work around 8:40 A.M. They break for lunch between 1 and 2 P.M. After lunch, most of them snooze for awhile and then go back to work until 5:00 P.M.

At five o'clock they usually all change into other clothes, splash a little water on themselves and use copious amounts of deodorant. They travel home by bus or first stop off at the cantina en route to home.

Whether they are remodeling or building from the ground up, they always build the wall without any provision for electrical conduit. When ready to install the electrical conduit, the electricians come in and knock a trench in the wall for the conduit and wires. Afterwards, of course, the albañiles come back through and re-do their work making the wall look finished again. A friend once asked why it was done this way without making provisions for the electrical conduit. The albañil's response was that it had to be done that way because no one knows where the wiring will go. In my last remodel job, there were plans indicating the location of all electrical outlets. Nevertheless, the albañiles still made the wall first, the electricians made trenches for the conduit, and the albañiles came back to re-do it all. I am mystified by it all but have learned it is best to let them do it their way.

While albaniles can do amazing things, they do not seem capable of making walls straight. I am amazed by this fact given the complexity and preciseness of construction in the Mayan pyramids and temples that were constructed one thousand years before by these same albaniles ancestors.

It is customary to leave a "security guard" on the property at nights and on weekends due to the rampant theft. At my first remodel job, the "security" was an old man who had to be about ninety. I have no idea how he could have stopped any would-be thieves. He would hang his hammock and sleep at night in silence, without electricity. For a good while, there were no working baths. But I did not want to know the solution he found to this problem, so I never asked.

Painters are even less punctual in terms of arriving to work than albañiles. Early for a painter is 10:00 A.M. Drop cloths to protect floors and doors from errant paint are an unknown concept. If you wish to ensure that the paint only goes on the walls, doors, where it is supposed to go, you better have paper, plastic, or drop cloths yourself. I learned the hard way. I remember on my first house I had a door repainted after I moved in. There was more paint on the floor and walls than on the door.

When remodeling, painters do not like to move obstacles in their way. I have a friend who said that her painters painted around a broom leaned up against the wall. That is, when they finished they left an area unpainted that was a vague outline of a broom. For them, this was satisfactory.

But painters are always enjoyable people to be around, like albañiles. My last painter was named Rey David, King David. King David is a nice looking, short and stocky guy with long curly hair. He could not be more agreeable. He always ends each conversation with the phrase, "Have an excellent day."

All contractors in Merida always quote jobs without including windows, doors, and any carpentry work that may be required. Since for thousands of years Mayans have worked with stone and concrete, albañiles are simply carrying on traditions of their ancestors. Carpentry is a relatively new trade in comparison to brick masonry. Therefore, carpenters are eyed as something really unique, and their trade is viewed as somewhat mysterious. The carpenters I have met are truly unique in many ways compared to their stateside counterparts.

For my first house, a friend recommended a carpenter named Pedro. Pedro did not have much work, but I have to say he was a good carpenter, at least by Yucatecan standards. Pedro's problem was that he did not feel compelled to come to work. So the house took much longer to complete than it should have.

Pedro also had a kidney problem. When his kidney gave him problems, he would disappear for days at a time and get checked into a Social Security hospital. He would not even tell his wife and children. It took me awhile to get used to that.

For my second house, I decided I would try a carpenter recommended by my architect, Juan.

Juan is rotund and works with his son, who is very nice but seems a bit retarded. Juan comes to work astraddle a motor scooter with his son balanced on back.

Both Juan and his son are extremely outgoing and pleasant. Both want to please beyond any reasonable expectation. But these guys make Pedro look like Speedy Gonzalez. They are always late in arriving and plan their work very inefficiently. They take at least five times longer than a U.S. carpenter, but they are probably five times more agreeable than a U.S. carpenter!

In Merida, all work is paid 50% in advance. Regardless of what you are buying, if it has to be built or installed, you will pay the 50% in advance. One reason is that most of these people live hand-to-mouth and do not have the money to buy materials. While this may not be true of contractors, the tradition is still pay some advance.

Obviously, this can be worrisome, given the fraud and lack of professional responsibility exhibited by many. Fortunately, I have not had a problem with this, although I know people who have lost their deposit when the individual never returned to do the work. And forget suing, as the Mexican justice and court system is non-functional except on rare occasions.

Ads for houses are interesting. As noted previously, phone lines go with homes. Because phone lines take so long to get installed, if you already have a phone line this is a benefit. Therefore, you will note that many ads for homes make mention of a phone line that stays with the house.

Also, some areas do not have utilities, such as water and electricity, even within the city limits.

Homes that have utilities are advertised as having all services, another advantage for the buyer. And this is not just in the poor housing areas.

In many new areas under development that have very expensive homes, the development may not have utilities or paved streets. For the buyer to get these amenities, he or she may have to pay the city to obtain them. This does not seem to be a problem that affects sales.

However, making a deal is not always easy. Last year I was trying to buy property on the beach. I negotiated four sales directly with the seller. All four ultimately did not go through. The first one because the person who represented himself as the owner was not the owner. I never found the real owner, but once it became clear I was negotiating with someone who had no right to sell the property, I moved on.

The second property was actually two small tracts adjoining one another with two separate owners. The two different owners were in-laws. I was paying the same for both properties although one was slightly larger. The slightly larger property was landlocked. When the in-law of the slightly larger, but landlocked, property heard from her brother-in-law that he was receiving the same amount as she, she demanded more money. We had not signed a contract so I just walked away from the deal.

In the other two deals, again no contract was signed but we agreed on amounts. Shortly after the verbal agreement, the sellers wanted to re-open negotiations. It is as I mentioned in the Introduction. It seems that if you agree to a price the seller assumes that he/she must be selling too cheaply and immediately wants to re-negotiate. Agreeing to the new higher price would only be the start of a new set of negotiations. Again, I had to walk away and ended up not buying anything on the beach.

Speaking of beach property, my friend Lyman bought three contiguous lots in a beach town near Merida called Celestun. He got them at a good price. He had a lawyer who reviewed the papers and closed the deal. The next time Lyman and his wife went to view their new beach property they noted that someone had built a shack on it. The person in the shack said he was the caretaker hired by the owner. Since Lyman knew he had not hired anyone, he began to wonder.

Lyman was not the only one wondering. It seems that about sixty lots in this same area had been sold by various individuals to many different people. These sixty lots were being claimed by someone else. The someone else had papers as well, reflecting that the someone else was the owner.

When Lyman hired another lawyer to look into it, the lawyer said the someone else was the owner with title issued directly from the Agrarian Reform Agency of the government. Making matters worse, the someone else was supposedly a partner with the governor's brother. In Mexico, the governor of any state is omnipotent.

To add insult to injury, research showed that the someone else paid one peso to the government for each lot. Further research showed that the property had been "interchanged" with other property at Catastro. That is, somehow the property bought for one peso from the government was actually physically located off the beach but through some kind of shenanigans at Catastro was re-described as beach property and drawn on the Catastro maps as Lyman's land. I know it seems strange to the uninitiated, but after having lived in Mexico, I do not doubt that this is what happened. Actually, I am told that this is not an uncommon practice. It simply takes a bribe of the right person in Catastro.

Over the course of several years Lyman has been fighting this "Lawsuit." I put lawsuit in quotes because no formal litigation has occurred. Each of Lyman's lawyers has taken the approach that the best thing to do is to go through administrative (political) channels to rectify the problem. Lyman has no legal basis for litigation against the seller for fraud, because the seller placed the fraudulent papers for the land that Lyman bought in the name of the seller's maid. His maid has not a cent to her name and, apparently, under Mexican law there is no basis for litigation against the real culprit in this case.

For three years the political channels have not been of much help. I feared this since it was rumored that the governor's brother was participating in the fraud. Nevertheless, one of the first lawyers kept telling Lyman that at any moment the governor was going to issue an order for the land to be returned to Lyman. I did not understand how the governor could do such a thing but the governor, apparently, can do anything he wants in the Yucatan.

After a lengthy wait, Lyman obtained another lawyer. This lawyer took the issue to some government agency in Mexico City. A decision has been "forthcoming any day now" for many months. I hope it comes in Lyman's favor, but I certainly have my doubts.

Another friend recounted his story of beach property in another part of Mexico that the governor of that state tried to "rob." The governor sent in armed police to occupy the land. My other friend hired a lawyer who did file an actual lawsuit in Mexican federal court. Fortunately, my friend won his lawsuit although it cost him a great sum of money. And in the process, the bad guys trumped up charges that required my friend to essentially become a fugitive and leave the state for about a year until he won both lawsuits.

This sort of wild west mentality I experienced after the purchase of my first property in Merida. I had not moved in and was taking a friend by to see it when I noticed two men digging up a beautiful palm out of my side yard. I asked what they were doing and they told me their boss, the lady next door told them to go dig it up and move it to her yard. They were simply following instructions.

I went to visit my neighbor-to-be who was a young lady of about thirty, attractive and clearly used to having her way. She was not the least bit embarrassed by being caught robbing my palm tree. An argument ensued. She seemed to think it her right to take whatever tree she wanted off my land because the house was not occupied. I disagreed and the palm stayed. Happily, she and her husband soon moved.

Buying and selling real estate, like nearly everything else in Mexico, is much harder than it should be. A lack of an organized market, coupled with a legal system that is more dysfunctional than our system in the States, creates fertile ground for opportunists. Nevertheless, property can be bought and sold without great risk if the proper care is taken prior to purchase and sale.

CHAPTER THIRTY-THREE

Chic[11] and Patricia

---
11   Chic is a nickname for Charles. I always thought this name was spelled with a "k" at the end. However, Chic spells it the same way as the French word chic.

Chic and Patricia are the All-American couple. Chic was the high school football star in St. Louis and Patricia a beauty queen from Nashville. They met on a blind date while Chic was attending Vanderbilt and Patricia was in school at Peabody College. I met them both at the bar in Pancho's in Merida.

They are both delightful people and very approachable. Chic is a retired aerospace engineer and Patricia continues her work as an artist. Chic has a great sense of humor and is constantly laughing his contagious laugh, which, of course, makes him a joy to be around.

Patricia is quite introspective and philosophical. Unlike many such people, she is not heavy and humourless; quite the contrary. She is very friendly.

After the two of them married, Chic obtained a job in aerospace research in Georgia. This launched his career in a trajectory of product development and marketing within the aerospace industry. He worked for a number of aerospace companies in Georgia, Canada, California and New York. Apparently, he had a successful career and retired about five years prior to our meeting.

While Chic was pursuing his aerospace engineering career, Patricia attended various art schools. While attending one such school she had several opportunities over time to go to France, Germany and Italy to study art and sculpture. While away on her studies, she fell in love with a small town in France called Flavigny. For the past twenty odd years they have been going to Flavigny and about twenty years ago bought a home that they remodelled.

After Chic retired, he soon became bored. While travelling in France, the couple found a monastery for sale that was in ruin in St. Jean de la Porte, which is located in the Savoie region of France, near the French Alps. The monastery was built in 1032. They bought it and remodelled it and it is now a beautiful chateau that I had the opportunity to visit. The initial construction phase took two years but the work continues.

Patricia's fame as an artist appears to be growing. She is obtaining more and more invitations to show her art around the U.S. She has done a series on Frankenstein that, even to my unsophisticated eyes, is clearly remarkable. Recently, she has begun a series of egg paintings. I am told by other artists that it is extremely difficult to paint eggs and to get the shape and the perspective correct.

For some reason, Merida is beginning to attract a number of artists. Galleries are springing up like weeds in the rainy season. I am told that one of the new galleries is owned by an artist from Monaco who is a close friend to Prince Albert and that he will visit within the year.

At any rate, Chic and Patricia are part of the Merida scene. They are very interesting and enjoyable people. Their living and work experiences have enriched their already interesting personalities. They remain intellectually curious and physically active. I am blessed to have known them and hope they remain in Merida for many years to come. I did my part of making sure they remain in Merida by selling them one of my former homes. They tell me that they sometimes catch themselves still referring to it as "Gus' house".

CHAPTER THIRTY-FOUR
The Governor's Visit

In Mexico, a State Governor is omnipotent. Perhaps within each state, the governor commands more respect than the president of the country. When we got a call that the Governor wanted to come for a plant tour, we knew it would be somewhat of a spectacle, but I was not really prepared for the grandness of the event.

A few days before the visit, the Governor's security detail came out to get the lay of the land. We have a parking lot in front of the factory for about twenty cars. Inside the factory grounds we have covered parking for top and mid-management. The Governor's security people said that on the day of the visit the entire outside parking lot would need to be vacated to make room for the Governor's entourage and their automobiles. The Governor's fleet of Suburbans would need to be parked with the rear facing the factory in the event that the Governor would need to make an emergency exit from our premises. In that unlikely event, the Governor and his entourage would exit the plant running toward the vehicles placed for fast get-away. They may have thought that some of our seamstresses were too aggressive. If they had come on a payday and seen the reaction of a sewer who felt he or she had been gypped out of a centavo, they would have had a right to prepare for all kinds of defensive security measures.

I was a bit surprised at the request. After all, the parking lot had only one entrance and exit on the other side of the parking lot from the factory entrance where the cars would be backed up. This meant that in the event of a real emergency the Governor, his entourage, and all of their vehicles could easily be trapped within the parking lot while chased around by lunatic employees who would have removed their sewing needles from their machines to use to shred the Governor and his security detail into small pieces. I would have thought it wiser to park the governor's vehicles on the street in front, which would have provided greater mobility and flexibility to the security detail.

Nevertheless, on the day of the visit we, of course, complied with the request and had any vehicles that were in the front parking lot removed and parked on the street. We awaited the Governor for his 10:00 A.M. visit. He arrived approximately one hour late, almost considered early by Yucatecan government standards. There was an army of press following him, and they all entered the factory.

We first showed the Governor our new employee induction video. He seemed appropriately pleased and asked sufficient questions about the company to give the impression he cared. Then the walking tour of the factory began. The Governor, the press, and the rest of his posse walked slowly through the factory listening to the explanation of our production processes and so forth.

Toward the end of the tour, he received a phone call on his cell. It was a personal call, and he talked for three or four minutes. Shortly after that call, I noticed him yawning an immense and prolonged yawn. He was not apologetic at all about the yawn. I guess it is fine to do this, especially since I seem to remember that President Reagan dozed a bit on the dais when the Pope was speaking.

The Governor at this time, Patricio Patron, had been elected on the coat tails of Vicente Fox. Vicente Fox was the first president of Mexico in over seventy years that did not come for the PRI Party. This was the first Governor elected from the PAN Party in the Yucatan. The Governor was young, good-looking, and aggressive in his speeches about how the Yucatan would prosper under his leadership. He was tall by our standards, but a giant by Yucatecan standards. He is about six foot seven inches tall. The average Yucatecan male is about five foot five inches tall. It was quite a sight to see him walking through the factory.

Upon leaving the factory building, he held an impromptu press conference at the entrance of the factory with the press corps. Thankfully, there was no need for emergency exits that would have tested the security detail's theory of rapid exits. However, the Governor probably wished that there had been a bomb threat or a crazed sewer wielding a sewing needle as the press had quite a few probing questions.

The Governor had recently proposed a new airport to be built outside of town on land that was rumoured to be owned by members of his family. This sort of government purchases with taxpayer money of property held privately by high-level government officials is more or less traditional in Mexico. However, there had been much opposition to this proposal. The existing airport had been remodelled in recent years and was sufficient to handle current and future levels of air traffic. Personally, I saw no need for a new airport, but I made it a point, as a foreigner, never to opine about political matters in public.

After the press finished (almost literally) with the Governor, a TV crew came back into the factory and asked for an interview with me. I had my fifteen seconds of fame in Mexico. The interview appeared not only on local TV but somehow made it to the national level.

In the TV footage, I was chagrined to see I was neither as handsome nor as articulate as I had always assumed myself to be. I was further chagrined to see that we were running a certain fairly sensitive federal agency's shirts with emblems at the time of the tour. I had neglected to tell the TV crew not to film this emblem. Given Mexico's general dissatisfaction with the War in Iraq, I now had visions of protests and bad press followed by my customer's decision to renege our contract. I was thinking it was I who may need to station my vehicle for a rapid exit. Thankfully, all of my concerns about possible problems were for naught.

CHAPTER THIRTY-FIVE

The Return of Lee Richards

While the manuscript was with the editor I am happy to report that I received an email from Lee. Lee had been sailing the Caribbean for the last seven years. The boat he bought the year after he sold me THE BLIND PIG, is now up for sale. I received all the particulars on the new boat. I responded to his email, and Lee wrote back that he wanted to visit Merida again.

Appropriately, we made a date to meet at Pancho's. Lee was there when I arrived for our appointment about a week later. He seemed a bit pale and thinner, but his big, eternal grin was intact.

Our easy friendship picked up right where we had left it about eight years before. His boat was in dry docks in Trinidad, and he had just arrived in Merida from a few weeks in Cartagena. Because I had been in Cartagena about four months previously, we began by exchanging stories of the fabled Colombian women. Since Lee has been going to Colombia for almost thirty years, he told me of a series of emails he had written over the years that he cobbled together as a story he called "Cartagena Adventure." He sent me a copy. It was very entertaining and full of "Lee-isms." The stories had to do with the same themes as always: drink, drugs, and women. All the stories were very well-written in Lee's descriptive and poetic style. One story reminded Lee of an earlier incident involving the famed war protestor, Abbie Hoffman. Apparently, Lee had known him, and he related the story as a diversion from the Cartagena Adventures.

I was curious to know if Lee was able to get his social security payments. "Yes," he responded.

"Lee," I wanted to know, "what name are you receiving it under?"

"Well, actually, I am receiving it under two names. When I went to the Social Security office to find out if I was going to receive anything, she looked me up and told me, 'Yeah, here it is. I asked her, 'I worked for awhile under this other name, would you mind checking that?' She told me, no problem and that name popped up too. So she simply added the two together and didn't ask any questions." He followed all this with his famous laugh.

From there we began talking about a number of things and went over old stories as well as some new stories. Lee is one of the most compassionate people I know, and one of his stories I did not know previously concerned the daughter of one of his former partners. This partner committed suicide and had a daughter who was two at the time. Lee committed to send her to college. She recently graduated from Michigan University.

I said, "Lee, that is very admirable. That had to have cost a good bit of money."

"Hey, money is the cheapest thing you can give away. There's about three or four trillion of it floating around in the United States, if you can't get a little of it. That's pretty pathetic."

Once again, Lee had a perspective that I had not considered before.

He went on, "You know I never worried about money. There were days, years ago, when I would wake up on the East Coast without a cent to my name. I just never worried. I would go out and start panhandling for breakfast and go on from there."

We discovered that we had been living in Austin, Texas at the same time in the late sixties. He was a protester and me a student.

We had one more dinner together on his last night in Merida. I was honored that he would want to spend it with me, as he had other friends in Merida. He called me that morning asking if we could have dinner his last night. I already had plans with another friend who is a sophisticated ex-pat businessman living in the Yucatan, a friend who, unfortunately, does not want his story told. Due to this man's sophistication, I was concerned that he might not mix well with Lee. Lee is very sophisticated, but people with closed minds would not have wanted to even talk with Lee. The dinner went well and my sophisticated friend called the next day explaining that he had been completely charmed by Lee, as everyone always is who spends time with him.

Then Lee was off to Miami where he would travel with an old girlfriend to Arkansas to buy land. Since Lee did not have a bank account, he mainly dealt in gold and gold coins. Holding gold over the last few years had been fortuitous, since gold had more than tripled in value over that time, and he now had a small fortune. Not worrying about money seemed to be a philosophy that works well for Lee. I hope I see him again soon.

CHAPTER THIRTY-SIX
EDUCATION

It is trite to say, but it is true: the quality of education represents the future potential of any country. Having been in higher education in the United States, I fear for the future of the United States. However, by comparison, Mexico's future is bleak.

To begin with, the hours of operation are minimal. While there seems to be no standard, some schools start at 7:00 A.M. and are out by 11:00 A.M. Four hours of school a day is not sufficient. It would not be sufficient even if students were taught historical facts during the four hours, but they are not taught Mexican history based on facts.

Since I am from Texas and something of a history buff, I was interested in what Mexicans thought of the Texas Rebellion from Mexico. I was shocked to learn that Mexicans knew nothing of the Texas Rebellion. They responded that Texas had been sold to the United States. I thought this might have been an isolated misunderstanding. It was not. Every Mexican I asked about it gave me the same answer, including highly educated professionals.

I understand patriotism and that it is a good thing to be patriotic toward your country. However, there are lessons to be learned from history. In this case, why Texas revolted in the first place might be an interesting introspective lesson for Mexican citizens.

No Mexican believed my "version" of Mexico-Texas history. The facts are undisputed in the rest of the world. Mexico gave land grants to whomever would come to Texas to settle it on the idea that the settlers would tame the Apaches and Comanches. The Mexican government did not want to spend the time, money, and energy in fighting these Indians, and thought it would be easier to entice others to do it.

Most of the land grant recipients were former citizens of the United States, but many were Mexican citizens and some were from Europe. At some point, these settlers were wanting more rights from Mexico City and when the government was not forthcoming, the revolt ensued.

Santa Anna, President of Mexico and General of the Mexican Army, amassed some six thousand troops to storm the Alamo inhabited by less than a hundred and fifty Texicans, as they were called in those days. All Texicans were killed and their bodies burned.

Later, Sam Houston surprised the Mexican Army during siesta at San Jacinto and routed Santa Anna's army. Santa Anna fled, dressed himself in a private's uniform to disguise himself, and was later captured. It was only when he entered under Texan guard with some other prisoners that the Texans realized who he was as the Mexican soldiers recognized him and began shouting for their leader.

Santa Anna agreed to sign over Texas to the Texans in exchange for his life. Texas became the Republic of Texas, with Sam Houston as its first president, and was admitted to the United States ten years later.

I have a portrait of Santa Anna hanging in my home. Despite the fact that Santa Anna was probably the most famous general in all of Mexican history, no Mexican visiting my home has ever recognized the man in the portrait. I also have one of Sam Houston.

So during the four hours of schooling, I am not sure what is being taught if Mexico-Texas history is representative. I do know that when students do not learn whatever is being taught, they are failed. However, this is not what you and I might expect. The students who fail are given second and third chances to pass before being retained in the same grade for the next year.

Furthermore, the four hours of schooling may not really be four hours. If the students don't arrive on time, there may be no penalty. Most schools have a policy of something like twenty minutes of grace period. Mexicans are taught from an early age that arriving late is not a problem. No wonder they are never on time as adults!

Also, it seems that many schools have socials on Friday. One friend's child tells me that a different student is required to bring a movie each Friday. There are no studies that day as everyone in the class, including the teacher, watch movies.

Each year when Day of the Teacher arrives, there are no classes. It has become tradition to take extra days and make a long weekend if Day of the Teacher falls on some day other than a Friday.

I get confused about schools sometimes. There is a public school system and also private schools. Those who can afford private schools, of course, go to them. However, I am not sure if public schools are free. There may be some fees that have to be paid, but there are no taxes imposed on the public specifically to operate public schools.

Within the private schools, there is something called "open schooling". This is a very informal type of schooling that takes place. I know that years ago I went to a language school for a refresher course. This was an open school without any credentials set up in a house that was rented for this purpose. Among the foreign students, learning Spanish would be done in a separate room where a Meridian student would be taught the traditional subjects such as math and science. I have no idea how this works except that when finished with this open schooling, the student received a certificate that doubled as a high school diploma.

My sense is that there is little in the way of certification done on schools or teachers. The teacher union has full sway essentially over what goes on. I have seen little discussion about educational standards or scandals. I believe that scandals are not discussed because there is very little emphasis placed on education.

It is my understanding that an individual with a college degree in education must pay union officials to obtain a teaching job. Further, I am told that if the money is paid to a union official, there is still no guarantee that the job will be obtained. And since the money was paid as a bribe, and bribes are illegal in Mexico, there will be no recourse for the individual who paid to obtain his or her teaching job.

Mexico boasts that the vast majority of its citizens are literate. That would really depend on how literate is defined. The spelling of most Mexicans is atrocious. But the same could probably be said for most Americans these days.

Merida has at least three universities. Two are public institutions, one of which is a technological school. There is a private university that has a good reputation. My experience with hiring engineers from the Tech has been good.

But I have noticed that the universities conduct classes in strange ways. The students are often given projects and do not have to come to class. One very good custom, in my opinion, is that they are all required to do a type of internship, which gives them the practical experience that they need.

Some of my American friends have speculated that the Mexican government wants the educational system to remain in a poor state. The theory is that if the populace is un-educated, they can more likely be duped by the political powers. It could be. However, a relatively much better educated populace in the U.S. seems to be constantly duped by politicians.

CHAPTER THIRTY-SEVEN
Legal and Tax Issues

Mexico has relatively high tax rates, given the economic plight of most of its citizens. I would have thought the tax rates would be lower than those in the U.S. Not so. Basically, the corporate and individual tax rates are very similar to the U.S. rates. Mexico does have the advantage of a much simpler system in the sense that there are not so many possible deductions as in the states, nor are there so many possible loopholes.

The U.S. Congress uses tax policy to affect economic actions. The congress can pass tax laws to promote certain industries. The U.S. Congress does this routinely. The Mexican Congress does not appear to be so proactive.

When the Mexican Congress becomes proactive with respect to tax policy, it is usually disastrous. However, there are those who argue that the same is true for the U. S Congress. Recently the Mexican Congress has proposed a new tax law that is additional to the regular income tax law. This tax re-defines taxable income in a way that excludes the deductions for salaries, payroll taxes and charitable donations. Taxable income, re-defined, will be taxed at 16 percent.

This will be disastrous for the maquila industry. Since, by definition, the industry assembles the product and usually does not own the raw materials for the product being assembled, normally about 70% of all expenses are represented by salaries and wages. This will cause the re-defined taxable income of maquilas to soar, since most formerly deductible expenses are no longer deductible. Presumably, this will cause tax revenues to do the same. The maquila industry already provides an enormous amount of tax revenue to the country. The proposed tax would be almost confiscatory, forcing many maquilas to re-think their investment in a country already becoming non-competitive. The lack of competitive advantage in Mexico vis a vis other countries has already created disinvestment and exacerbated the problem of lack of tax revenues. Further disincentives to operate in Mexico will only create additional reduction in tax revenues. Nevertheless, this widely known fact has not caused the Mexican Congress any pause in its quest for more taxes.

Mexico is short on tax revenues due to the large underground economy already discussed. This problem is aggravated by corruption. A Mexican friend told me a story of meeting outside the offices of an HACIENDA (Mexican IRS) employee to "negotiate" the payment of taxes. The negotiation ended in a relatively small payment to the Hacienda and a larger payment (bribe) to the employee to settle the problem.

To me, this type of situation is a recurring theme in Mexican society. Those who follow the law are punished in a relative sense while those who pursue illegal or unethical solutions, although traditional, suffer no consequences as the probability of getting caught is virtually nil. In the case of maquiladoras, which are normally foreign-owned, the vast majority pay taxes. But an inordinately large group of potential taxpayers simply evade taxes. The government finds it easier to simply raise taxes, which are paid by the law-abiding citizens, rather than find and punish wrongdoers. So, the good guys bear the costs.

Because the government is short on money, it looks for any way to rob Peter to pay Paul. I once had a tax refund coming for my personal taxes. The Hacienda handles these refunds by depositing them directly into your bank account, if you have one. I was at first impressed by this efficiency. But not for long.

This efficiency is interrupted by the constant and incredible Mexican need for paperwork and signatures. Before the refund can be electronically transferred to your account, you must sign a form of acknowledgement. The form of acknowledgement is delivered to the address you have given on your tax return.

In my case, my refund was approximately one year late in coming. I received a form delivered by personnel of the Hacienda stating that the acknowledgement form could not be delivered to me as they were unable to locate me at the address I had given. I was immediately struck by the irony that the form that I did receive, essentially stating that they could not find me, had the same address as the acknowledgement form I needed to sign to receive my refund that I never received. In other words, I was found where I could supposedly not be found. It seems like a Zen Buddhist koan.

When presented with these facts, Hacienda was unable to provide an answer as to how this could happen. Nevertheless, they responded that they would resend the acknowledgement form. Unbelievably, the cycle repeated. After an appropriately lengthy Mexican bureaucratic delay of several months, I was delivered another form advising me that the address given was un-locatable. The third try was charmed, and I eventually obtained my refund.

Again, Hacienda had no explanation. My accountant believed it was a strategic move by Hacienda to play the float. That is, the government was short of money and solved the problem by coming up with pretexts as to why refunds were not given.

The same kind of strategy is used for IVA refunds. IVA is a value-added tax that must be paid on nearly all products and services. If you are in business, the IVA is refundable if you apply for it. It should be a simple matter, but the Hacienda makes life difficult for those wanting refunds.

First, in order to apply for the refund, you must make an appointment. At the time of the appointment you have the right to deliver the papers asking for the refund. Hacienda does whatever it does to check that the IVA was actually paid. If the Hacienda is satisfied, and they almost never are, the refund appears in your company account after several weeks.

But normally the Hacienda is not satisfied with the original set of papers; they typically find some "i" not dotted, or "t" left uncrossed. At which point you are notified and given another appointment. Then you are required to show proof of payment of the facturas (invoices) in question where the IVA was supposedly paid. This, of course, will require another appointment and perhaps more requests for proof.

IVA is required to be collected on all facturas. Recall that a factura is the only legal proof for a deductible expense. IVA collected is reported to the Hacienda. Everything should match up.

However, due to rampant fraud the Hacienda is often skeptical, so delays in receipt of IVA reimbursements are somewhat understandable. An example of fraud with IVA is facturas that are false that can be bought. I had the son of a friend of the famous J.W. Barnes who called me one day and offered me the purchase of false facturas at a discount. For example, if the facturas show a total of 50,000 pesos in IVA that is refundable, the facturas could be bought for 20,000 pesos. I declined, but thanked him for thinking of me. In an incredulous tone, he asked me if I understood what he was offering, as if he was offended that I did not take him up on this offer to participate in a fraud. I guess he had never been turned down before for the chance to defraud the government in a way that is probably foolproof.

Since no one trusts anyone in Mexico and as there is no reliable mail service, any document that is delivered must have an original and a copy. This concept includes facturas. The original factura is delivered to the recipient, and the recipient is required to stamp the factura copy with the date and the company stamp, proving it was delivered. The copy is taken back to the company that is issuing the factura. To ensure that it is delivered, most companies have their own DILIGENCIERO, which is an errand boy. No one uses the Mexican postal system.

This creates problems with bill paying and getting paid for bills. If you have sold something and the buyer wants to use the expense as a tax deductible expense, he will need a factura. He will not pay until he receives the factura. Since the seller does not want to give the factura without receiving payment, something of a Mexican standoff, if you will, is initiated. If the factura is given before payment, the seller, knowing other Mexicans, realizes he is now at a disadvantage as the buyer has what he wants, and the seller does not have his money.

The problem is solved as follows. The seller sends his diligenciero to the buyer with the merchandise and the factura. The diligenciero is instructed to not give up the merchandise or the factura until he receives a contra RECIBO, which is the buyer's signature on a form indicating that he has received the factura. Most companies write checks on Mondays and the diligenciero is asked to return the following Monday for his check. At that time the diligenciero has to sign a form indicating he received the check and turn back the contra recibo to the buyer and the cycle is closed.

This situation is clearly inefficient. It also creates unnecessary costs to the untrained eye. But these costs and inefficiencies are considered necessary in Mexico as preventive measures against fraud. Due to the apparently ineffective legal system, you really have no recall against fraud. If there are problems, in most cases forget about litigation. I don't understand the system at all. It is different from our system, which is based on common law. However, Mexico and all of Latin America uses the Napoleonic system. As I understand it, the legislature is the sole source of law and judges cannot set precedents. So defensive measures are the only recourse you have.

Furthermore, it seems to me that many lawyers really don't like to litigate. Their solution seems to be to go to a politician in the government and request that he issue an edict to solve the problem.

There is a government-sponsored legal office that handles small claims. This office is known by its acronym, PROFECO. As was reported earlier, we did have success in this forum.

An interesting legal idiosyncracy in Mexico involves elections. By law, at some point prior to election day, and on election day, no beer or alcohol can be sold. The government apparently wants no one voting who is intoxicated. But, obviously, this law is easily circumvented by stocking up on beer and alcohol before the cut off point. And, of course, vendors simply sell in surreptitious ways.

In the last presidential election, another curious prohibition occurred. For several days prior to the election, the INSTITUTO FEDERAL DE ELECCIONES (Federal Election Insitute) prohibited the broadcast of Fox News, which is received by satellite TV. Since Fox News only broadcasts in English, I was somewhat perplexed by the prohibition. I never discovered the reason for this.

I had a strange experience replacing license plates. A car I owned spent several weeks in a mechanic's shop undergoing repairs. In the process, the mechanic somehow lost the front license plate.

My assumption was that the replacement would be a relatively simple process. I was wrong. It turned out to be a serious legal proceeding. The first trip to the office responsible for issuing the new license plates took thirty minutes in line to discover that

I needed a long list of paperwork to prove that I was the owner; the title in my name was insufficient proof.

For the second trip I took every conceivable paper I could that pertained to the car. I waited in line again and the clerk then informed me that I would need copies as he was going to keep the copies, and the office did not make copies. He said that for the citizens' convenience, a copy shop was located in this particular government building. There, another interminable line had formed.

However, the "line" turned out not to be a line, but a grouping of people who all wanted copies. I have often noticed in Mexico, that otherwise warm and congenial people who do not wish to wait in a line like civilized people, simply go to the front of the line and start shoving papers at the clerk. Amazingly, the clerk accepts the papers, and no one complains that it is not fair. Again, those who follow the rules are those who get punished, while those who break them suffer no consequences.

After another thirty minute wait for my "turn," I obtained approximately fifteen copies and returned to the original line for the clerk to issue the license plates. Of course, I dutifully took my place at the end of the line. Once the clerk started working with me and my copies again, he began to type a long legal decree. I signed it and he went off to get another signature from his boss. It turns out that his boss left for lunch and would return in two to two and a half hours (typical lunch break). No one else was empowered to sign the form, and the plates could not be issued without that signature.

The clerk agreed I could come back the next day instead of waiting two and a half hours. When

I returned the next day, the boss had still not signed and was out of the office again "running errands." On the fourth trip, the next day, I received my signed decree and my new plates.

I, and others, have had similar experiences with obtaining the FM3, a work visa. It is illegal to have revenues in Mexico without this visa. While one would think that the government would have a policy to make this an easy document to obtain for foreigners employing Mexicans, it appears that the government really wants to put obstacles in the path of foreign investors. A friend who employs about 300 people began her visa renewal on time. But due to the delays similar to those described above for license plates, it was not completed by the government office by the deadline. She was deported while the government slowly finished the visa, at which time she was allowed to return to the country. One can see why many Mexicans simply skirt the law and pay bribes. It is much easier and not that costly.

CHAPTER THIRTY-EIGHT

MISCELLANEOUS MUSINGS ON MERIDA AND MEXICO

There are many interesting aspects to living in Merida that should be mentioned, especially if you are considering a move. One thing that will drive you crazy is the noise level. Mexicans have an incredible tolerance for noise. They seem to actually prefer to live on busy streets and will pay a premium for a house so situated despite the racket that buses and other vehicles, with and without mufflers, make.

Parties in residential neighborhoods will go on to all hours of the night. A "disturbing the peace" concept does not exist; the Police will not do anything about your partying neighbors. A friend once called the police about a party at 3 AM but the police said the partying neighbors had obtained some type of party permit that allowed them to make all the ruckus they wanted. The Police refused to go see them.

Another friend who was giving English lessons asked her students about why there was no outrage over neighbors who partied all night. Her students, all Mexicans, really did not understand the point of her question. They could not understand why someone would complain about neighbors. After all, they said, neighbors have rights. Besides, maybe next weekend they would want to do the partying, and their neighbors should not have a say in when they decide to stop or how loud they should put the music.

To some extent, I admire the attitude. Everyone has a right to do as he pleases. But the idea that doing as you please should have limits in terms of adverse effects on others is not part of the equation.

Speaking of music, any time a store is having a sale or even just a normal day, the store may rent a huge sound system that is set up on the sidewalk blaring music at ear-splitting levels. The huge speakers, placed on the sidewalk, are usually taller than most Mayans. I have noticed the same at car dealerships. It drives me away, but it attracts potential buyers like a magnet as if loud music puts them all in a buying mood. I have no idea how they can even hold a conversation with the music at those levels.

There is a fascination with loud firecrackers. For no known reason, powerful firecrackers and rockets will be set off in the neighborhoods on any night. That is, it will not be a holiday or any particular reason for celebrating. Sometimes these shows will last for as long as fifteen minutes. It sounds like a small war. No one but me seems to mind.

Don't be offended by all the warmth and touching, hugging and kissing. Once you have met someone, even if briefly, it is not uncommon to kiss the ladies on the cheek, often simultaneously shaking their hand. I kind of like the tradition. This is normal when you are greeting and when you are parting.

Men normally shake hands and give an ABRAZO – a hug. The abrazo is given on both sides of the head; that is, two abrazos, one to the left and one to the right after or during shaking hands. Again, this may be done upon greeting and upon parting.

Mexicans, especially males, have their own set of gestures that are somewhat effeminate. I find this a bit ironic since many Mexican males still cling to the tradition of MACHO. The universal come-over-here-signal made by males in Mexico is to place your arm out in front and crooked at the elbow to the point that your hand, palm pointing down, is at the middle of your chest about eighteen inches in front of your body. Then with a limp wrist the fingers are flicked inward. Don't interpret this in any other way other than come over here.

Then there is the QUE PASO? gesture. Que paso is translated basically as, what's up? Or what's going on? This is usually given when you are seeing a friend from a distance. Instead of yelling, "What's going on?" you simply pull your elbow into the body and stick your arms up from there at forty five degrees, perpendicular to your body and palms up. At the same time you hunch your shoulders up and place a very quizzical look on your face. The person to whom you are gesturing most probably will do the same to you. All is well and both of you can keep going on your separate ways without wasting breath. There is, at least, this one area of Mexican efficiency.

Then there is the Hey-I-don't know or I-didn't do-it gesture. This gesture also leans toward the effeminate side. Both arms go up, parallel to the body, pivoting at the elbow, which is held tightly against the torso, palms facing in front and fingers spread pointing up. At the same time, the mouth is distorted down at the corners and the eyebrows go up. The shoulders usually hunch at the same time.

If you are able to master these three gestures, you are on your way to integrating with Mexican society.

◦✼◦

Throughout Merida, wherever you park you are most likely to encounter a VIENE-VIENE, which translates as come-come. These are guys who supposedly help you park and leave from your parking space by directing you with little red rags, which they wave around or twirl in the air.

My opinion is that these guys add absolutely no value. However, they do expect tips. And they are everywhere, not just on the sidewalk. For example, if you park in Walmart's parking lot, you will see a number of viene-vienes. They apparently have designated areas within the parking lot or on the street in which they work.

I have always wondered how they get the spots on the street. They seem to have fixed and undisputed areas that they work, even though they are not employees of any entity. For example, at a specific area on Paseo Montejo the same vien-viene is there each day. I have heard that they are allowed into the business parking lots by permission. But the street is public. I have never seen a disagreement between viene-vienes about who has the right to certain public areas. I have heard that the first one to stake out the area is the one who gets the uncontested right to direct parking. Given the almost lawless air of Mexico, I am amazed that there never seems to be viene-vienes in disagreements over who has the rights to a specific area.

In years past in Mexico, these guys extorted tips. As you parked, there would be subtle hints that the neighborhood was bad, and you might want to agree to pay a small fee for the viene-viene to look after your auto. Those who did not agree in advance would often return to a damaged auto, most surely inflicted by the spurned viene-viene.

However, at least now in Merida, there are no subtle threats. Nevertheless, I would estimate that the vast majority of parkers pay a tip for this non-value added service. Actually, describing it as a non-value added is a generous description. I have seen situations where the viene-viene creates near accidents by directing a car leaving a parking spot into approaching traffic.

Merida, which claims to be the oldest city in the Americas having been founded in 1541, quite naturally is full of very old homes. (In point of fact, I believe both Cartegena and Panama City were founded prior to Merida.) At least they are old by standards in the Americas. Most of the existing old homes come from the Colonial Period.

One of the most distressing aspects to the culture is the lack of respect and care given to these old homes by Mexican families. In their defense, many Mexicans simply cannot afford to maintain these homes. All of the old homes were built with thick stone walls and are in constant need of repair.

As a general rule, Mexicans who can afford to maintain the older homes do not care to live in them. Most wealthy Mexicans in Merida prefer to live in the northern part of the city in the new developments and in modern homes.

There just is not the pride in the heritage represented by these homes among Mexicans. It is quite a contrast to Europe where homes are much older, and the pride reflected by Europeans in these older structures is evident. As a result, a large number of very old homes in Merida are simply deteriorating into dust.

Thankfully, many foreigners are moving to Merida and buying these homes and remodeling them so that they are returned to the elegant splendor of the past. All of the infrastructure has to be replaced, but the beautiful architecture is maintained.

Unfortunately, the influx of foreigners who pay prices well above the local market have created an asymmetrical market. Locals who hear of a neighbor's home selling at an astronomical price, put their own homes on the market at the same price without regard to size or condition of their own home. Then, they do not budge from the price they have set, despite the reality of the market.

One of the more fascinating things about Mexico is BRUJERIA. Brujeria is sorcery. Many Mexicans believe in sorcery. A sorcerer can be a BRUJO OR BRUJA, depending on sex.

Carlos Cateñeda wrote a series of books in the 1960s about a Yaqui Indian in the north of Mexico that was a brujo. There is much speculation about whether the story is true. The brujo, known as Don Juan, in the books was a serious brujo who supposedly caused some supernatural events in the life of Casteñeda. Some of those events were aided by the use of organic plants with halucenagenic properties, such as PEYOTE.

Most brujos, as I understand it, are not involved in halluconegenic aids, although they believe they have supernatural cures based on the use of plants and herbs. Out of curiosity, I went to a brujo once in *Ucu*, a little pueblo just outside Merida.

This brujo had developed some fame, and there was a waiting line to see him. As far as I know, this brujo was not as serious a brujo as Don Juan in the sense that I was not asked to ingest any substance. Lyman and I went in order to get a LIMPIEZA, which is a cleansing. I wanted to see a brujo in action.

Each person entered into the brujo's house/office, which was a CHOZA, a typical Mayan house that is oval in shape and with a thatched roof. Chozas are sometimes made from cement block, but are traditionally made of mud and sticks with a thatched roof.

Once alone with the brujo in the choza, we sat across from one another in old wooden chairs. I explained that I wanted a limpieza, and he told me to wait while he walked out into his backyard. He returned carrying a small branch of a tree showing recent signs of having been ripped from a larger branch. The small branch he was carrying still had leaves on it.

He began to chant in Maya and lightly touch me with the branch over my entire body. This procedure and chant lasted some two to three minutes.

I was charged the equivalent of about $10 and left with the confidence that I had been cleansed.

Ecology is an unknown science in Mexico. As already mentioned, buses and trucks spewing contamination are commonplace. Pueblos don't have normal trash collection as we know it. Therefore, by tradition in the pueblos, one area is used to throw trash that is not burned. This location is usually on the side of the highway entering the pueblo. So the first thing a visitor sees is a trash pit that serves as the municipal trash dump by default. Of course, the area is infested with flies, vultures, and who knows what else.

It would seem more prudent to take a few steps into the jungle to discard the trash behind a buffer of jungle. However, this would take a bit more time and effort and, apparently, a trash-strewn breeding ground for germs, that also serves as an invitation to wild animals at the entrance to the town, does not bother the residents.

Merida does have organized trash collection by private companies. The cost for this service is incredibly low. Some companies have the trucks that compact the trash. Other companies just use big trucks, like dump trucks. You don't want to get behind one of these trucks in traffic. A trail of stench wafts behind them that would gag a maggot.

Although the cost trash collection service is incredibly low, this does not prevent your neighbors from deciding they don't have to pay it. I was astonished to find that one (or more) of my neighbors have decided to simply place their trash along side of mine on trash days. Since I live alone, I don't have much trash and the added volume of a neighbor does not cause the trash collectors a problem normally. However, sometimes the trash collectors demand that Doña Tere pay them extra if my (and my neighbor's) trash exceeds a certain limit. I don't know who is doing it, and I know from experience everyone would deny it so I have not bothered to investigate.

A couple of years ago, Merida required residents to separate their garbage between organic and inorganic. Different-colored bags would indicate which was which. The city maintained that bags would be taken to different sites for disposal. A big deal was made in the press and unless separated, the trash was not to be collected.

By experience, I knew that the bags would most likely all be taken to the same location and dumped there whether organic or inorganic. It would be more costly for the owners of the trash companies to take to two different locations. They would know that there would never be any consequence to dumping all in one location. I am sure that is what happened. The tradition of the authorities to not follow up on these kinds of potential problems would be respected and everyone knows it.

Over time, there were no more stories about being ecologically correct with trash. Now I notice everyone uses the black garbage bags for all types of trash as was done in the past before the new ecologically correct rules.

The city of Merida places trash cans in parks and around the city with signs identifying organic and inorganic trash. Again, I would be willing to bet that both types of receptacles are taken to the same place for disposal.

Recently, the trash company with the concession in Progreso, the nearest port, suffered a scandal in the news. This company was caught illegally dumping trash in the mangrove. For several days it was front page material in the newspaper. I would suspect that no one will be prosecuted; that certain officials will be rewarded for their assistance in making the problem go away.

The issue of time is confusing. As we all know, to Mexicans time is a relative concept. But in matters that can be measured precisely, there is still a confusing difference. For example, what we call a week, or seven days, is called 8 days in Merida. We normally think of fourteen days as two weeks. Mexicans refer to two weeks as fifteen days. This was confusing until I figured out they were always counting the current day as a complete day.

Often when you ask someone how long something will take or how long they will take to arrive they use the word "rato," which is basically translated as "a while." We usually interpret "a while" to mean a relatively short time period. A rato covers both short and relatively long periods in Mexico. So again, I get confused. I often ask Mexican friends, "How much is a rato?" They think this very funny, like why would I even want to know how long a rato is? Mexicans are much more comfortable leaving that sort of thing undefined, while we Americans are a bit more obsessed with measuring time. Both philosophies certainly have their merit.

The same is true of other time-related concepts. Like the word AHORRITA, which is translated as "right now." It is supposed to be something that is on the verge of being done or occurring at the moment. But it doesn't. It means something like, "My intention is to do it right now, but I will do it when I feel a stronger urge and I am not sure when that urge might strike me; it could be right now or it could be at some point in the future." You can see why it is shorter to just say "ahorrita."

I believe saying "ahorrita" when you really don't meant right now is all part of the idea of pleasing the person to whom you are talking, as I have mentioned before. Mexicans love to please in the moment; they are not concerned about the fact that at some point in the future, and maybe near future, the person to whom you are speaking is most likely not going to be pleased. Oh, well, we'll cross that bridge when we get there.

It is like the phrase YA VOY, which is translated literally as, "I am already going". The phrase often means, "It is my intention to be already going." Even after all these years, when I hear these words, I know what they really mean, but I still get aggravated.

Another confusing phrase is "TU CASA." We all know this means "your house." However, Mexicans have a warm, pleasant and charming way of referring to their own house as "tu casa," meaning that "my house is your house." When Mexicans want to say, "My house is your house," we all know the phrase, MI CASA ES TU CASA, and it is sometimes used.

However, often Mexicans say "tu casa" when they mean "my house." For example, one might describe where one lives and at the end of the sentence say, "ALLA TIENES TU CASA," translated as "There you have your house" which means "There is my house". So you can imagine the times that Mexicans have said to the un-indoctrinated some thing like, "Let's get a party together" and the un-indoctrinated agrees, only to then hear the Mexican state, "A LAS NUEVE EN TU CASA" (9:00 P.M. at your house). The poor soul is taken aback by the unaccustomed Mexican rudeness thinking that the Mexican has said something to the effect that, "Let's have a party and I will ask people to come to your house—get all the food and drink together." The Mexican has referred to "tu casa," meaning his own home. Then, of course, both the Mexican and the American prepare for parties at their own home, each expecting the other to show up.

CHAPTER THIRTY-NINE
Industrial Infrastructure

The Yucatan is quite different from the rest of Mexico. It is also somewhat isolated, and so it is possible that comments about the industrial infrastructure cannot be extrapolated to Mexico in general.

I am still dismayed that the loss of electrical power is relatively frequent. While the frequency of problems is much less than it was, it continues to be a disappointing feature of industrial life in Yucatan. When any construction is under way near our plant, electrical loss is almost weekly. Recently the highway in front of the Industrial Park was being widened. This created power outages at least once a week for awhile, presumably through carelessness on the part of the construction workers who must have been constantly cutting cables.

During the rainy season, we get active storms full of lightning and thunder and torrential rains. While they usually only last for a short time, power outages are a common occurrence as a result of these storms. There must be some kind of a solution to this, as the same thing happens at certain times of the year in the Houston area without such dire consequences.

The loss of power creates enormous potential for damage to equipment. For expensive electronic equipment, we have spent as much as a thousand dollars or more on voltage regulators and circuit breakers that are dedicated to only one machine. This is a form of insurance that protects the machine against the seemingly uncontrollable power outages.

Another problem with the electrical supply is that it is not stable. While we may not completely lose power we often experience wild fluctuations in the voltage coming into our lines. These relative spikes in electrical current have damaged equipment, even when protected by regulators and breaks.

I am perplexed by the government's apparent lack of interest in solving this problem. One of the government economic agencies asked if they could bring a representative of a well-known Italian fashion designer to our plant to get an example of an operating sewing factory in the Yucatan. While on the tour of our plant, we lost all power.

Once this happens there are the excited screams of all the operators like you would hear if you were listening to over 500 people on a roller coaster ride in an amusement park. This coupled with the relative darkness of the interior of the factory seemed to frighten the Italian, despite the emergency lighting that automatically powers up with the loss of electricity. In a way, this was poetic justice to the government for not improving the infrastructure. I understand that the Italian company is subcontracting on a small scale in the Yucatan.

I am surprised at the cost of potable water supplied by the government agency that is the equivalent of the water company. The Yucatan promotes itself as a region of more than ample supplies of water, despite the absence of lakes and rivers.

It is true that there are no lakes or rivers and, oddly, there is ample water. This is due to the large underground aquifers that exist in the limestone bedrock. Actually, it has been described to me that there are large amounts of water flowing beneath the Yucatan in what amounts to underground rivers connected by cenotes and the porous limestone bedrock. Basically, anywhere you excavate in the Yucatan to a depth of about four meters, you are going to hit water.

Therefore, one would think that a solution to the relatively high cost of potable water would be to simply dig a water well. The problem is that the government presumes to have rights to all water below your land, as it does to oil. Therefore, to dig a water well legally, you first need permission from the COMMISION NACIONAL DEL AGUA, National Water Commission, known as the CNA.

Once that permission is obtained, then you must measure the water flowing from the well and pay the government for the use of the water. It is true that the cost of this water is less than the cost of potable water supplied through the city infrastructure. Nevertheless, I was struck by the government's legal claim to water under your own property. We have a water well on our factory grounds and report water usage each month. Since the factory was bought from a previous owner, to make the water well legal we had to submit copious reams of paperwork to the CNA and pay fees for the right to extract water for our own personal use.

The way most people deal with an onerous legal requirement in Mexico, such as legalizing water wells and paying for the water, is simply to not obtain permission for water wells. Then, if caught, one simply pays the appropriate bribe, and all is resolved. However, this is not an option we considered.

I will have to say that the roads have improved immensely over the last ten years. They are much wider and better-paved. Accidents I believe have been diminished in number. Since driving habits are no better, I assume this decreased accident rate is due to the greater flexibility in driving maneuvers afforded by wider and better-paved roads.

However, the freight trucks, if anything, have become greater death traps than before, although I never would have thought this possible. I know that the Mexican government has complained that the U.S. was being unfair by not allowing Mexican trucks to cross the border and deliver Mexican cargo within the U.S. Mexico retaliated by not allowing U.S. trucks to cross the border. Believe me, the U.S. government was correct and making a decision with the best interests of pedestrians and other drivers in mind when Mexican freight trucks were denied entry into the U.S.

I presume that Mexican freight trucks have some type of inspection that is mandated. But, as should be obvious by now, inspections and restrictive regulations merely provide opportunities to government bureaucrats in Mexico to obtain bribes, thereby thwarting the purpose of any inspections, if in fact, required.

One advantageous aspect to freight trucks and drivers in Mexico is the fact that drivers will come to the plant with an empty container and stay all day without charging. The truck may arrive at 8:00 A.M. and leave at 7:00 P.M. without any extra charges. This works out well for us if we have rush orders not yet finished; we simply load what we have and tell the driver to wait until we complete the lagging production without any additional cost. He usually opens both doors to his cab and easily drifts off to sleep. I doubt that any trucking company in the States would allow a driver to stay with his rig and container all day without extra charges.

At the end of the day, I will have to say that the infrastructure is sufficient. Nevertheless, it is not without its challenges as described in the foregoing.

CHAPTER FORTY
Cuba

While clearly Cuba is not part of the Yucatan, the story of my adventures in paradise would not be complete without a few words on Cuba. This is especially true after the J.W. Barnes story. Furthermore, the Yucatan has had quite a bit of migration and immigration with Cuba. Cuba is separated from the peninsula by the Yucatan Channel, and at its closest point, Cuba lies only about 100 miles offshore.

There is evidence that contact between the two land masses goes back to ancient times and is even possible that there was a land bridge at one time. The remains of an underwater city was recently discovered through some sophisticated technology. Archaeologists claim it has features of some of the ancient Mexican civilizations.

The Yucatan has become the entrance to a human smuggling route from Cuba to the US. Once on land in Mexico, those fleeing Cuba for the U.S. apparently find it easier to enter the U.S. through the border. They make it over land with the help of coyotes, human traffickers, who transport their human cargo to the border for a fee.

Some Cubans entering Mexico illegally in the Yucatan find it easy to obtain false Mexican papers through corrupt officials. Some of them stay in Mexico and enter the drug trade. Recently, a Cuban, who reportedly was part of a drug mafia, was gunned down in broad daylight, gangland style.

Before Castro, there was more commerce, in all senses, between Cuba and the Yucatan. Under Communism, Cuba really never produced much of anything and commerce with Mexico slowed significantly. About ten years ago there were a number of scandalous stories concerning Cuban women and Yucatecan men married to Yucatecan women. In vogue at this time were Cuban shows with singers and dancers visiting the Yucatan from Cuba. These were great spectacles. I saw one once. It was a cross between a concert with Vegas-style show room dancers and a Circus. Performers would hang from ropes, form human pyramids, and dive and tumble around in nimble ways on the stage, all the while singing and dancing.

Many of the performers, both male and female, were interested in escaping Cuba and the only safe way to do so was to marry a foreigner. So the performers viewed the shows as opportunities to meet someone of the opposite sex and seduce them into marriage. Of course, to the performers it made little difference if their seducee was already married or not.

Therefore, many Cuban performers, females especially, were wooing Yucatecan men from their wives. Yucatecan women viewed these Cubans as a scourge to be eradicated before every available Yucatecan male succumbed to their Cuban charm. And, I must say, Cuban women are perhaps the most "charming" in all the world. I was told that as a result of this famed charm, there was some sort of political intervention, no doubt promulgated by furious Yucatecan women, which prohibited Cuban shows and saved Yucatecan men from their doom. It must have been a successful intervention, as for the past ten years I sadly note that I have not seen one Cuban show advertised in Merida.

I have always had a fascination with Cuba. In the 1950s and 60s, impressionable young minds like mine were bombarded by romantic notions of revolutionaries such as Fidel Castro and Che Guevarra who were said to be fighting evil dicatators in the name of the people. Then, in the early and mid 1960s, many Cuban refugees came to Texas to make a new life. I met some of them, and they told me stories that were not so grounded in romanticism. Nevertheless, my fascination continued.

In college I minored in Political Science and spent one entire semester researching and writing papers on Cuba. I learned quite a bit about Cuba that was based in statistics and objective research. It became clear to me that perhaps Fidel was fighting against an evil dictator, Batista. But, in the end, Fidel himself has shown much more imagination as an evil dictator than what Batista could have imagined. Despite my understanding of the realities of Cuba, my interest in Cuba continued over the years.

As related in the J.W. Barnes story, I obtained a contact with a large U.S. chicken producer. I also learned that since around 2000, the U.S. does not have an economic embargo against food and medical supplies sold to Cuba. I realized I could finally combine my interest in Cuba with a business purpose. Furthermore, the U.S. government provided travel licenses for legal travel to Cuba by U.S. citizens if there was a legitimate business purpose. Fortuitously, at least I thought so at the time, I learned of J.W., who had business dealings in Cuba on a supposedly grand scale.

I soon met with J.W. for the purpose of learning more about doing business in Cuba. J.W. was clearly knowledgeable about the ins and outs and claimed to have the high-level government contacts that would be necessary. As the reader recalls, J.W. suggested that I attend a conference in Cuba in the coming weeks in order to make my contacts on the Cuban side. I soon obtained my travel license from the U.S. government making my trip legal under U.S. statutes. I also paid the fees for the conference and in a matter of weeks was on my way.

The conference was quite interesting. There were a number of representatives from very large companies. However, the vast majority of attendees seemed to be there only as an excuse to travel to Cuba. From talking to them, it was obvious they really had no business purpose to their trip. I think some of them did not even have travel licenses and therefore were on Cuban soil breaking U.S. law in much the same way that J.W. had done.

As I recall, the conference lasted several days. The highlight of the conference was Fidel's speech to the attendees. Conference officials herded us into an auditorium. We were probably about two hundred and fifty in number and were told that Fidel would arrive in minutes. After about forty-five minutes, we were told to all take a break and return in an hour, at which time Fidel would grace us with his presence.

We returned in an hour and after only another twenty minutes of waiting EL LIDER MAXIMO arrived. This was 2004, and Fidel had earlier taken a bad spill while leaving the stage after another speech. In that fall, he had broken an arm and a leg. Therefore, Fidel was wheeled to the stage from a side door seated in a wheel chair with his broken leg propped up and sticking straight out.

Fidel immediately began speaking, and we all braced for his normal, interminable speech. After about fifteen minutes (he was only getting warmed up), a young aide came in with a cell phone in one hand and whispered something to Fidel. Fidel told us all, "Excuse me, I have to take this call." Naturally, I assumed that some emergency similar to another Bay of Pigs invasion was underway. However, Fidel had a warm smile on his face and began speaking in very familiar terms with the caller. The mike was still on and I heard him say, "Well, I am in a room with some friends." At some point he explained to us all that he was speaking with another friend, Hugo Chavez. They spoke for another ten minutes while we all waited. From what I could hear of the conversation, it was a friendly chat with no particular purpose like we all might have with a friend, really just shooting the breeze. It was a very bizarre scene. The Cubans in the room seemed to think nothing of it, but the rest of us were amazed that the president of a country would receive an obviously personal phone call in the midst of a speech that he was delivering.

Once he finished his conversation with fellow dictator Hugo Chavez, he resumed his speech. His speech was typical Fidel. The speech brimmed with statistics about the economic wonders of the Cuban economy. I am certain none of the statistics were real or correct. According to Fidel, Cuba was an economic paradise. He was very careful to not be overly critical of the U.S., which I thought showed some discretion, since the purpose of the conference was to create commerce between the U.S. and Cuba.

The speech turned out to be fleeting by Fidel's standards; it lasted approximately two and a half hours. We all felt as if our butts had turned to concrete by the end. However, I truly felt for the interpreters who were housed in a glass room overlooking the auditorium. There were three interpreters who you could watch as they attempted to stay up with Fidel. Since Fidel speaks without prepared remarks, the interpreters are completely without preparation either. Fidel speaks rapidly and hardly seems to take breaths. There were three interpreters who worked in shifts of about ten minutes each. They must have learned that it would be an impossible task for one interpreter to maintain enough energy to last through even a short Fidel speech. I noticed that after about an hour, when one interpreter would pass off to the next one, the interpreter finishing his or her turn would literally drop their head to the desk and cradle it in their arms in exhaustion.

During the conference, I met some of the high-ranking officials with Alimport, the government "company" that does the importing from the U.S. I was also able to obtain a meeting with the buyer responsible for buying U.S. chicken. At this meeting I was introduced to another buyer who represented Venezuela. I was hoping to sell in relatively small quantities, as my capital would not have been sufficient to buy an entire boat load of chicken. I could have signed a contract for an entire boat, but did not have the capital and did not want to borrow money for such a risky venture. Although Cuba had never failed to pay, the risk and concerns about when title passed to Cuba had some legal implications that the U.S. government had not totally worked out at the time. Therefore I passed on this opportunity.

Approximately three months after the conference, I did receive a phone call from the Venezuelan buyer requesting a quote on chicken to be delivered to Venezuela. There were no U.S. government complications with selling to Venezuela and, therefore, the normal international legal traditions were maintained and known. However, oddly this buyer quit returning phone calls, and so I was unable to make the deal.

I made several trips to Cuba over the next year and a half for the purpose of selling chicken. I discovered on these trips that the Cuban people were in dire straits. Mexico is to Cuba as the United States is to Mexico in terms of economic advancement; Cuba makes Mexico look like an advanced country with a sophisticated economy and infrastructure.

It was a surrealistic experience. All business and economic activity of any size goes through the government, which means through Fidel. Fidel is rumoured to personally be worth billions. He has allowed some entrepreneurial activity at the smallest level in recent years.

As a result of European and Canadian tourism, many Cubans were able to obtain U.S. dollar currency. Also, relatives of Cubans living in the U.S. sent dollars to their family members. Castro did not like the fact that there were perhaps millions of cash dollars in the hands of private Cuban citizens. Therefore, abut the time I first went to Cuba, a law was passed that outlawed the use of U.S. dollars. Fidel gave a certain time period for all Cuban citizens to legally exchange their dollars for Cuban pesos, which are worthless. After the deadline, it would be illegal for any Cuban to be found with U.S. dollars in his or her possession.

At the same time, Fidel made it illegal for tourists to use U.S. dollars or Euros. Therefore, when entering the country, all foreign currency by law must be changed into a special currency called the Cuban Convertible Peso (CUC). Cuban citizens may not use the CUC. The CUC is tied one-to-one to the dollar, but the Cuban government charges a commission to exchange the foreign currency for the CUC of approximately 20%. Therefore, if you expect to spend, say, $1000 you must take $1,200 in order to have the 1000 to spend. Fidel makes 20% off the top. Since the CUC has no value outside of Cuba, when leaving the country you must convert any CUCs left over to dollars. Fidel is kind enough to charge no commission for going from CUCs to dollars.

It is illegal for Cubans to use CUCs. They must use the Cuban peso. Cubans may not use facilities for foreigners, such as hotels. Of course, Cubans don't have the money to pay the prices that the hotels charge anyway. There are special taxis that foreigners are required to use that charge much more than taxis that Cubans use. And so forth. Essentially, there are two economies and two currencies—one for Cubans and one for foreigners.

While living costs for Cubans are incredibly low, living costs for foreigners are relatively expensive. I was surprised by this fact. I had assumed that due to the deplorable state of the Cuban economy, that Cuba would be relatively inexpensive. For example, the rent on a modest house in Cuba might be the equivalent of $50 per month, while the cost of a medium-priced hotel, exclusively for foreigners, might be $170.

The only Cubans who are legally employed are employed by the government. This is true even though the employer may be a legally organized corporation, such as the aforementioned Alimport. The owner of the company is the Cuban government. Salaries paid by the government to its employees are incredibly low.

For example, I met an anaesthesiologist who claimed to be paid something in the range of the equivalent of $300 per month. This was supposedly a very good anaesthesiologist. I say this as the government would not allow him to travel outside of the country. He said he was prohibited from doing so because the government feared he would defect, and the country would lose his expertise. Nevertheless, his wife had permission to travel and had been out of the country at various times.

I have always heard that Cuban medicine is one of the most advanced and sophisticated in the world. This is apparently another one of the myths promoted by Fidel. I met a Cuban friend who had a bad virus, and the Cuban doctors were certain that if they extracted a certain tooth that the virus would be cured. Apparently, there is some prevailing medical theory in Cuba that all illness stems from the teeth.

One of the reasons that Cubans are able to survive physically is that Fidel provides the equivalent of food stamps to every Cuban. With the monthly coupons, Cubans can go to special stores and buy just enough food to survive. However, the quality of this food is very bad.

I took a trip once to the countryside. I was struck by the fact that the fields lay fallow. I asked my Cuban companions why that is, especially since Cuba was so well-known for its sugar cane. The response was that there was no incentive to grow foodstuffs because the government would be the only buyer, and the price would be insufficient to make a decent living. Besides, food was furnished by the government, although it was of incredibly low quality. And since the Russians quit buying sugar cane, there were no buyers in the world market. I did occasionally see relatively small plantings of sugar cane.

Basically, all foodstuffs are imported. Most of the imports come from the United States. This is true for rice and beans also, which I found amazing. Metric ton after metric ton of rice and beans arrives from the United States to Havana.

Internet is illegal in Cuba for private residences. The government does not wish that its citizens receive any information not authorized by it for dissemination. However, illegal internet exists. Through official corruption, internet signals can be obtained and installed in private homes. Every so often government inspectors come through neighbourhoods, checking on such illegal activity. Normally, the provider of the internet is advised in advance and has time for his customers to hide their cables that bring internet into the homes.

The communist "block spy" concept is alive and well in Cuba. The residents of each block have a general idea of who he or she is and are very careful about what they say around this individual. I have been told that oftentimes, it is the block spy who is providing the illegal internet! So many of the spies are playing both sides of the street—earning favors by reporting non-approved behaviour and/or speech and earning money by selling illegal internet. Satellite TV is also illegal. However, the statements above about internet also apply to satellite Television.

The state of poverty can be illustrated by an experience I had one day while jogging. After I was cooling down, a resident came up to me to ask for my sweaty t-shirt. I gladly agreed and we began talking. One of the things he told me was that it was easier to get marijuana than it was to get clothes for the average Cuban. He claimed he did not have toothpaste or toilet paper.

The infrastructure in Cuba is well below inadequate. This is not true in the tourist hotels, but it is true in the rest of the country. Electricity is intermittent. Many homes in Havana do not have running water. The old, gracious and beautiful buildings in Old Havana are all crumbling into pieces. The Spanish government supposedly has provided a grant to restore Old Havana. This restoration project was underway on my last visit.

The level of repression experienced by Cubans is amazing to me in that it is only ninety miles offshore from the U.S. I would not be surprised by such repression in a faraway land such as China.

Fear of the government is everywhere. While they speak in hushed tones about Fidel and their fears, they are terrified to do anything about it. Weapons do not exist outside of the military. I had one Cuban tell me that she wished the U.S. would invade again and take over the country. I quickly assured her that there was no chance of that happening.

I told the story in the J.W. Barnes chapter about being stopped by the Cuban Police while in a private car with friends. All were interrogated, including me. The owner of the car was dragged to the police station and interrogated until early in the morning of the next day. His error was helping a friend who had promised to pick me up at the Havana Airport. This man was not authorized to transport foreigners.

Despite this intolerable situation, I find the Cuban people with a JOIE DE VIVRE and a naturally happy spirit that is inspirational. They endure hardships that are not necessary in a modern age because their leader is too stubborn to accept Communism as a failure. Or perhaps it is because he supposedly profits personally and immensely from the situation as it is structured.

An example of Cuban hardships, their manner of dealing with it, and their friendly and giving attitude is shown by my experience when a friend invited me to a party. I did not wish to attend the party since I knew the neighbourhood where they lived was truly poverty-stricken. Only because I was so taken by the gracious offer did I accept.

I arrived by taxi to the hilly outskirts of Havana on a street littered with pot holes and barely passable by car. We walked down the hill between some small houses in terrible shape and arrived at the house of Omar. Omar's house has a living room that is the size of a tea kettle and is attached to the kitchen by a narrow hall. Off the hall is a tiny bathroom in which just barely fit a shower, a lavatory, a toilet and a fifty gallon plastic drum of water. The drum of water was in the bathroom because there was no running water. A bucket in the drum was used to gather water, which would then be poured into the toilet to flush the water out. There was one bedroom off the kitchen.

About fifty friends were gathered in this tiny house and spilled out into a relatively large yard that held a number of coconut trees. Omar is white and married to quite a large black lady, Nora. They have a child who at that time was about three years old.

One of the interesting characteristics of the Cuban people is the complete lack of prejudice. Or at least this is my impression. Blacks and whites mix without any problem. There are many bi-racial couples. Cubans are a handsome people and often the mix of black and white genes produces an astonishingly beautiful offspring.

Omar is a butcher by trade. He, of course, works for a government-owned operation. To obtain meat for the party, Omar stole it from the government butcher shop. I am told that all government employees steal and that the government is aware of it. The citizens believe that the government turns a blind eye to let off some of the pressure of such a dire economic situation.

Another party-goer was a chef at one of the fine tourist hotels. Because they all knew that a foreigner was coming, they decided to make the party special by stealing lobster from the hotel, also, of course, owned by the government. They stole just enough lobster for a plate for me and one other foreigner who was there. The chef cooked it, and it was indescribably delicious.

Besides being given one of the two available plates of melt-in-your mouth lobster, I was treated with incredible respect. I was very touched that such economically humble people accepted me completely into their homes without any strings attached.

Everything about Cuba is a bit exotic. I have a friend who wanted to become a "Santo" in the SANTERIÁ religion. This is a religion that originated with the slaves who came from Africa. While it is not the Voodoo cult from Haiti, it does have similar characteristics.

I don't know much about their belief system, but my friend explained what she had to do to become a Santo. First, there is a ceremony conducted by a person she called "the Padre," or priest. During this ceremony, there is a series of animal sacrifices that occur. The ceremony goes on for quite awhile apparently. Before the end of the ceremony, all of her hair was cut off. Then my friend had to stay reclined on a mat in the corner of one of the rooms in the priest's home for a week. She was given special food to eat.

Then she began a period that was to last a year where she could only wear white. She also had to have her head covered in white at all times. She was to visit the priest once a week. She asked me if I wanted to meet the priest, and I accepted her invitation.

The priest was a very tall black man who had an imposing presence. He had a series of beads strung around his neck. He did not seem very friendly at first. They discussed various issues and things that she had to do for the coming week. Then she asked him to give me a reading. He requested that I sit in a chair in the room where my friend had spent a week on the floor. He kneeled on the floor in front of me and began to shake some shells in his hand and threw them out on the floor like dice. He seemed to pick them up in a certain order and ask me questions. It was a bit uncanny. He asked me about certain aspects of my life that no one in Cuba would have known.

My friend indicated when the reading was over and suggested that I leave some money on a small altar of sorts that had been erected in the corner of the room. I did so and asked if my friend would take a picture of me and the priest together. It was at this point that he seemed to loosen up and become more friendly. I invited him to join us for lunch later in the day, and he accepted. At this time he also presented me with a string of beads that he was wearing.

    I have to say that Cuba is the most interesting country I have ever visited. I am glad I was able to visit while Castro was still in power. I am sorry for the Cuban people that Castro was in power in order to give me the opportunity to see Communist Cuba. As I write this, Fidel finally ceded power the week before and his brother, Raul, has taken over control of the country. I doubt much will change in the near future. I hope that the Cuban spirit and fun-loving attitude will not change. But I also hope that Cuba will soon no longer be the one remaining example of Communist economic failure in this hemisphere.

CHAPTER FORTY-ONE
Leaving OGA

The experience of managing OGA has certainly taught me more about my weaknesses than my strengths. Several years ago, between the time Joe Toste left and Luis came, I found that I was patting myself on the back quite a bit. I think I had fallen into the trap of thinking I could not be wrong. After all, we had done pretty well, and I was the CEO and majority stockholder. I probably was not very easy to live with during that time and, no doubt, full of myself. I am not sure what made me realize that, but at some point I came to realize I was more than capable of making a mistake and should remember that possibility each time I make a decision.

Discussing much more about my weaknesses would not be very entertaining for me or for the reader. Suffice it to say that I have learned a lot about myself and not all of it was favorable.

The whole experience of starting and running OGA has been a laboratory of learning. One of the most important lessons I think I learned was the responsibility that goes with being an entrepreneur. I always thought that running a business was about the boss. So, running OGA would be about me, and I liked the idea of something being about ME. From the outside looking in, I always thought it would be exhilarating to be the boss.

Running a business showed me what the other side of the entrepreneur coin is like. While it is always exhilarating, it is not always fun. And, at some point, it became clear to me that it was not really about me. It was a sobering experience to realize that the decisions our team and I made not only affected our future but also the future of about 500 other families. Those five hundred families were depending upon us to make the right decisions—that's an awesome responsibility.

In some sense, I came to feel like a proud father. I felt that Claudia and I had five hundred children for whom we wanted the best and knew that our decisions would impact their future, not just ours. As Luis had honored me in telling me he would like to consider me as a father figure, I thought of how closely the upper management group of thirteen resembled my professional children. I believe many times I was an inadequate "father" and teacher for them, but I also believe I have made some positive impact on their personal and professional lives. I know they all have enormous potential to take OGA to even higher altitudes.

I feel some guilt for knowing that I am going to leave them alone in their daily battle to make OGA better. I know this guilt contributes to the melancholy I feel at the thought that my leaving will become a reality over the next year or so. I know that I am going to miss them immensely, but I also know that the time is right and that they are more than capable of continuing the flight of the Ganso.

I will be forever grateful for my experience and for the individuals and their efforts that contributed to OGA's success. The experience has been priceless;

it cannot ever be taken from me, nor will I ever lose it. It will forever be a part of me and has helped shape who I am. This experience, unlike money and wealth (assuming I obtain them), I will take to the grave.

The day of reckoning, when I was going to announce to the team that I was leaving, was fast approaching. I was quite worried about controlling my own emotions and knew that if their emotions were not controlled, I would lose it for sure. It was reassuring in a way to watch Brett Favre announce his retirement on TV and lose control in the process. Somehow this relaxed me to know that a tough guy like him could also become emotional.

Of course, Claudia already knew of the decision, but not the exact timing. I told her it was time to announce my decision in March of 2008 and that I wanted to tell the profit-sharing group first. She told me that she thought both Wendy and Mary were going to cry, and this concerned me. I began to steel myself.

We met in the conference room, and it was hard for me to get started. I stuttered around for awhile. There was a knot in my throat that could have choked an elephant. Once I finally got the words out, everyone was surprised, despite the fact that I had told them for years that at some point I was going back to the States to live. Claudia, Wendy, and Mary did cry. This caused a lot of watering in my own eyes, and I noted the same in the eyes of Luis, Sergio, and Santiago.

Luis spoke first. He was clearly upset but said that he was committed and would stay and continue seeking the company goals. Both Santiago and Sergio spoke in order and essentially said the same. This was very reassuring to me. Finally, the same came from Wendy and Mary. I appreciated all of their comments.

Over the next few months, I had a number of private conversations with each of them. The tone of the talks we had was very reassuring to me and, frankly, convinced me beyond a shadow of a doubt that I had become the father figure to them. This knowledge created an incredible pride that I felt for myself and I felt the same for them, as a real father would for his children. It is difficult to explain. But it is as if these people who made up the profit-sharing group were confirming to me that they were going to continue the legacy of Ganso Azul. I was left with the sensation that fathers must have when their children indicate they are planning to procreate and extend the branches of the family tree.

Claudia gave me a special pride. She had matured immensely and was realizing the potential created by her intelligence and charisma. We had a heart-warming conversation in her office one day that created some striking sensations for me. I realized I was going to miss them more than I had anticipated.

Just before my announcement to the team, the customer decided to give us another product line—outerwear. Outerwear consists of a special type of high-added-value garments such as raincoats. We would have to expand the factory to accommodate more inventory of the special fabrics used by these garments. We would probably be hiring another hundred to a hundred and fifty people to produce this product line and expand the factory another 12,000 square feet.

The expansion would result in greater profits, assuming we were successful in the implementation. For awhile, I began to question my decision to leave.

This would be an exciting challenge. However, I knew my decision had been made, and it was best to follow through.

Prior to leaving, Claudia and I began to work the State Government for financial assistance in the expansion. A new state government had come in recently. Fortunately, the political appointment in the economic development office who was responsible for promoting expansion in the Yucatan was a friend. He was also from the private sector and was very understanding of our situation.

I am happy to say that he carried the ball for us in the government and obtained a sizeable sum for financial assistance. This restored my faith in the government. Until this point, I had determined that the government was simply not interested in increasing employment in the Yucatan. After all, a number of maquilas had closed, reducing employment by several thousand, and the only reaction by the government that I could discern was a figurative yawn. Hopefully, this will mark the turning point in the government's attitude about economic development.

I have to say that I am leaving on a high note in every respect. The business is still growing thanks to the extraordinary efforts of the team. We won some financial concessions from the state government that will help alleviate the financial pain in starting a new product. Finally, and most importantly, I am leaving feeling pride and respect for every member of our team and receiving similar sentiments from them.

I just wonder about my ability to adapt in the U.S. without the adrenalin rush that I get from the challenges that present themselves every day at OGA. Only time will tell.

Made in the USA
Lexington, KY
25 October 2011